JOURNALS

OF

RALPH WALDO EMERSON

1820–1872

VOL. VI

Waldo Emerson

JOURNALS
OF
RALPH WALDO EMERSON

WITH ANNOTATIONS

EDITED BY
EDWARD WALDO EMERSON
AND
WALDO EMERSON FORBES

1841–1844

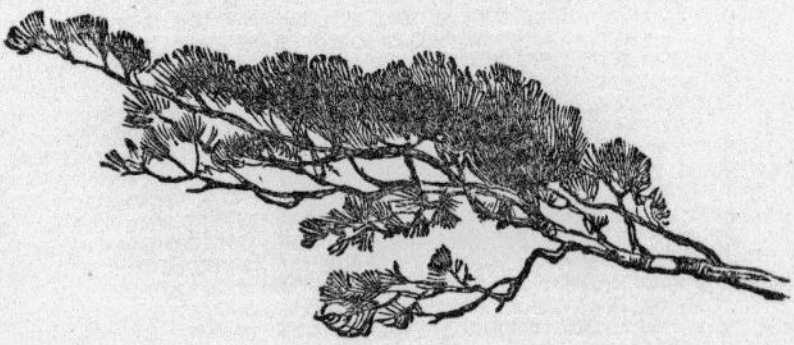

BOSTON AND NEW YORK
HOUGHTON MIFFLIN COMPANY
The Riverside Press Cambridge
1911

CONTENTS

JOURNAL XXXII

(Continued)

1841

CONTENTS

stock in Nations. Kinds of corn. G. W. Tyler ; his
prowess. Temperance elegant. Inaptitude. *De Clifford* and *Pericles and Aspasia* teach behavior. Self-
seekers' Nemesis. Friendship in communities. Deep
natures have latitude. Real gentility. Mrs. Ripley's
eager scholarship. Two or three persons. The marriage institution ; woman's ideal place. Writing ;
autobiographical. Emerson, Thoreau, Alcott. Poetry
to come ; now too conscious ; should sweep away
the poet ; the instinct. Sky and earth. The man
in black ; the Swedenborgian. Indirection. Nature's
symbolism. Talk with Margaret Fuller. Stories il-
lustrating the times. The startled German. Shakspeare as metaphysician. Editors and Webster. The
Soul's two directions ; does Love reconcile these ?
Good courage. Exclusives. The Champion. Riches
a meter. Speeches and protocols also in God's
scheme. Artists' models. The great Harlequin.
Man and expression in books. Elizabeth Hoar, the
sister. Life's repetitions grateful. Genius. Hope.
My book. Life's sum. Daguerreotype. Margaret
Fuller. Tone ; Whiggery is secondary, timid. Fanny
Elssler's dancing is new expression ; the moral.
Effect of music. Webster ; the change. Water.
Good expression rare. Insanities. Right aristocracy ;
infernal infantry of Fashion. The Moment in writing ; its relief. The unrecognized great. The opening firmament. Jesus at a club ? Two doors to
high life. Fashion. Inhumanity and geniality in company. Margaret Fuller's unsettled rank. Trade and
holiness. Unfinished literary work. The Transcen-

CONTENTS

Garrison thunders for Peace ; the wrong way ; take
man as he is, and give a better way. Society hates
unmaskers. The Divinity School. Fight Slavery on a
high plane. The Webster boys. Untrained American
writing. Our contemporaries. Conscience. Reform
is elegance. Aunt Mary. Bitterness talks itself out.
Thought immature not spirit. Basis of ideals. Ad-
vanced arithmetic transcendental. Village explains
world ; greatness near. Daguerre's guess. The Composer needs the underparts also. Youth of Nature.
The three wants. The acquiescent attitude. Heed the
hints and miracles. The resplendent day. The man
contrasted with his works. Shelley. A test. Soldiers.
Inspiration must make its own way. Skepticism. Heroes of sickness. Dandies of moral sentiment. Time
conquerable. Poet must work a miracle. Workers and
their critics. New thought out of ruins of old.
America lost in her area. Men magnetizable. Great
causes belittled by converts ; need long perspective.
Wonder before genius. Strength wasted in denial.
Nature ignores our language. Heart fears no uncover-
ing to the better and wiser. Beauty in world of
thought. Originality. Miracle of Poetry, God, from
commonest materials. Self-help. Anti-Transcendentalists, their reasons. Believe in your work. Affirmative.
The writings of Ancient world sacred. Man still returns to the old words. Our base of granite. The

CONTENTS

JOURNAL XXXIII

1842

(From Journals E, J, K, and N)

The happy household. Death of Waldo ; the vacancy,
relics ; his happy life and friends ; his sayings. Mass
in writing ; advancing steps ; perspective. Mass in
friendship. Boy and violets. Seeing without eyes.
Facts as horses. Proclus. Bores. Jonson and Tennyson. Optical life. Ignore the declaimer, speak the
thought. Proclus, magnificent suggestion. Lady
turned church-member. Accept not persons. Experi-

CONTENTS

CONTENTS xiii

lured by politics. Trick in conversation. Walk with
Hawthorne to Harvard and visit to Shakers. Landor;
Scott ; piety; Wordsworth; Culture from Europe;
travel without a call. London a magnet. Young preachers. Coleridge at Andover. The little girls. Hosmer
on farm animals. Health and rules. Sons. Economy.
Supremacy of classic authors. Divinity behind man's
institutions. Steam's lift to Boston. Bargaining. Man's
one way to freedom. Doctor Channing's strength.
Mourning gradual; Reform's value appears late. *La
Peau d' Ane*. Life's goods by the highway. Impo-
sition. Take turns. Words mere suggestions; beautiful facts. Spectatorship. Democrats and Whigs. Useless genius. Infants teach cheerfulness. Underlying
seriousness; the Soul's safeguards. Margaret Fuller;
gypsy talent and Custom; Rabelais. Merchants;
nothing new. Thoughts on tedious visitors. Mary
Rotch on guidance of the Friends. Indian summer.
Homer's value to Americans. Rabelais again. Books
to read. Society must not be overdone. God offers
alternatives. Truth gives good utterance; Richter.
The human housedog. Alcott's risky imports. Letter
on Doctor Channing's death; the minister and author.
Poets; Tennyson, Burns, Browning, Bailey, verse
inspired and uninspired. The poor stove. Classics.
Talking on Life. Boston's hospitality. Jones Very's
influence. The Greaves Library; Charles Lane and
Henry G. Wright; Alcott. Suggestive writers; Cornelius Agrippa and Robert Burton. Basal mistake of
communities. Persons are not ideas. Literary justice.
Paracelsus. The Reformers claim they bring all that

CONTENTS XV

JOURNAL XXXIV

1843

(From Journals Z, R, and U)

JOURNAL XXXV

1844

(From Journals U and V)

CONTENTS

ILLUSTRATIONS

JOURNAL

NANTASKET
WATERVILLE ADDRESS
LECTURES ON THE TIMES

JOURNAL XXXII

(Continued)

1841

(From Journal G)

[All page references to passages from the Journals used by Mr. Emerson in his published works are to the Centenary Edition, 1903–05.]

[DURING this year it is evident that Mr. Emerson's forces had ebbed, in spite of the gardening hours with his friend Henry Thoreau, and the change to the lonely hostelry on Nantasket Beach, whither he went to write his "Waterville Address," was important.

In Mr. Cabot's Memoir of Emerson he gives several letters written from Nantasket to Mr. Emerson's wife and friends with pleasant mention of that fortnight's sojourn.[1]]

1 On July 13 he wrote : —

DEAR LIDIAN, . . . I find this place very good for me on many accounts. . . . I read and write, and have a scheme of my speech in my head. I read Plato, I swim, and be it known unto you I did verily catch with hook and line yesterday morning two haddocks, a cod, a flounder, and a pollock,

NANTASKET BEACH, *July* 10.

You shall not love beautiful objects ardently: you will not, if you are beautiful. He who is enamoured of a statue, a picture, a tune, or even of the stars and the ocean, finds in them some contrast to his own life. His own life is ugly, and he sickly prefers some marble Antinous or Cupid to the living images of his father and mother, and whole towns of his countrymen dwelling around him. But when a man's life is concordant with Nature, he will behold all that is most beautiful in the universe with a fraternal regard unsurprised.

(From loose sheet)

[The following, though undated, was evidently written in July at Nantasket.]

and a perch. . . . The sea is great, and reminds me all the time of Malta, Sicily, and my Mediterranean experiences, which are the most that I know of the ocean; for the sea is the same in summer all the world over. Nothing can be so bland and delicious as it is. I had fancied something austere and savage, a touch of iron in it, which it hardly makes good. I love the dear children and miss their prattle. Take great care of yourself, and send me immediate word that you are well and hope everything good. That hope shall the Infinite Benevolence always justify.

Your affectionate husband,

WALDO E.

We have two needs, Being and Organization. See how much pains we take here in Plato's dialogues to set in order the One Fact in two or three or four steps, and renew as oft as we can the pleasure, the eternal surprise of coming at the last fact, as children run up steps to jump down, or up a hill to coast down on sleds, or run far for one slide, or as we get fishing-tackle and go many miles to a watering-place to catch fish, and having caught one and learned the whole mystery, we still repeat the process for the same result, though perhaps the fish are thrown overboard at the last. The merchant plays the same game on 'Change, the card-lover at whist, — and what else does the scholar? He knows how the poetry, he knows how the novel or the demonstration will affect him, — no new result but the oldest of all, yet he still craves a new book and bathes himself anew with the plunge at the last. The young men here, this morning, who have tried all the six or seven things to be done, namely, the sail, the bowling-alley, the ride to Hull and to Cohasset, the bath, and the spyglass, they are in a rage just now to do something: these itching fingers, this short activity, these nerves, this plasticity or creativeness accompanies forever and ever the Profound Being.

And yet the secret is kept.

It is only known to Plato that we can do without Plato. Being costs me nothing. I need not be rich, nor pay taxes, nor leave home, nor buy books for that. It is the organizing that costs. And the moment I *am*, I despise city and the seashore, yes, earth and the galaxy also.

"When Nature is forsaken by her lord, be she ever so great, she doth not survive." — VEESHNOO SARMA.

Too feeble fall the impressions of our sense upon us to make us artists. Every touch should thrill: now 't is good for life, not for poetry. It seems as if every man ought to be so much an artist that he could report in conversation what has befallen him.

Aristotle defined Space as a certain immoveable vessel in which things were contained.

Every sensual pleasure is private and mortal: every spiritual action is public and generative.

The Church aërates my good neighbors and serves them as a somewhat stricter and finer ablution than a clean shirt or a bath or a sham-

pooing. The minister is a functionary and the
meeting-house a functionary : they are one and,
when they have spent all their week in private
and selfish action, the Sunday reminds them of
a need they have to stand again in social and
public and ideal relations beyond neighborhood,
— higher than the town-meeting — to their fellow men. They marry, and the minister who
represents this high public, celebrates the fact ;
their child is baptized, and again they are published by his intervention. One of their family
dies, he comes again, and the family go up publicly to the church to be publicised or churched
in this official sympathy of mankind. It is all
good as far as it goes. It is homage to the Ideal
Church, which they have not : which the actual
Church so foully misrepresents. But it is better
so than nohow. These people have no fine arts,
no literature, no great men to boswellize, no fine
speculation to entertain their family board or
their solitary toil with. Their talk is of oxen
and pigs and hay and corn and apples. Whatsoever liberal aspirations they at any time have,
whatsoever spiritual experiences, have looked
this way, and the Church is their fact for such
things. It has not been discredited in their eyes
as books, lectures, or living men of genius have

been. It is still to them the accredited symbol
of the religious Idea. The Church is not to be
defended against any spiritualist clamoring for
its reform, but against such as say it is expedi-
ent to shut it up and have none, this much may
be said. It stands in the history of the present
time as a high school for the civility and man-
suetude of the people.[1] (I might prefer the
Church of England or of Rome as the medium
of those superior ablutions described above, only
that I think the Unitarian Church, like the
Lyceum, as yet an open and uncommitted organ, free to admit the ministrations of any inspired man that shall pass by : whilst the other
churches are committed and will exclude him.)

I should add that, although this is the real
account to be given of the church-going of the
farmers and villagers, yet it is not known to
them, only felt. Do you not suppose that it is
some benefit to a young villager who comes out
of the woods of New Hampshire to Boston and
serves his apprenticeship in a shop, and now
opens his own store, to hang up his name in
bright gold letters a foot long ? His father could
not write his name: it is only lately that he could:

1 The passage in parentheses was written a day or two
later, but referred to this place.

the name is mean and unknown: now the sun shines on it: all men, all women, fairest eyes read it. It is a fact in the great city. Perhaps he shall be successful and make it wider known: shall leave it greatly brightened to his son. His son may be head of a party: governor of the state: a poet: a powerful thinker: and send the knowledge of this name over the habitable earth. By all these suggestions, he is at least made responsible and thoughtful by this public relation of a seen and aërated name.

Let him modestly accept those hints of a more beautiful life which he meets with; how to do with few and easily gotten things: but let him seize with enthusiasm the opportunity of doing what he can, for the virtues are natural to each man and the talents are little perfections.

Let him hope infinitely with a patience as large as the sky.

Nothing is so young and untaught as time.

Cities of men are like the perpetual succession of shells on the beach.

This world is a palace whose walls are lined with mirrors.

[*Of a*] *Preacher*. " There he has been at it, as tight as he could spring for an hour and a half."

A vulgar man in leaving the eaves of his house has left the moral law and the gods. At Paris, at New Orleans he gives himself up to his appetite.

The theory of the Whig, carried out, requires that government should be paternal, and teach Paddy where is land, and how he should till it, that he may get bread. But the governments that now are, are improvident. The Spiritualist who goes for principles, and for the high and pure self, has none of this tenderness for individuals.

Do not waste yourself in rejection ; do not bark against the bad, but chant the beauty of the good.

I take pleasure only in coming near to people. What avails any conversation but the sincere? Uncover thy face, uncover thy heart to me, be thou who thou may, and the purpose of purposes is answered to us both. We may well play

together, or eat or swim or travel or labor together, if this is the result: if this is not, all
that we have accomplished together is naught.
Is plain dealing the summit of human well-being?
What serenity and independence proceed out
of it! Then I have not lost the day: then I
have not lived in vain. To be a lover with a
lover, to be a god with a god, seems to be only
this happiness, no more, namely, the being truer:
with a broader and deeper Yes and No. Is this
also a fortune, a felicity, coming by the grace
of God, and not to be compassed by any effort
or genius, when it does not descend on us like
beauty or light? I cannot establish it with all,
or with most, or with many; then I could be
happy with all: no, but only with a few.

Travel, I think, consists really and spiritually
in sounding all the stops of our instrument. If
I have had a good indignation and a good complacency with my brother, if I have had reverence and compassion, had fine weather and good
luck in my fishing excursion, and profound
thought in my studies at home, seen a disaster
well through, and wrought well in my garden,
nor failed in my part at a banquet, then I have
travelled, though all was within the limits of a

mile from my house. Domestication consists in the unique art of living in the fact, and not in the appearance. Who has learned to root himself in being, and wholly to cease from seeming, he is domestic, he is at the heart of Nature. He must be sustained by the sense of having labored, or nothing can yield him cheerfulness.

Facts. All is for thee; but thence results the inconvenience that all is against thee which thou dost not make thine own. Victory over things is the destiny of man; of course, until it be accomplished, it is the war and insult of things over him. He may have as much time as he pleases, as long as he likes to be a coward, and a disgraced person, so long as he may delay to fight, but there is no escape from the alternative. I may not read Schleiermacher or Plato, I may even rejoice that Germany and Greece are too far off in time and space than that they can insult over my ignorance of their works, I may even have a secret joy that the heroes and giants of intellectual labor, say, for instance, these very Platos and Schleiermachers are dead, and cannot taunt me with a look: my soul knows better: they are not dead, for the nature of things is alive, and that passes its fatal word to me that these men shall yet meet me and shall yet tax me line for line, fact for fact, with all my pusillanimity.

All that we care for in a man is the tidings he gives us of our own faculty through the new conditions under which he exhibits the common soul. I would know how calm, how grand, how playful, how helpful, I can be.

Yet we care for individuals, not for the waste universality. It is the same ocean everywhere.[1] . . . So can Dante or Plato call the nations about them to hear what the Mind would say of those particulars which it happened to meet in their personality.

> Lobster-car, boat, or fish-basket,
> Peeps, noddies, old-squaws, or quail,—
> To Musketaquid what from Nantasket,
> What token of greeting and hail?
>
> We cannot send you our thunder,
> Pulse-beat of the sea on the shore,
> Nor our rainbow, the daughter of Wonder,
> Nor our rock, New England's front door.
>
> White pebbles from Nantasket beach
> Whereon to write the maiden's name,

1 The substance of what follows is in "The Method of Nature" (p. 205).

Shells, sea-eggs, sea-flowers, — could they teach
Thee the fair haunts from whence they came ! [1]

Shall I write a sincerity or two ? — I, who
never write anything else, except dullness? And
yet all truth is ever the new morn risen on noon.
But I shall say that I think no persons whom
I know could afford to live together on their
merits. Some of us, or of them, could much
better than others live together, but not by
their power to command respect, but because
of their easy, genial ways : that is, could live
together by aid of their weakness and inferiority.

Understand that the history of modern improvements is good as matter of boast only for
the twelve or twenty or two hundred who made
them, not for those who adopted them and said
We. The smallest sign of moral force in any

1 On the last day of July Mr. Emerson wrote to Carlyle,
who in many letters was preaching Silence to him : —

"As usual at this season of the year, I, incorrigible, spouting
Yankee, am writing an oration to deliver to the boys in one of
our little Country Colleges. . . . You will say that I do not
deserve the aid of any Muse. O, but if you knew how natural it is to me to run to those places ! Besides, I am always
lured on by the hope of saying something which shall stick
by the good boys." (*Carlyle-Emerson Correspondence*, vol. ii,
Letter LXII.)

person countervails all the models in Quincy Hall. The inventor may indeed show his model as sign of a moral force of some sort, but not the user.

I only need to meet one agreeable person, boy or man or woman, to make my journey a happy one. But lately it has been my misfortune to meet young men with a certain impudence on their brow, and who speak and answer with that offensive assumption, that what I say I say to fill up the time, and not that I mean anything. Not so with that fair and noble boy, whom I saw at Nantasket, and whom all good auguries attend !

Ascending souls sing a pæan. We will not exhort, but study the natural history of souls, and congratulate one another on the admirable harmonies.

Rich, say you? Are you rich? how rich? rich enough to help anybody? [1] rich enough to suc-

---

[1] This passage is essentially printed in " Manners " (*Essays*, Second Series, pp. 153, 154), but it so truly represents Mr. Emerson's human kindness and hospitality to souls in trouble that it is here given to offset the many theoretical utterances of impatience or of exclusion, which he entered in the Journal of this period when the mood was on him.

cor the friendless, the unfashionable, the eccentric, rich enough to make the Canadian in his wagon, the travelling beggar with his written paper which recommends him to the charitable, the Italian foreigner with his few broken words of English, the ugly, lame pauper hunted by overseers from town to town, even the poor insane or half-insane wreck of man or woman, feel the noble exception of your presence and your house, from the general bleakness and stoniness; to make such feel that they were greeted with a voice that made them both remember and hope? What is vulgar but to refuse the claim? What is gentle but to allow it?

He is very young in his education who needs distinguished men in order to see grand traits. If there is grandeur in you, you will detect grandeur in laborers and washerwomen. And very fine relations are always established between a clear spirit and all the bystanders. Do you think there is no tie but your dollar between you and your landlord or your merchant? Have these made no distinction between their customers or guests?

Be calm, sit still in your chair, though the company be dull and unworthy. Are you not there? There then is the choir of your friends;

for subtle influences are always arriving at you from them, and you represent them, do you not? to all who stand here.

It is not a word, that " I am a gentleman and the king is no more," but is a fact expressed in every passage between the king and a gentleman.

With our faith that every man is a possessed person having that admirable Prompter at his ear, is it not a little superfluous to go about to reason with a person so advised?

We treat him as a detachment.

Do people expect the world to drop into their mouths like a peach.

I wish I could see a child go to school or a boy carrying a basket without a feeling of envy, but now I am so idle that everybody shames me.[1]

1 Mr. Emerson wrote to Mr. Ward at this time : —

" Is it the picture of the unbounded sea, or is it the lassitude of this Syrian summer, that more and more draws the cords of Will out of my thoughts, and leaves me nothing but perpetual acquiescence and perpetual thankfulness ? . . . I find no emblems here that speak any other language than the sleep and abandonment of my woods and blueberry pastures at home. . . . Ah, my friend, I fear you will think it is to little purpose that I have for once forsaken my house and crept

Tropes. The metamorphosis of Nature shows itself in nothing more than this, that there is no word in our language that cannot become typical to us of Nature by giving it emphasis. The world is a Dancer ; it is a Rosary ; it is a Torrent ; it is a Boat ; a Mist ; a Spider's Snare ; it is what you will ; and the metaphor will hold, and it will give the imagination keen pleasure. Swifter than light the world converts itself into that thing you name, and all things find their right place under this new and capricious classification. There is nothing small or mean to the soul. It derives as grand a joy from symbolizing the Godhead or his universe under the form of a moth or a gnat as of a Lord of Hosts. Must I call the heaven and the earth a maypole and country fair with booths, or an anthill, or an old coat, in order to give you the shock of pleasure which the imagination loves and the sense of spiritual greatness? Call it a blossom, a rod, a wreath of parsley, a tamarisk-crown, a cock, a

down hither to the water side, if I have not prevailed to get away from the old dreams. Well, these too have their golden side, and we are optimists when the sun shines. . . . You have been here ? It is a sunny, breezy place with delicious afternoons and nights to such as can be delighted." (*Letters from Emerson to a Friend.*)

sparrow, the ear instantly hears and the spirit leaps to the trope.

The doctrine of Necessity or Destiny is the doctrine of Toleration, but every moment, whilst we think of this offending person that he is ridden by a devil and go to pity him, comes in our sensibility to persuade us that the person is the devil, then the poison works, the devil jumps on our neck, and back again wilder on the other: jumps from neck to neck, and the kingdom of hell comes in.

The Age. What is the reason to be given for this extreme attraction which persons have for us but that they are the Age?[1] Well, now we have some fine figures in the great group and many who promise to be fine. I think the nobility of the company or period is always to be estimated from the depth of the ideas. Here is great variety and great richness of mysticism. . . . But how many mysticisms of alchemy, magic, second sight and the like, can a grand genius like Leibnitz, Newton, or Milton dispose of amongst his shining parts, and be never the worse?

1 The passage thus beginning is found in "Lecture on the Times" (*Nature, Addresses, etc.*, p. 262).

Motley assemblage on the planet; no conspiring as in an anthill. Every one his own huckster to the ruin of the rest, for aught he cares. In perspective one may find symmetry, and unconscious furtherance. . . .

As soon as a man gets his suction-hose down into the great deep he belongs to no age, but is eternal man. And as soon as there is elevation of thought we leave the Times.

I will add to the portrait of Osman that he was never interrupted by success: he had never to look after his fame and his compliments, his claps and editions. In very sooth shall I not say that one of the wisest men I have known was one who began life as fool, at least, with a settled reputation of being underwitted?

"To me men are for what they are,
They wear no masks for me."

When I was praised I lost my time, for instantly I turned round to look at the work I had thought slightly of, and that day I made nothing new.

The dissipation of praise, the dissipation of newspapers, and of evening parties.

It is the blue sky for background that makes the fine building.

Ideal. I think there are better things to be said for the conservative side than have yet been said. Certainly the *onus* of proving somewhat striking and grand should be with the Idealist. His defects are the strength of the man of the world.

Nothing but God can root out God. The whole contest between the Present and the Past is one between the Divinity entering and the Divinity departing. Napoleon said that he had always noticed that Providence favored the heaviest battalion.

Optimates. Elizabeth Hoar says that the fine young people break off all their flowers and leave none to ripen to fruit. So we have fine letters and a too imaginative and intellectual period, but no deep and well adapted character.

Scholar. We all know enough to be endless writers. Those who have written best are not those who have known most, but those to whom writing was natural and necessary.

Let us answer a book of ink with a book of flesh and blood.

All writing comes by the grace of God.

Character. I do not wish to appear at one time great, at another small, but to be of a stellar and undiminishable light.

Superlative. The greatest wit, the most space. It is the little wit that is always in extremes and sees no alternative but revelry or daggers.

Scale. We are to each other results. As your perception or sensibility is exalted, you see the genesis of my action and of my thought, you see me in my debt and fountains, and to your eye instead of a little pond of the water of life I am a rivulet fed by rills from every plain and height in nature and antiquity and deriving a remote origin from the foundation of all things.

August 22.

Measure is a virtue which society always appreciates, and it is hard to excuse the want of it.[1] . . .

Society may well value measure, for all its law and order is nothing else. There is a combat of opposite instincts and a golden mean, that is Right. What is the argument for marriage but this? What for a church, a state, or any existing

1 The substance of what follows is found in " Manners " (*Essays,* Second Series, p. 139).

institution, but just this — We must have a mean?

Genius unsettles everything. It is fixed (is it?) that after the reflective age arrives there can be no quite rustic and united man born. Yes, quite fixed. Ah, this unlucky Shakspeare! and ah, this hybrid Goethe! Make a new rule, my dear, can you not? and to-morrow Genius shall stamp on it with his starry sandal.

"Then it is very easy to write as Mr. Pericles writes. Why, I have been reading the books he read before he wrote his Dialogue, and I have traced him in them all and know where he got the things you most admire." Yes, and the turnip grows in the same soil with the strawberry; knows all the nourishment that it gets, and feeds on the very same itself; yet is a turnip still.

All histories, all times, equally furnish examples of the spiritual economy; so does every kitchen and hen-coop. But I may choose then to use those which have got themselves well written. The annals of Poland would be as good to a philosopher as those of Greece, but these last are well composed.

Portableness. The meaner the type by which a spiritual law is expressed, the more pungent it is, and the more lasting in the memories of men, just as we value most the smallest box or case in which any needful utensil can be carried.

The telescope is a screen: that is all. " And when Adam heard the voice of the Lord God in the garden he hid himself."

" Remember to be sober and *to be disposed to believe*; for these are the nerves of wisdom." The reformer affirms the tendency, the law. Vulgar people show much acuteness in stating exceptions. He is not careful to answer them or to show that they are only exceptions. Enough for him that he has an advocate in their consciences also declaring the law. They ought, instead of cavilling, to arm his hands, to thank him in the name of mankind, to see that he is the friend of humanity against their foolish brawling.

Humoring. I weary of dealing with people, each cased in his several insanity. Here is a fine person with wonderful gifts, but mad as the rest, and madder, and, by reason of his great genius,

which he can use as weapon too, harder to deal
with. I would gladly stand to him in relation
of a benefactor as screen and defence to me,
thereby having him at some advantage and on
my own terms — that so his frenzy may not
annoy me. I know well that this wish is not
great but small, is mere apology for not treating
him frankly and manlike: but I am not large
man enough to treat him firmly and unsympa-
thetically as a patient, and, if treated equally and
sympathetically as sane, his disease makes him
the worst of bores.

Quarrels are not composed on their own
grounds, but only by the growth of the character which subverts their place and memory.
We form in the life of a new idea new relations
to all persons; we have become new persons
and do not inherit the wars or the friendships
of that person we were.

"If the misunderstanding could be healed, it
would not have existed," added L.[1]

Unity. Ἓν καὶ πᾶν.[2] Nature is too thin a
screen: the glory of the One breaks through
everywhere.[3]

1 Lidian ?   2 One, yet all.
3 This sentence, first written in the Journal of 1837, is

I remember, when a child, in the pew on Sundays amusing myself with saying over common words as "black," "white," "board," etc., twenty or thirty times, until the word lost all meaning and fixedness, and I began to doubt which was the right name for the thing, when I saw that neither had any natural relation, but all were arbitrary. It was a child's first lesson in Idealism.

August 27.

How noble in secret are the men who have never stooped nor betrayed their faith! The two or three rusty, perchance wearisome, souls, who could never bring themselves to the smallest composition with society, rise with grandeur in the background like statues of the gods, whilst we listen in the dusty crowd to the adroit flattery and literary politics of those who stoop a little. If these also had stooped a little, then had we no examples, our ideas had been all unexecuted: we had been alone with the mind. The solitary hours — who are their favorites? Who cares for the summer fruit, the "sopsavines" that are early ripe by help of the worm at the core? Give me the winter apple, the rus-

printed in "The Preacher" (*Lectures and Biographical Sketches*, p. 223).

settin and pippin, cured and sweetened by all the heat and all the frost of the year.

In regard to H—— I suppose we all feel alike that we care very little what he says, provided only that he says it well. What he establishes with so much ingenuity to-day, we know he will demolish with equal ingenuity to-morrow, not valuing any position or any principle, but only the tactics or method of the fight. Intellectual play is his delight, the question is indifferent. He is a warrior, and so only there be war, he is not scrupulous on which side his aid is wanted. In his oration there was universal attack, chivalry all round the field, but he cut up all so fast and with right good will that he left himself no ground to stand on ; universal offence, but no power of retreat or resistance in him, so that we agreed it was a triumphant success for his troop, but no sincerity, a devastation and no home. It was the profoundness of superficiality, the most universal and triumphant seeming. The sentence which began with an attack on the conservatives ended with a blow at the reformers : the first clause was applauded by one party, and the other party had their revenge and gave their applause before the period was closed.

It is not to be denied that the pious youth who in his closet espouses some rude and harsh reform, such as Anti-slavery or the abstinence from animal food, lays himself open to the witty attacks of the intellectual man; is partial; and apt to magnify his own: yes, and the prostrate penitent also, he is not comprehensive, he is not philosophical in those tears and groans. Yet I feel that under him and his partiality and exclusiveness is the earth and sea and all that in them is, and the axis around which the eternal universe revolves passes through his body there where he stands, while the outcast that affects to pity his narrowness and chains is a wanderer, free as the unloved and the unloving are free and independent of the state, just as bachelors and beggars are homeless, companionless, useless. The heart detects immediately, whether the head find it out or not, whether you exist for purposes of exhibition or are holden by all the force of God to the place you occupy and the thing you do. This abuse of the conservative to win the reformer, and abuse of the reformer to win the conserver, may deceive the head, but not the heart. The heart knows that it is the fear and love of Beacon Street which got this bottle-green flesh-fly, and that only the love and the terror of the Eternal God begets the Angel which it waiteth for.

There is no depth to the intellectual pleasure which this speculation gives. But let in one of those men of love in the shade there, whom you affect to compassionate, and you shall feel instantly how shallow all this entertainment was, for he shall exercise your affection as well as your thought, and confront you with the realities that analyze Heaven and Hell.

Long ago I said, I have every inch of my merits allowed me, and was sad because my success was more than I deserved, — sad for others who had less. Now the beam trembles, and I see with some bitterness the slender claims I can make on fortune and the inevitable parsimony with which they will be answered.

Robin went to the house of his uncle, who was a clergyman, to assist him in the care of his private scholars. The boys were nearly or quite as old as he and they played together on the ice and in the field. One day the uncle was gone all day and the lady with whom they boarded called on Robin to say grace at dinner. Robin was at his wits' end; he laughed, he looked grave, he said something, nobody knew what, and then laughed again, as if to indemnify himself with the boys for assuming one moment the cant of a man. And yet at home perhaps Robin had often said grace at dinner.[1]

The woman spoken of to-day who finds beauty in every household work is right. And why not beauty in the Sunday church? I never wonder that the people like to go thither. I am interested in every shoe that goes into the meeting-house.

Yes, love relieves us of all timidities and superstitious fears by the most confident, mutual prophecy of each other: so that it is suicidal to this extent, that it can do without interviews, which once it existed for.

[Here follows much that is printed in "Manners" (*Essays*, Second Series).]

Character is the one counterpoise to all artificial, or say rather surface distinctions. Let a man be self-reposed and he shames a whole

[1] A reminiscence, no doubt, of the time just before he entered college, when Mr. Emerson was allowed by his uncle, Rev. Samuel Ripley, to assist in his private school at Waltham.

court, a whole city, who are not so. Do not care
for society, and you put it away into your pocket.

I saw a young man who had a rare gift for
pulpit eloquence : his whole constitution seemed
to qualify him for that office, and to see and
hear him produced an effect like a strain of
music : not what he said, but the pleasing efflux
of the spirit of the man through his sentences
and gesture, suggested a thousand things, and
I enjoyed it as I do a painting or poetry, and
said to myself, " Here is creation again." I was
touched and taken out of my numbness and unbelief, and wished to go out and speak and write
all things. After months I heard the favored
youth speak again. Perhaps I was critical, perhaps he was cold. But too much praise I fancied
had hurt him, had given to his flowing gesture
the slightest possible fixedness; to his glowing
rhetoric an artful return. It was later in the season, yet the plant was all in flower still, and no
signs of fruit. Could the flowers be barren, or
was an artificial stimulus kept upon the plant
to convert all the leaves and fruit-buds to flowers? We love young bachelors and maidens, but
not old bachelors and old maids. It seemed to
me that I had seen before an example of the
finest graces of youthful eloquence, hardened by

the habit of haranguing, into grimace. It seemed that if, instead of the certainty of a throng of admirers, the youth had felt assured every Sunday that he spoke to hunger and debt, to lone women and poor boys, to grief, and to the friends of some sick or insane or felonious person, he would have lopped some of these redundant flowers, and given us with all the rest one or two plain and portable propositions. Praise is not so safe as austere exactors, and of all teachers of eloquence the best is a man's own penitence and shame.

There are some public persons born not for privacy, but for publicity, who are dull and even silly in a *tête-à-tête*, but the moment they are called to preside, the form dilates, the senatorial teeth appear, the eye brightens, a certain majesty sits on the shoulders, and they have a wit and happy deliverance you should never have found in them in the closet.

August 31.

I know not why Landor should have so few readers. His book seems to me as original in its form as in its substance. He has no dramatic, no epic power, but he makes sentences, which, though not gravitation and electricity, is still vegetation. After twenty years I still read his strange dialogues with pleasure, not only sentences, but, page after page, the whole discourse.[1] . . .

I value a book which like this or Montaigne proves the existence of a literary world. What boundless leisure, what original jurisdiction, what new heavens and new earth! The old constellations have set, new and brighter have arisen: we have eaten lotus, we have tasted nectar. O that the dream might last! There is no man in this age who so truly belongs to this dispensation as Landor. To the performer this appears luxury; well, when he has quite got his new views through, when he sees how he can mend the old house, we will quit this entertainment. Until then, leave us the land where Horace and Ovid, Erasmus and Scaliger, Izaak Walton and Ben Jonson, Dryden and Pope had their whole existence.

> "In the afternoon we came unto a land
> In which it seemed always afternoon."

But consider, O Reformers, ere you denounce the House of Fame and the land whose intoxi-

[1] Almost the whole of what follows was used by Mr. Emerson in the *Dial* paper, "Walter Savage Landor," printed in *Natural History of Intellect*.

cations Homer and Milton, Plato and Shakspeare have partaken, that a shade of uncertainty
still hangs over all that is actual. Alas, that I
must hint to you that poverty is not an unmixed
good; that labor may easily exceed. The sons
of the rich have finer forms and in some respects a better organization than the sons of the
laborer. The Irish population in our towns is
the most laborious, but neither the most moral
nor the most intelligent: the experience of the
colleagues of Brook Farm was unanimous, " We
have no thoughts."

He who serves some, shall be served by some:
he who serves all, shall be served by all.[1]

When we quarrel, O then we wish we had
always kept our appetites in rein, that we might
speak so coolly and majestically from unques-
tionable heights of character.

Black and White Art. The sibyl[2] treats every
person with some art, flatters them, respects
popular prejudices, accuses rum and slavery, and

---

1 He that feeds men serveth few;
    He serves all who dares be true.
          — *Poems*, " The Celestial Love."
2 Probably his Aunt Mary.

so appears cunning. The little boy who walks with me to the woods, has no design in his questions, the question which is asked in his mind he articulates to me, — over him, over me, — we exist in an element of awe and singleness. Not all children do so. Some have a fraud under their tongue before they can speak plain. But the art of the artist, how differs that from the art of sin? He too has a design on us, but it is not for his benefit, but for ours. That which first charms him and still charms him, he endeavors to convey, so that it shall work on us its legitimate effect. That is worship still.

Well for us that we cannot make good apologies. If I had skill that way, I should spend much of my time at that. Not being able, I leave it with Nature, who makes the best; meantime I am doing something new, which crowns the apology.

Whitewashing. We embellish involuntarily all stories, facts, and persons. In Nature there is no emphasis. By detaching and reciting a fact, we already have added emphasis to it and begun to give a wrong impression, which is inflamed by the new point given every time it is told. All persons exist to society by some shining trait of beauty or utility they have. We borrow the proportions of the man from that one fine feature we see, and finish the portrait symmetrically, which is false; for the rest of his body is small or deformed.

Concord Fight. I had occasion, in 1835, to inquire for the facts that befel on the Nineteenth April, 1775. Doctor Ripley carried me to Abel Davis and Jonas Buttrick and Master Blood. The Doctor carried in his mind what he wished them to testify, and extorted, where he could, their assent to his forewritten History. I, who had no theory, was anxious to get at their recollections, but could learn little. Blood's impression plainly was that there was no great courage exhibited, except by a few. I suppose we know how brave they were by considering how the present inhabitants would behave in the like emergency. No history is true but that which is always true. It is plain that there is little of "*the two o'clock in the morning courage*" which, Napoleon said, he had known few to possess.

These thoughts of which the Universe is the celebration are, no doubt, as readily and thor-

oughly denoted in the nature and habits of animals and in those of plants as in men. The words
dog and snake and crocodile are very significant
to us.

At Cambridge, the last Wednesday, I met
twenty members of my college class and spent
the day with them. Governor Kent of Maine
presided, Upham, Quincy, Lowell, Gardner,
Loring, Gorham, Motte, Wood, Blood, Cheney,
Withington, Bulfinch, Reed, Burton, Stetson,
Lane, Angier, Hilliard, Farnsworth, Dexter,
Emerson. It was strange how fast the company
returned to their old relation, and the whole
mass of college nonsense came back in a flood.
They all associated perfectly, were an unit for
the day — men who now never meet. Each resumed his old place. The change in them was
really very little in twenty years, although every
man present was married, and all but one fathers.
I too resumed my old place and found myself
as of old a spectator rather than a fellow. I
drank a great deal of wine (for me) with the wish
to raise my spirits to the pitch of good fellowship, but wine produced on me its old effect,
and I grew graver with every glass. Indignation
and eloquence will excite me, but wine does not.

One poor man came whom fortune had not favored, and we carried round a hat, and collected one hundred and fifteen dollars for him in two minutes.

Almost all these were prosperous men, but there was something sad and affecting in their prosperity. Very easy it was to see that each owed his success to some one trait or talent not supported by his other properties. There is no symmetry in great men of the first or of the tenth class. Often the division of talents is very minute. One man can pronounce well; another has a voice like a bell and the "orotund tone." Edward Everett's beautiful elocution and rhetoric had charms for the dull. I remember Charles Jarvis in my class, who said "he did not care what the subject was; he would hear him lecture on Hebrew or Persian."

There is this pleasure in a class meeting. Each has been thoroughly measured and known to the other as a boy, and they are not to be imposed upon by later circumstances and acquisitions. One is a governor of a state, one is a president of a college, one is president of a senate, two or three are bank presidents. They have removed from New Hampshire or from Massachusetts or from Vermont into the State where they live. Well, all these are imposing facts in the new neighborhood, in the imaginations of the young men among whom they come; but not for us. When they come into the presence of either of their old mates, off goes every disguise, and the boy meets the boy as of old. This was ludicrously illustrated in the good story Wood told us of his visit to Moody in his office among his clients at Bangor. "How are you, Moody?" with a slap on the back. — "How do you do, sir?" with a stare and a civil but formal bow. "Sir, you have the advantage of me." — "Yes, and I mean to keep it. But I am in no hurry. Go on with your business. I will sit here and look at this newspaper until your client is gone." M. looked up every now and then from his bond and his bondsman, but could not recollect the stranger. By and by they were left alone. "Well," said Wood, "and you have not found me out?" — "Hell!" cried Moody, with the utmost prolongation of accent, "it's Wood!"

What you owe to me — you will vary the phrase — but I shall still recognize my thought. But what you say from the same idea, will have to me also the expected unexpectedness which belongs to every new work of Nature.

Amongst us only the face is well alive : the trunk and limbs have an inferior and subsidiary life, seeming to be only supporters to the head. The head is finished, the body only blocked. Now and then in a Southerner we see a body which is also alive, as in young Eustis. So is it with our manners and letters.

A beautiful woman varies her dress with her mood, as our lovely Walden Pond wears a new weather each time I see it, and all are so comely that I can prefer none. But there must be agreement between the mood and the dress. Vain and forgotten are the fine things if there is no holiday in the eye.

Tropes. Every gardener can change his flowers and leaves into fruit and so is the genius that to-day can upheave and balance and toss every object in Nature for his metaphor, capable in his next manifestation of playing such a game with his hands instead of his brain. An instinctive suspicion that this may befal, seems to have crept into the mind of men. What would happen to us who live on the surface, if this fellow in some new transmigration should have acquired power to do what he now delights to say ? He must be watched.

For me, what I may call the autumnal style of Montaigne keeps all its old attraction.

Your reading you may use in conversation, but your writing should stop with your own thought.

The whole history of Sparta seems to be a picture or text of self-reliance.

Waldo's diplomacy in giving account of Ellen's loud cries declares that she put her foot into his sandhouse, and got pushed.

Democracy. Caius Gracchus, Plutarch says, first among the Romans turned himself in addressing the people from facing the senate-house, as was usual, and faced the Forum.

The trumpet-like lowing of a cow — what does that speak to in me? Not to my understanding. No. Yet somewhat in me hears and loves it well.

I am glad to have guests who can entertain each other, and if I cannot find a second guest in our narrow village to keep the first in play, then I would have pictures, statues, an observ-

atory and telescope, a garden, — somewhat that
can bear the brunt of the stranger's arrival and
allow me to play a second part and be a guest in
my own house. But when the friend shall come,
then the smallest closet in my house is wide
enough for our entertainment.

Has not Pedantry been defined, a transfer-
ence of the language of one district of thought
or action to another district, not in the way of
rhetoric, but from a bigoted belief that it is in-
trinsically preferable? I remember some remark
of Coleridge that is tantamount to this. I easily see that the spirit of life finds equal exercise
in war, in chemistry, or in poetry. I see the law
of Nature equally exemplified in bar-room and
in a saloon of philosophers. I get instruction
and the opportunities of my genius indifferently
in all places, companies and pursuits, so only
that there be antagonism. Yet there would be
the greatest practical inconvenience, if, because
the same law appears indifferently in all, we
should bring the philosophers of the bar-room
and of the saloon together. Like to like.

[Here follows most of the matter printed in
the first two pages of " Character " (*Essays*, Second Series).]

Character is that reserved force which acts only by *Presence*, and not by visible or analysable methods. Samuel Hoar accomplishes everything by the aid of this weapon, not by talent, not by eloquence, not by magnetism. We feel that the largest part of the man has never yet been brought into action. As modern warfare is war of posts and not of battles, so these victories are by demonstration of superiority and not by conflict.

If one should go into State Street or much lower places, he would find that the battle there also is fought and won by the same grand agents.[1] . . .

Lord Bacon's method in his books is of the Understanding, but his sentences are lighted by Ideas.

The fame of Burns also is too great for the facts.

Lotus-eaters. I suppose there is no more abandoned epicure or opium-eater than I. I taste every hour of these autumn days. Every light from the sky, every shadow on the earth, ministers to my pleasure. I love this gas. I grudge to move or

---

1 Here follow other sentences printed in "Character."

to labor or to change my book or to will, lest I should disturb the sweet dream.

Our people are easily pleased: but I wonder to see how rare is any deviation from the routine. . . . If Mr. and Mrs. Wigglesworth go to walk with their family in the mornings they are the speculation of Boston.

The moment is all. The boys like to have their swing of peaches once in the season, and it suffices them; or of plums, or cherries. We like to be rested; we like to be thoroughly tired by labor; I sit on a stone and look at the pond and feel that having basked in a nature so vast and splendid I can afford to decease, and yet the antecedent generations have not quite lost their labor. "In the heat of the battle Pericles smiled on me, and passed on to another detachment." [1]

I find a few passages in my biography noticeable. But it is the present state of mind which selects those anecdotes, and the selection characterizes the state of mind. All the passages will in turn be brought out.

1 Quoted from Landor's *Imaginary Conversations*.

Dr. Osgood said of P's sermon that it was patty cake.

In history the soul spreads itself, enormous, eccentric and allows no rash inductions. The men who evince the force of the moral sentiment and of genius are not normal, canonical people, but wild and Ishmaelitish — Cromwells, Napoleons, Shakspeares, and the like.

The fine doctrine of *availableness* which gave the Whig party John Tyler for their President reaches into the politics of every parish and school district.

In Plutarch's Life of Demosthenes it is quoted from the philosopher that through all his orations runs one idea, that Virtue secures its own success.

Dandies of Moral Sentiment. I, credulous, listened to his fine sentiment and wondered what must be the life of which the ornaments were so costly: and coming again, he lived there no longer: he was now such a tradesman as other tradesmen are, and he recognized my face with patronage and pity.

The fancies of the boy exceed a hundredfold the fruitions of the man.

(From E)

September.

A poet is very rare. I spoke the other day to Ellery's ambition and said, Think that in so many millions, perhaps there is not another one whose thought can flow into music. Will you not do what you are created to do? . . . But Ellery, though he has fine glances and a poetry that is like an exquisite nerve communicating by thrills, yet is a very imperfect artist, and, as it now seems, will never finish anything. He does not even like to distinguish between what is good and what is not, in his verses, would fain have it all pass for good,—for the best,—and claim inspiration for the worst lines. But he is very good company, with his taste, and his cool, hard, sensible behaviour, yet with the capacity of melting to emotion, or of wakening to the most genial mirth. It is no affectation in him to talk of politics, of knives and forks, or of sanded floors, if you will; indeed, the conversation always begins low down, and, at the least faltering or excess on the high keys, instantly returns to the weather, the Concord Reading Room, and Mr. Rice's shop. Now and then something appears that gives you to pause and think. First, I ask myself if it is real, or only a flitting shade of thought, spoken before it was half realized; then, if it sometimes appears, as it does, that there is in him a wonderful respect for mere humours of the mind, for very gentle and delicate courses of behaviour, then I am tempted to ask if the poet will not be too expensive to the man; whether the man can afford such costly self-denials and finenesses to the poet. But his feeling, as his poetry, only runs in veins, and he is, much of the time, a very common and unedifying sort of person.

(From G)

September 4.

Rightly says Elizabeth, that we do not like to hear our authors censured, for we love them by sympathy as well as for cause, and do not wish to have a reason put in the mouth of their enemies. It is excellent criticism and I will write it into my piece.

September 11.

The Poet, The Maker. It is much to write sentences: it is more to add method, and write out the spirit of your life symmetrically. Of all the persons who read good books and converse about them, the greater part are content to say, I was pleased; or I was displeased; it made me active or inactive; and rarely does one eliminate [1] and express the peculiar quality of that life which the book awoke in him. So rare is a general reflection. But to arrange many general reflections in their natural order so that I shall have one homogeneous piece, a *Lycidas*, an *Allegro*, a *Penseroso*, a *Hamlet*, a *Macbeth*, a *Midsummer-Night's Dream*, — this continuity is for the great. The wonderful men are wonderful hereby. The observations that Pythagoras made respecting sound and music are not in themselves unusually acute; but he goes on: adds fact to fact, makes two steps, three, or even four, and every additional step counts a thousand years to his fame.

September 12.

Osman said that when he went a-berrying the devil got into the blueberries and tempted him to eat a bellyful, but if he came to a spring of water he would wash his hands and mouth and promise himself that he would eat no more. Instantly the devil would come to him again in the shape of larger and fairer berriers than any he had

1 It is a curious fact that in many places Mr. Emerson uses *eliminate* as meaning *to separate for use* instead of *to get rid of*.

yet found, and if he still passed them by, he would
bring him blackberries, and if that would not
serve, then grapes. He said, of one thing he was
persuaded, that wisdom and berries grew on the
same bushes, but that only one could ever be
plucked at one time.[1]

Optimates. Sir, said Heavenborn, the amount
of labor you have spent on that piece is disgraceful. For me, not even my industry shall violate
my sentiment. I will sit down in that corner and
perish, unless I am commanded by the universe
to rise and work.

And what became of Heavenborn? What a
pragmatical question! Nothing to tell of: yet I
suppose the new spirit that animates this crop of
young philosophers, and perhaps the fine weather
at this very hour, this thoughtful autumnal air,
may be some of his work, since he is now, as we
say, dead.

Osman. Our low and flat experiences have no
right to speak of what is sacred. Out of a true
reverence, which is all the good we have left us,
we do not recognize the existence of God and
Nature, but do what we can to exterminate them

1 Compare the little poem "Berrying" (*Poems*, p. 41).

from the category of being. If I should ever be better, I will grant you their existence.[1]

But I sympathize with all the sad angels who on this planet of ours are striking work and crying, O for something worthy to do![2] . . .

Life. Osman. We are all of us very near to sublimity. As one step freed Wordsworth's Recluse on the mountains from the blinding mist and brought him to the view of " Glory beyond all glory ever seen," so near are all to a vision of which Homer and Shakspeare are only hints and types, and yet cannot we take that one step. It does not seem worth our while to toil for anything so pitiful as skill to do one of the little feats we magnify so much, when presently the dream will scatter and we shall burst into universal power. The reason of all idleness and of all crime is the same. Whilst we are waiting, we beguile the time, one with jokes, one with sleep, one with eating, one with crimes.

It is pedantry to give such importance to property. Whoso does shows how much he desires

1 This difficult passage Mr. Emerson bracketed. It seems to mean that a tide of doubt may be a humility.

2 The rest of this passage is in "The Transcendentalist" (*Nature, Addresses, etc.,* p. 341).

it. Can I not play the game with these counters
as well as with those? with land and money as
well as with brown bread and serge? A good
wrestler does not need the costume of the ring,
and it is only indifferent writers who are so hard
to be suited with a pen.

"I will not sign any petition that Mr. D. may
hold his office: he and his party have been doing
all they could to destroy my business, and drive
me to saw wood for a living, and now he may saw
wood himself," said my neighbor the manufac-
turer. And that is the repute in which "the solid
part of the community" hold labor. To such
men no wonder that the fact of George Ripley's
association should appear wonderful, men of the
highest cultivation leaving their libraries and going out in blue frocks and cowhide boots into
the barnyard and peat-bog. They think it a
freak, but when they find it lasting, and that the
plans of years are based on it, they revise their
own positions. Antony and Cleopatra, and old
King George III drest themselves in kersey and
went out *incogniti*.

Jones Very told George Bradford that "he
valued his poems, not because they were his, but
because they were not."

"The Transcendentalists do not err in excess, but in defect, if I understand the case. They do not hold wild dreams for realities : the vision is deeper, broader, more spiritual than they have seen. They do not believe with too strong faith : their faith is too dim of sight, too feeble of grasp, too wanting in certainty." (Rev.) Thomas T. Stone's letter to M. M. E., June, 1841.

September 21.

Dr. Ripley died this morning.[1] The fall of this oak of ninety years makes some sensation in the forest, old and doomed as it was. He has identified himself with the forms at least of the old church of the New England Puritans, his nature was eminently loyal, not in the least adventurous or democratical; and his whole being leaned backward on the departed, so that he seemed one of the rear-guard of this great camp and army which have filled the world with fame, and with him passes out of sight almost the last banner and guidon flag of a mighty epoch. For

1 Mr. Emerson's interesting account of his good and hospitable step-grandfather, who had always welcomed him and his mother and brothers to the ancestral home, is printed in *Lectures and Biographical Sketches*, but most of what is printed there is here omitted.

these Puritans, however in our last days they have declined into ritualists, solemnized the heyday of their strength by the planting and the liberating of America.

Great, grim, earnest men, I belong by natural affinity to other thoughts and schools than yours, but my affection hovers respectfully about your retiring footprints, your unpainted churches, strict platforms, and sad offices; the iron-gray deacon and the wearisome prayer rich with the diction of ages.

Well, the new is only the seed of the old. What is this abolition and non-resistance and temperance but the continuation of Puritanism, though it operate inevitably the destruction of the church in which it grew, as the new is always making the old superfluous? . . . He was a punctual fulfiller of all duties. What order, what prudence! No waste, and no stint, always open-handed; just and generous. My little boy, a week ago, carried him a peach in a calabash, but the calabash brought home two pears. I carried him melons in a basket, but the basket came home with apples. He subscribed to all charities; he was the most public-spirited citizen in this town. He gave the land for the monument. He knew the value of a dollar as

well as another man. Yet he always sold cheaper
than any other man. . . .

> " Woe that the linden and the vine should bloom
> And a just man be gathered to the tomb."

But out of his own ground he was not good for
aught. To talk with the insane he was as mad
as they ; to speculate with the thoughtful and
the haters of forms he was lost and foolish. . . .
Credulous and opinionative, a great browbeater
of the poor old fathers who still survived from
the Nineteenth of April in order to make them
testify to his history as he had written it. A
man of no enthusiasm, no sentiment. His hor-
ror at the doctrine of non-resistance was amusing. . . .

He was a man very easy to read, for his whole
life and conversation was consistent and transparent. . . . In college, F. King told me from
Governor Gore, who was the Doctor's classmate, he was called " Holy Ripley," perhaps in
derision, perhaps in sadness, and now in his old
age when all the antique Hebraism and customs
are going to pieces, it is fit he too should depart,
most fit that in the fall of laws a loyal man should
die.

Shall I not say in general of him, that, given

his constitution, his life was harmonious and perfect?

His body is a handsome and noble spectacle. My mother was moved just now to call it " the beauty of the dead." He looks like a sachem fallen in the forest, or rather like "a warrior taking his rest with his martial cloak around him." I carried Waldo to see him, and he testified neither repulsion nor surprise, but only the quietest curiosity. He was ninety years old the last May, yet this face has the tension and resolution of vigorous manhood. He has been a very temperate man. A man is but a little thing in the midst of these great objects of Nature, the mountains, the clouds, and the cope of the horizon, and the globes of heaven, yet a man by moral quality may abolish all thoughts of magnitude and in his manners equal the majesty of the world.

September 28.

Temperament. Every man, no doubt, is eloquent once in his life. The only difference betwixt us is that we boil at different degrees of the thermometer. This man is brought to the boiling-point by the excitement of conversation in the parlor; that man requires the additional caloric of a large meeting, a public debate; and

a third needs an antagonist, or a great indignation; a fourth must have a revolution; and a
fifth nothing less than the grandeur of absolute
Ideas, the splendors of Heaven and Hell, the
vastness of truth and love.

The whole state of society of course depends
on that law of the soul which all must read
sooner or later, — as I am, so I see; my state
for the time must always get represented in my
companion's nuptial, mercantile, or municipal,
as well as in my face and my fortunes.

"A new friend is like new wine; when it is
old thou shalt drink it with pleasure." (Eccle-
siasticus ix, 10.)

(From H)

"One avenue was shaded from thine eyes
    Through which I wandered to eternal truth."

Acquiescence, patience, have a large part to
play. The plenty of the poorest place is too
great, — the harvest cannot be gathered. The
thought that I think excludes me from all other
thoughts. Culture is to cherish a great susceptibility, to turn the man into eyes, but as the
eye can see only that which is eye-form, or of

its own state, we tumble on our walls in every
part of the universe, and must take such luck
as we find, and be thankful. Let us deserve to
see. Too feeble and faint fall the impressions
of Nature on the sense. Let us not dull them
by intemperance and sleep. Too partially we
utter them again : the symbols in which I had
hoped to convey a universal sense are rejected
as partial. What remains but to acquiesce in the
faith that by not lying, nor being angry, we
shall at last acquire the voice and language of a
man.

Sun and moon are the tablets on which the
name and fame of the good are inscribed.

Nature is a silent man.

It would be well if at our schools some course
of lessons in Idealism were given by way of
showing each good Whig the gunpowder train
which lies under the ground on which he stands
so firmly. Let him know that he speaks to
ghosts and phantasms, let him distinguish between a true man and a ghost.

" We do not wake up every morning at four
to write what all the world thinks," said the good
German.

The Inevitableness of the new Spirit is the grand fact, and that no man lays to heart, or sees how the hope and palladium of mankind is there; but one blushes and timidly insinuates palliating circumstances, and one jeers at the foible or absurdity of some of its advocates, — but on comes the God to confirm and to destroy, to work through us if we be willing, to crush us if we resist. No great cause is ever defended on its merits.

If I should take the sum of the Annual Registers, of the Red Books, of the Scientific Associations, of the Lloyds' Lists, and Bicknell's Reporters, I should not get the Age which this pine wood speaks of.

Boston. Natural History Society; Athenæum and Galleries; Lowell Institute; Lyceum; Mechanics' Fair; Cambridge College; Father Taylor; Statehouse; Faneuil Hall; Bookshops; Tremont Theatre.

Men. Taylor, Webster, Bancroft, Frothingham, Reed, Ward.[1]

There is a great destiny which comes in with

1 Rev. Edward Taylor, Rev. Nathaniel L. Frothingham, Sampson Reed, the Swedenborgian, and Samuel Gray Ward.

this as with every age, which is colossal in its
traits, terrible in its strength, which cannot be
tamed, or criticised, or subdued. It is shared
by every man and woman of the time, for it is
by it they live. As a vast, solid phalanx the generation comes on, they have the same features,
and their pattern is new in the world. All wear
the same expression, but it is that which they do
not detect in each other. It is this one life which
ponders in the philosophers, which drudges in
the laborers, which basks in the poets, which
dilates in the love of the women. Fear not but
this is full of romance, the wildest sea, or mountain, or desert — life is not more instinct with
aboriginal force. This is that which inspires
every new exertion that is made. It is this which
makes life sweet to them; this which the am-
bitious seek power that they may control; this
they wish to be rich that they may buy; when
they marry, it is out of love of this; when they
study, it is this which they pore after, and would
read, or would write. It is new in the universe,
it is the attraction of time: it is the wonder of
the Infinite: this is the last painting of the
Creator: calm and perfect it lies on the brow of
the enormous Eternity, and if, in the superior re-
cesses of Nature there be any abode for perma-

nent spectators, what is there they would study but this, — the cumulative result, the new morning with all its dews, rich with the spoils of all foregoing time? Is there not something droll to see the first-born of this age ignorant of the deep, prophetic charm that makes the individual nothing; interrupting the awe and gladness of the time with their officious lamentations that they are critical, and know too much? Are they not torn up in a whirlwind, — borne by its force, they know not whence, they know not whither, yet settling their robes and faces in the moment they fly by me with this self-crimination of *ennui*? If ever anybody had found out how so much as a rye-straw is made! Feeble persons are occupied with themselves, — with what they have knowingly done, and what they propose to do, and they talk much hereof with modesty and fear. The strong persons look at themselves as facts, in which the involuntary part is so much as to fill all their wonder, and leave them no countenance to say anything of what is so trivial as their private thinking and doing. I can well speak of myself as a figure in a panorama so absorbing.

The whole game at which the philosopher busies himself every day, year in, year out, is to find the upper and the under side of every block in his way. Nothing so large and nothing so thin but it has two sides, and when he has seen the outside, he turns it over to see the other face. We never tire of this game, because ever a slight shudder of astonishment pervades us at the exhibition of the other side of the button, — at the contrast of the two sides. The head and the tail are called in the language of philosophy *Finite* and *Infinite*. Visible and Spiritual, Relative and Absolute, Apparent and Eternal, and many more fine names.

The Poet. I was astonished one morning by tidings that Genius had appeared in a youth who sat near me at table.[1] . . .

It is strange how fast *Experience* and *Idea*, the wonderful twins, the Castor and Pollux of our firmament, change places ; one rises and the other instantaneously sets. To-day and for a hundred days Experience has been in the ascendant, and Idea has lurked about the life merely to enhance sensation, the firework-maker, master of the revels, and hired poet of

[1] Here follows the imaginary story told in "The Poet" (*Essays,* Second Series, p. 10).

the powers that be: but in a moment a revolution! the dream displaces the working day and working world, and they are now the dream and this the reality. All the old landmarks are swept away in a flood, and geography and history, the laws and manners, aim and method of society are as fugitive as the colors which chase each other when we close our eyes. All experience has become mere language now. Idea drags it now, a chained poet, to adorn and sing his triumph.

Chilmark. Sir, I have your note for a small debt, can you pay it to-day?

Hyannis. Far otherwise: perhaps you have brought me money.

Chil. No.

Hy. I contracted that debt when I bought and sold; now I protest against the market. The word *pay* is immoral.

Chil. "It is best to be off wi' the old love,
    Before ye be on wi' the new."

In Berlin it was publicly reported at the tea-tables that Fichte had declared his disbelief in the existence of Heinrich Schlossen, who was worth two hundred thousand thalers. Nay, it

was currently whispered that he did not credit
the existence of Madame Fichte.

I stood one day in the Court House talking
with Luther Lawrence when the sheriff introduced through the crowd a number of women
who were witnesses in the trial that was pending.
As they filed rapidly through the crowd, Mr.
Lawrence said, "There go the light troops!"
Neither Plato, Mahomet, nor Goethe have said
a severer thing on our fair Eve. Yet the old
lawyer did not mean to be satanic. The ridicule
lies in the misplacement of our good Angel, in
the violence of direction with which this string
of maids and matrons are coming with hot heads
to testify what gossip they know about Mr.
Gulliver or Mrs. Veal, — being quite dislodged
from that shrine of sanctity, sentiment, and solitude in which they make courts and forums
appear absurd.[1] . . .

I remember Edward Taylor's indignation at
the kind admonitions of Dr. P. The right answer is, 'My friend, a man can neither be praised
nor insulted.'

[1] Here follow sentences printed in "Character" (*Essays,*
Second Series).

On rolls the old world, and these fugitive colors of political opinion, like doves' neck lustres, chase each other over the wide encampments of mankind, Whig, Tory; Pro- and Anti-slavery; Catholic, Protestant; the clamor lasts for some time, but the persons who make it change; the mob remains, the persons who compose it change every moment. The world hears what both parties say and swear, accepts both statements, and takes the line of conduct recommended by neither, but a diagonal line of advance which partakes of both courses.

Aster solidagineus or *solidago bicolor*.[1]

1 Many of the botanical names used by Mr. Emerson are not to be found in Gray's Botany. His manual probably was Dr. Jacob Bigelow's book on the plants in the neighbourhood of Boston.

Scattered through this Journal are notes of flowers or birds probably pointed out by Mr. Thoreau as Nature's Calendar. Compare in "May Day" the lines: —

> Ah! well I mind the Calendar,
> Faithful through a thousand years,
> Of the painted race of flowers,
> Exact to days, exact to hours,
> Counted on the spacious dial
> The broidered zodiac girds, etc.
>
> *Poems*, p. 176.

The Poet. The Idealist at least should be free
of envy ; for every poet is only a ray of his wit,
and every beauty is his own beauty reflected.
He is ever a guest in his own house and his
house is the biggest possible.

Exaggeration is a law of Nature. As we have
not given a peck of apples or potatoes, until we
have heaped the measure, so Nature sends no
creature, no man into the world without adding
a small excess of his proper quality.[1] . . . Every
sentence hath some falsehood of exaggeration in
it. For the infinite diffuseness refuses to be epi-
grammatized, the world to be shut in a word.
The thought being spoken in a sentence becomes by mere detachment falsely emphatic.

G. W. Tyler patronizes Providence.[2] . . . The
Whig party in the Universe concedes that the
Radical enunciates the primal law, but makes no
allowance for friction, and this omission makes
their whole doctrine impertinent. The Whig assumes sickness, and his social frame is a hospi-

1 Then follows a passage thus beginning in "Nature"
(*Essays*, Second Series, pp. 184, 185).

2 Here follow sentences printed in "The Conservative"
on the absence of long sight and elevation of purpose among the
Whigs (*Nature, Addresses, etc.*, p. 319).

tal, his total legislation is for the present distress,
—a universe in slippers and flannels, with bib
and pap-spoon, swallowing pills and herb-tea.
Whig preaching, Whig poetry, Whig philosophy, Whig marriages. No rough, truth-telling
Miltons, Rousseaus.

Blue Heron, loon, and sheldrake come to
Fairhaven Pond; raccoon and otter to Walden.

The merchant will not allow a book in the
counting-house, suspects every taste and tendency but that for goods, has no conversation,
no thought but cotton, qualities of cotton, and
its advance or fall a penny or a farthing. What
a cramping of the form in wooden cap, wooden
belt, and wooden shoes, is this, and how should
not the negro be more a man than one of these
victims? — the negro, who, if low and imperfect
in organization, is yet no wooden sink, but a
wild cedar swamp, rich with all vegetation of
grass and moss and confervæ and ferns and flags,
with rains and sunshine; mists and moonlight,
birds and insects filling its wilderness with life
and promise.

It is plain that none should be rich but those
who understand it. Cushings and Perkinses

ought to be rich, who incline to subscribe to college and railroad, to endow Athenæums, and open public gardens, and buy and exhibit pictures, liberalities which very good and industrious men, who have earned their money a penny or a shilling at a time, would never think of. Yet what are rich men for? It is a most unnecessarily large and cumbrous apparatus for anybody who has not a genius for it to produce no other result than the most simple contrivance of an acre and a cabin.

Every nation, to emerge from barbarism, must have a foreign impulse, a graft on the wild stock, and every man must. He may go to college for it, or to conversation, or to affairs, or to the successes and mortifications of his private biography, war, politics, fishing, or love, — some antagonism he must have as projectile force to balance his centripetence.

Master Cheney [1] says there is the eight-rowed corn, and the twelve-rowed, and the brindled, and the Badger corn, and the Canada corn, and the sweet, and the white, and the Missouri.

1 An old schoolmaster turned farmer, in Concord, father of Mr. Emerson's friend and classmate, John Milton Cheney.

Fifty pounds to the bushel makes corn merchantable, and he weighed a bushel of the Bigelow (?) corn and there were seventy pounds. O Master Cheney! I catch the tune in your talk, and see well that you have no need of poetry. I see its silver thread gleaming in your homespun. You do not break off your flowers. You plough your crops in.

G. W. Tyler [1] came here with all his rattle. The attributes of God, he said, were two, power and risibility. It was the duty of every pious man, he said, to keep up the hoax the best he could, and so to patronize Whiggism, Piety, and Providence, and wherever he saw anything that would help keep the people in order, schools or churches, or poetry, or what-not, he must cry Hist-a-boy! and urge the game on. It was like Eli Robbins's [2] theory of amusements. He sleeps four hours, from three to seven. He outwitted Mr. Greenleaf in the courts. He practised medicine somewhere in the barracks, and, at St. Johns, having in a freak called himself a Free-will Bap-

1 George Washington Tyler. Part of this passage is used in "The Conservative," p. 322.

2 Perhaps one of Mr. Emerson's friendly hearers when he filled the pulpit at East Lexington.

tist, he was immediately carried off to preach at
a meeting, which he did for fifty-five minutes,
and left the audience in tears, and got up a revi-
val. A pound and a half of coffee to a pint of
water, he drinks every night, of the thickness of
molasses, and when he had headache, he piled
a peck of ice on his head, by means of an iron
hoop.

" Fame is the spur that the clear spirit doth raise
  To scorn delights and live laborious days."

The philosopher sat with his face to the East
until cobwebs were spun over the brim of his
pot of porridge. Intemperance is the only vulgarity.

Inaptitude. I will never wonder at Mr. Pick-
ens, who said " he would not go to Mr. R——'s
church until the interesting times were quite
over " (i.e., until the ordination and personal
topics were exhausted). People's personality,
their biography, their brother and sister, uncle
and aunt, are sadly in the way.

The novel of *De Clifford* gave me to think
of aristocracy. I should like to have this and
Pericles and Aspasia circulate freely in this country as lessons in the beauty of behavior which

we greatly need, — lessons on personal merit and manners; but this book is superstitious and has no conception of the despotic power of character.[1] . . . But, in Miss Edgeworth, and in this story of *De Clifford*, the hero in the crisis speaks with the utmost spirit and nature, and so the scene is blood-warm, and does your heart good.

This hold we have on the selfish man, that he always values consequences, reputation, or after-clap of some sort; but the benevolent man never looks so far. Let the self-seeker be never so sharp, this unlucky trick of Nature is sharper than he, and has him on the hip. False connections have some good in them. All our solitudes yield a precious fruit, and this is the most remarkable of all our solitudes. I value the tenderness of a stern nature more than all the tenderness of the susceptible. When such a one is moved, the tears are precious. The only bribe the " community " has for us, is that it permits the association of friends without any compromise on any part, as our other hospitalities do not. We see now sundry persons whose slowness of friendship makes it plain that life is not

1 Here follows a passage printed in " Manners " (*Essays*, Second Series, p. 148).

long enough, with its rare opportunities, that we and they should ever be anything valuable to each other. They are constitutionally good and great, yet only by living in the house with them for years, could we realize the promise we read in their eye. They now are only the Lord's pledge to us that worth exists, and will some-where be available to us. What has life more to offer me than assurance?

I can forgive anything to a deep nature, for they outlive all their foibles and pedantries, and are just as good ten years hence and much bet-ter. Strange it is so hard to find good ones: the profound nature will have a savage rudeness, the delicate one will be shallow or have a great crack running through it, and so every piece has a flaw. I suppose that, if I should see all the gentry of England pass in review, I should find no gentleman and no lady.[1] . . . It must be genius which takes that direction [i.e., friendship]: it must be not courteous, but courtesy; not taste-ful, but taste; not gilt, but gold. O men of buckram and women of blonde, is civilization buckram and is gentleness blonde?

1 The rest of the paragraph is printed in "Manners" (*Essays*, Second Series, pp. 147, 148).

Sarah Alden Ripley is a bright foreigner : she signalizes herself among the figures of this masquerade. I do not hope when I see her to gain anything, any thought : she is choked, too, by the multitude of all her riches, Greek and German, Biot and Bichat, chemistry and philosophy. All this is bright obstruction. But capable she is of high and calm intelligence, and of putting all the facts, all life aloof, as we sometimes have done. But when she does not, and only has a tumultuous time, it is time well wasted. I think her worth throwing time away upon.

Eupatorium, white and red.

I see only two or three persons and allow them all their room : they spread themselves at large to the horizon. If I looked at many, as you do, or compared these habitually with others, these would look less. Yet are they not entitled to this magnificence ? Is it not their own ? And is not munificence the only insight?

We cannot rectify marriage, because it would introduce such carnage into our social relations, and it seems the most rabid Radical is a good Whig in relation to the theory of marriage.

Yet perhaps we can see how the facts stand in Heaven. Woman hides her form from the eyes of men in our world: they cannot, she rightly thinks, be trusted. In a right state the love of one, which each man carried in his heart, should protect all women from his eyes as by an impenetrable veil of indifference. The love of one should make him indifferent to all others, or rather their protector and saintly friend, as if for her sake. But now there is in the eyes of all men a certain evil light, a vague desire which attaches them to the forms of many women, whilst their affections fasten on some one. Their natural eye is not fixed into coincidence with their spiritual eye.

Spiræa tomentosa.

Why do I write another line, since my best friends assure me that in every line I repeat myself? Yet the God must be obeyed even to ridicule. The criticism of the public is, as I have often noted, much in advance of its invention. The ear is not to be cheated. A continuous effect cannot be produced by discontinuous thought, and when the eye cannot detect the juncture of the skilful mosaic, the spirit is apprised of disunion simply by the failure to affect the spirit. This other thing I will also concede, — that the man Fingal¹ is rather too swiftly plastic, or, shall I say, works more in the spirit of a cabinetmaker, than of an architect. The thought which strikes him as great and Dantesque, and opens an abyss, he instantly presents to another transformed into a chamber or a neat parlor, and degrades ideas.

I told Henry Thoreau that his freedom is in the form, but he does not disclose new matter. I am very familiar with all his thoughts, — they are my own quite originally drest. But if the question be, what new ideas has he thrown into circulation, he has not yet told what that is which he was created to say. I said to him what I often feel, I only know three persons who seem to me fully to see this law of reciprocity or compensation, — himself, Alcott, and myself : and 't is odd that we should all be neighbors, for in the wide land or the wide earth I do not know another who seems to have it as deeply and originally as these three Gothamites.

Poetry. But now of poetry I would say, that when I go out into the fields in a still sultry day,

1 Himself, or some other?

in a still sultry humor, I do perceive that the
finest rhythms and cadences of poetry are yet un-
found, and that in that purer state which glim-
mers before us, rhythms of a faery and dreamlike music shall enchant us, compared with which
the finest measures of English poetry are psalm-
tunes. I think now that the very finest and
sweetest closes and falls are not in our metres,
but in the measures of eloquence, which have
greater variety and richness than verse. . . .
Now, alas, we know something too much about
our poetry, — we are not part and parcel of it:
it does not descend like a foreign conqueror from
an unexpected quarter of the horizon upon us,
carry us away with our flocks and herds into a
strange and appalling captivity, to make us, at
a later period, adopted children of the Great
King, and, in the end, to disclose to us that he
was our real parent, and this realm and palace is
really our native country. Yet I please myself
with thinking that there may yet be somewhere
such elation of heart, such continuity of thought,
that a man shall see the little sun and moon
whisk about, making day and night, making
month and month, without heed, in the grandeur of his absorption. Now we know not only
when it is day, and when night, but we hear the

dinner-bell ring with the most laudable punctuality. I am not such a fool but that I taste the joy which comes from a new and prodigious person, from Dante, from Rabelais, from Piranesi, flinging wide to me the doors of new modes of existence, and even if I should intimate by a premature nod my too economical perception of the old thrum, that the basis of this joy is at last the instinct, that I am only let into my own estate, that the poet and his book and his story are only fictions and semblances in which my thought is pleased to dress itself, I do not the less yield myself to the keen delight of difference and newness.

I think that the importance of fine scenery is usually greatly exaggerated, for the astonishing part of every landscape is the meeting of the sky and the earth.[1] . . .

A man in black came in while I spoke and my countenance fell. Then I said, Surely I see that the Swedenborgian finds a sweetness in his church and is enveloped by it in a love and society that haunts him by night and by day, but if the Uni-

1 The rest of this passage, and also the one about "the cool, disengaged air" of natural objects which follows, are printed in "Nature" (*Essays*, Second Series, p. 176 and p. 183).

tarian is invited to go out and preach to Unitarians at Peoria, Illinois, I see no question so fit or inevitable as that he should ask whether they will pay the expense of his journey and maintain him well.[1] . . .

In good society, — say among the angels in Heaven, — is not everything spoken by indirection and nothing quite straight as it befel?[2]

It seems as if the day was not wholly profane, in which I have seen with interest a natural object.[3] . . . At least these things are not drenched in our personalities and village ambition, pay no tax, own no City Bank stock, and need not engage their wood to be sawed. And yet whilst they rescue me from my village, I know that they attract me for somewhat which they symbolize:

1 Here follow long passages which occur in "The Transcendentalist" (*Nature, Addresses, etc.*, pp. 352–354).

2 When visitors, young or old, came with their questions to Mr. Emerson, he never gave categorical answers, but looking beside the questioner, spoke the thought that suggested itself, as Thoreau said, "Listening behind me for my wit," and thus showed new proportions to the problem and set the visitor thinking anew.

3 A sentence or two here is printed in "Nature" (*Essays, Second Series*, p. 172).

that they are not foreign as they seem, but related. Wait a little, and I shall see the return even of this remote and hyperbolic curve.

Margaret Fuller talked of ballads, and our love for them: strange that we should so value the wild man, the Ishmaelite, and his slogan, claymore, and tomahawk rhymes, and yet every step we take, everything we do, is to tame him. It is like Farley's pioneer hatred of civilization, and absconding from it to cut down trees all winter and comfort himself that he was preparing for civilization! Margaret does not think, she says, in the woods, only " finds herself expressed."

One of my stories promised above to embody the history of the times — ' A Life and Times ' — should be that of little Edward Webster, who asked his father one day, after grace had been said at dinner, " Who would say *wis-wis* at dinner when he should be gone to Washington? "

Another of like import in the Chapter of Religion would be Lieutenant Bliss's reply to me when I asked him if they had morning prayers at West Point as at a college? He said, " We have *reveille* beat, which is the same thing."

Of the best jokes of these days is that told of

poor Bokum, that when he went to hire a horse
and chaise at a stable in Cambridge, and the man
inquired whether he should put in a buffalo?
"My God! no," cried the astonished German,
"put in a horse!"

I value Shakspeare, yes, as a Metaphysician,
and admire the unspoken logic which upholds
the structure of Iago, Macbeth, Antony, and the
rest. Is it the real poverty at the bottom of all
this seeming affluence, the headlong speed with
which in London, Paris, and Cochin China, each
seeing soul comes straight through all the thin
masquerade on the old fact, is it the disgust at
this indigence of Nature which makes these rag-
ing livers like Napoleon, Timour, Byron, Tre-
lawney, and John Quincy Adams drive their
steed so hard, in the fury of living to forget the
soupe maigre of life? . . .

It is a bad fact that our editors fancy they
have a right to call on Daniel Webster to resign
his office, or, much more, resign his opinion and
accept theirs. That is the madness of party. I
account it a good sign, indicative of public virtue
in the Whigs, that there are so many opinions
among them, and that they are not organized
and drilled.

There are two directions in which souls move: one is trust, religion, consent to be nothing for eternity, entranced waiting, the worship of Ideas: the other is activity, the busybody, the following of that practical talent which we have, in the belief that what is so natural, easy, and pleasant to us and desirable to others will surely lead us out safely:[1] in this direction lies usefulness, comfort, society, low power of all sorts. The other is solitary, grand, secular. I see not but these diverge from every moment, and that either may be chosen. When I was in college John L. Gardiner said one day that " he had serious thoughts of becoming religious next week, but perhaps he should join the Porcellians." It is no joke: I have often thought the same thing. Whether does Love reconcile these two divergencies? for it is certain that every impulse of that sentiment exalts, and yet it brings all practical power into play. Here I am in a dark corner again. We have no one example of the poetic life realized, therefore all we say seems bloated. If life is sad and do not content us, if the heavens are brass, and rain no sweet thoughts on us, and especially

1 Compare a similar passage in *Natural History of Intellect*, p. 56, in which, however, "the education of the man" takes the place of Trust here.

we have nothing to say to shipwrecked and self-
tormenting and young-old people, let us hold
our tongues. . . . And if to my soul the day
does not seem dark, nor the cause lost, why
should I use such ruinous courtesy as to concede
that God has failed, because the plain colors or
the storm-suit of grey clouds in which the day
is drest, do not please the rash fancy of my companions? Patience and truth, patience with our
own frosts and negations, and few words must
serve. . . . If our sleeps are long, if our flights
are short, if we are not plumed and painted like
orioles and Birds of Paradise, but like sparrows
and plebeian birds, if our taste and training are
earthen, let that fact be humbly and happily
borne with. The wise God beholds that also
with complacency. Wine and honey are good,
but so are rice and meal. Perhaps all that is not
performance is preparation, or performance that
shall be.

October 8.

Exclusives. The close communion Baptists
have a crowded communion: the open communion Unitarians have an empty table. If you
wish to fill your house, make the door so narrow that a fat man cannot get in, and you shall
be sure to be crammed with company.

The " Champion of England " is never called
on until what new boxer has appeared has beaten
all others who have met him in the ring. Then
the existing " Champion " must appear, or for-
feit his dignity and his pension. So the wise man
need never trouble himself about the writings of
the philosophers of the day until they have hit
the white, and come within his bolt.

> " O golden lads and lasses must,
> Like chimney sweepers come to dust."

Riches. Few may be trusted to speak of
wealth. Quicksilver is our gauge of temperature
of air and water, clay is our pyrometer, silver
our photometer, feathers our electrometer, cat-
gut our hygrometer, — but what is our meter
of man, our anthropometer? Poverty is the
mercury. Wealth seems the state of man.

The view taken of Transcendentalism in
State Street is that it threatens to invalidate con-
tracts.

Plutarch's heroes are my friends and rela-
tives.

As we drive it, the artist is in some degree
sacrificed. Michel Angelo, to paint Sistine fres-

coes, must lose for a time the power to read without holding the book over his head, and Doctor Herschel, to keep his eyes for nocturnal observation, must shield them from daylight.

Thomas H. Benton's speeches, and the Protocols of Vienna and St. Petersburg are as much in the circuit of to-day's Universe — have got to be accounted for as are the most vital and beautiful appearance; and the theory of Heaven and Earth can be equally established on the lowest and the highest fact. The permissive as much characterises God as the beloved.

As I looked at the Madonnas and Magdalens in the Athenæum, I saw that for the most part the painter seemed to draw from models, and from such beauties, therefore, as models are likely to be, flesh and color and emotion; but from lordly, intellectual, spiritual beauties, "the great seraphic lords and cherubim" of the sex, no sign but in Raphaels. Yet two or three Greek women, clear, serene, and organically noble as any forms which remain to us on vase or temple, adorn my group and picture of life. And we demand that character shall have nothing muddy or turbid, but shall be transparent, — sublime as God pleases, but not eccentric.

Saturday, *October* 9.

Hippomachus knew a good wrestler by his gait in the street, and an old stager like myself will recognize the subtle Harlequin in his most uncouth frocks, in an Olmsted stove, in a horned ox, in a parliamentary speech, or a bushel of cranberries.

Hurrah for the camera obscura! the less we are, the better we look.

Books, — yes, if worst comes to worst: but not yet. A cup of tea, or a cup of wrath, or a good book will kindle the tinderbox. The poultry must have gravel or egg shells, the swallow and bluebird must have a thread or a wisp of straw for his nest. Have you got the whole beaver, before you have seen his amphibious house? The man is only half himself. Let me see the other half, namely, his expression. Strange, strange, we value this half the most. We worship expressors; we forgive every crime to them. Full expression is very rare. Music, sculpture, painting, poetry, speech, action, war, trade, manufacture is expression. A portrait is this translation of the thing into a new language. What passion all men have to see it done for themselves or others. Now see how small is the list of memorable expressions by book, picture, house, or institution, after so many millions have panted under the Idea!

Elizabeth Hoar consecrates. I have no friend whom I more wish to be immortal than she, an influence I cannot spare, but must always have at hand for recourse. When Margaret mentioned " an expression of unbroken purity," I said, " That is hers." M. replied, " Yes, but she knows." I answer, — Know or know not, the impression she makes is that her part is taken, she has joined herself irrevocably to the sanctities, — to the Muses, and the Gods. Others suggest often that they still balance; their genius draws them to happiness; they contemplate experiment; they have not abdicated the power of election. Opium and honey, the dagger and madness, they like should still lie there in the background, as shadows and possibilities. But Elizabeth's mind is made up, and she has soared into another firmament, and these exist not for her. Bonaparte did not like ideologists : Elizabeth is no poet, but her holiness is substantive and must be felt, like the heat of a stove, or the gravity of a stone: and Bonaparte would respect her.

Life. Is identity tedious? Not if we can see to the life. That always stupefies us with sweet astonishment. A million times since the sun rose have the words "I thank you" been spoken. Yet are they just as graceful and musical in my ear when spoken with living emotion as if now first coined.

Riches. People say law, but they mean wealth.

Genius. The observations of talent are punctures; but, of genius, shafts which unite at the bottom of the mine. But ah! this scud of opinions.

Hope. We sit chatting here in the dark, but do we not all know that the sun will yet again shine, and we shall depart each to our work? God will resolve all doubts, fill all measures.

I would have my book read as I have read my favorite books, not with explosion and astonishment, a marvel and a rocket, but a friendly

ELIZABETH HOAR

and agreeable influence stealing like the scent of a flower, or the sight of a new landscape on a traveller. I neither wish to be hated and defied by such as I startle, nor to be kissed and hugged by the young whose thoughts I stimulate.

Partridge berry, white alder or *Prinos*.

The sum of life ought to be valuable when the fractions and particles are so sweet.

The Daguerreotype is good for its authenticity. No man quarrels with his shadow, nor will he with his miniature when the sun was the painter. Here is no interference, and the distortions are not the blunders of an artist, but only those of motion, imperfect light, and the like.

October 12.

I would that I could, I know afar off that I cannot, give the lights and shades, the hopes and outlooks that come to me in these strange, cold-warm, attractive - repelling conversations with Margaret, whom I always admire, most revere when I nearest see, and sometimes love, — yet whom I freeze, and who freezes me to silence, when we seem to promise to come nearest.[1]

1 See Cabot's *Memoir of Emerson*, pp. 275–279.

October 14.

(From a loose sheet in G)

It is not the proposition, but the tone that signifies. Is it a man that speaks, or the mimic of a man? Universal Whiggery is tame and weak. Every proclamation, dinner-speech, report of victory, or protest against the government it publishes betrays its thin and watery blood. It is never serene nor angry nor formidable, neither cool nor red hot. Instead of having its own aims passionately in view, it cants about the policy of a Washington and a Jefferson. It speaks to expectation, and not the torrent of its wishes and needs, waits for its antagonist to speak that it may have something to oppose, and, failing that, having nothing to say, is happy to hurrah. What business have Washington or Jefferson in this age? . . . They lived in the greenness and timidity of the political experiment. The kitten's eyes were not yet opened. They shocked their contemporaries with their daring wisdom : have you not something which would have shocked *them* ? If not, be silent, for others have.

Passion, appetite, seem to have self-reliance and reality ; but Whiggery is a great fear.

(From H)

I saw in Boston Fanny Elssler in the ballet of
Nathalie. She must show, I suppose, the whole
compass of her instrument, and add to her softest
graces of motion or "the wisdom of her feet,"
the feats of the rope-dancer and tumbler: and
perhaps on the whole the beauty of the exhibition is enhanced by this that is strong and
strange, as when she stands erect on the extremi-
ties of her toes or on one toe, or "performs the
impossible" in attitude. But the chief beauty is
in the extreme grace of her movement, the variety and nature of her attitude, the winning fun
and spirit of all her little coquetries, the beautiful erectness of her body, and the freedom and
determination which she can so easily assume,
and, what struck me much, the air of perfect sympathy with the house, and that mixture of deference and conscious superiority which puts her in
perfect spirits and equality to her part. When she
courtesies, her sweet and slow and prolonged
salaam which descends and still descends whilst
the curtain falls, until she seems to have invented
new depths of grace and condescension, — she
earns well the profusion of bouquets of flowers
which are hurled on to the stage.

As to the morals, as it is called, of this exhibition, that lies wholly with the spectator. The basis of this exhibition, like that of every human talent, is moral, is the sport and triumph of health or the virtue of organization. Her charm for the house is that she dances for them or they dance in her, not being (fault of some defect in their forms and educations) able to dance themselves. We must be expressed. Hence all the cheer and exhilaration which the spectacle imparts and the intimate property which each beholder feels in the dancer, and the joy with which he hears good anecdotes of her spirit and her benevolence. They know that such surpassing grace must rest on some occult foundations of inward harmony.

But over and above her genius for dancing are the incidental vices of this individual, her own false taste or her meretricious arts to please the groundlings and which must displease the judicious. The immorality the immoral will see; the very immoral will see that only; the pure will not heed it, — for it is not obtrusive, — perhaps will not see it at all. I should not think of danger to young women stepping with their father or brother out of happy and guarded parlors into this theatre to return in a few hours to the same; but I can easily suppose that it is not

the safest resort for college boys who have left
metaphysics, conic sections, or Tacitus to see
these tripping satin slippers, and they may not
forget this graceful, silvery swimmer when they
have retreated again to their baccalaureate cells.

It is a great satisfaction to see the best in each
kind, and as a good student of the world, I desire to let pass nothing that is excellent in its own
kind unseen, unheard.

In town I also heard some admirable music.
It seemed, as I groped for the meaning, as if I
were hearing a history of the adventures of fairy
knights, — some Wace, or Monstrelet, or Froissart, was telling, in a language which I very im-
perfectly understood, the most minute and laugh-
able particulars of the tournaments and loves
and quarrels and religion and tears and fate of
airy adventurers, small as moths, fine as light,
swifter than shadows, — and these anecdotes
were illustrated with all sorts of mimicry and
scene-painting, all fun and humor and grief, and,
now and then, the very persons described broke
in and answered and danced and fought and sung
for themselves.

I saw Webster on the street, — but he was
changed since I saw him last, — black as a thun-

der-cloud, and careworn; the anxiety that withers this generation among the young and thinking class had crept up also into the great lawyer's chair, and too plainly, too plainly he was one of us. I did not wonder that he depressed his eyes when he saw me, and would not meet my face. The cankerworms have crawled to the topmost bough of the wild elm and swing down from that. No wonder the elm is a little uneasy.

WATER

The water understands
Civilization well —
It wets my foot, but prettily;
It chills my life, but wittily;
It is not disconcerted,
It is not broken-hearted.
Well used, it decketh joy,
Adorneth, doubleth joy.
Ill used, it will destroy;
In perfect time and measure
With a face of golden pleasure
Elegantly destroy.

On the great Rarity of good Expressions. Fanny Elssler is a good expression. She can say in her language what her neighbors cannot say in theirs.

Part of the reason why Elssler is **so** bewitch-

ing to the gay people is, that they are pinched
and restrained by the decorums of city life, and
she shows them freedom. They walk through
their cotillions in Papanti's assemblies, but
Fanny's arms, head and body dance as well as
her feet, and they are greatly refreshed to see.

I rode to town with some insane people: the
worst of such company is that they always bite
you, and then you run mad also.

The aim of aristocracy is to secure the ends
of good sense and beauty without vulgarity, or
deformity of any kind, but they use a very
operose method. What an apparatus of means
to secure a little conversation.[1] . . .

It would give me no pleasure to sit in your
house, it would give me none to be caressed
by you, so long as this infernal infantry [fine
clothes, dinners, and servants] hinder me from
that dear and spiritual conversation that I desire. There will come a time when these ob-
structions, arising from I know not what cause,
will pass away; if it is a poorness of spirit in me,
I shall be warmed with the wine of God, and

[1] The passage beginning thus is printed in "Nature"
(*Essays*, Second Series, p. 190).

shall walk with a firmer step; if it is some un-
reasonable demand in you, experience will have
reduced your terms to the level of practicability.
The tone, the tone is all. . . .

In writing, the casting moment is of greatest
importance, just as it avails not in Daguerre
portraits that you have the very man before you,
if his expression has escaped.

October 21.

Yet is it not ridiculous, this that we do in this
languid idle trick that we have gradually fallen
into of writing and writing without end? After
a day of humiliation and stripes, if I can write it
down, I am straightway relieved and can sleep
well. After a day of joy, the beating heart is
calmed again by the diary. If grace is given me
by all angels and I pray, if then I can catch one
ejaculation of humility or hope and set it down
in syllables, devotion is at an end.

When the great man comes, he will have that
social strength which Doctor Kirkland or Doctor Franklin or Robert Burns had, and will so
engage us to the moment that we shall not suspect his greatness until late afterward in some
dull hour we shall say, I am enlarged: how dull

was I! Is not of late my horizon wider and new? This man! this man! whence came he!

One thing more. As the solar system moves forward in the heavens, certain stars open before us, and certain stars close up behind us. So is man's life.[1] . . .

October 22.

Would Jesus be received at Almacks? Would the manners of Adam and Eve be admired at the Thuilleries? In the lonely woods I remember London, and think I should like to be initiated in the exclusive circles. There are two ways: one, to conquer them and go as Attila to Rome, or as Napoleon married into the House of Austria: it has this condition that it be of the greatest kind, such conquest as grand genius makes, and so the individual demonstrates his natural aristocracy, best of the best.[2] . . . It must hold its place subject to this condition of refreshing instantly old merits with new ones or making its first stroke one of those strokes for empire which perpetuates position. . . .

1 In this and the next pages, passages are omitted which are printed in the "Lecture on the Times" (*Nature, Addresses, etc.*, pp. 264–267).

2 Here occurs the long passage printed in "Manners" (*Essays*, Second Series, pp. 143, 144).

Fashion is a large region and reaches from the precincts of Heaven to the purlieus of Hell. Mr. Philip Sidney is the presiding deity.

Inhumanity. You come into this company meanly. How so? We have come for the love of seeing each other and of conversing together. You have come to give us things which are written already in your note-books (and when you have told them, you are spent). The best of our talk is invented here, and we go hence greater than we came by so much life as we have awakened in each other; but you, when your quiver is emptied, must sit dumb and careful the rest of the evening. Everything you say makes you poorer, and everything we say makes us richer: you go home, when the company breaks up, forlorn: we go home (without a thought on ourselves) full of happiness to pleasant dreams.

To be sure there is a class of discreet citizens like secret-keeping men, good providers for their households, whom you know where to find: but do not measure by their law this wild influence which I found, to be sure, in space and time, but knew at once it could not be there imprisoned; a nature that lay enormous, indefinite, hastening every moment out of all limitation and to be treated like oxygen and hydrogen, of a diffusive, universal, irrevocable elasticity. He could keep no secret, he could keep no property, he could keep no law but his own.

Margaret is "a being of unsettled rank in the universe." So proud and presumptuous, yet so meek; so worldly and artificial and with keenest sense and taste for all pleasures of luxurious society, yet living more than any other for long periods in a trance of religious sentiment; a person who, according to her own account of herself, expects everything for herself from the Universe.

October 23.

Milton describes religion in his time as leaving the tradesman when he goes into his shop to meet him again when he comes out. . . . In so pure a church as the Swedenborgian I cannot help feeling the neglect which leaves holiness out of trade. These omissions damn the church.[1]

We forget in taking up a contemporary book that we see the house that is building and not the

1 The passage thus beginning and much that is omitted below are printed in the "Lecture on the Times" (*Nature, Addresses, etc.*, pp. 273–275).

house that is built. A glance at my own manuscripts might teach me that all my poems are unfinished, heaps of sketches but no masterpiece, yet when I open a printed volume of poems I look imperatively for art.

I think Society has the highest interest in seeing that this movement called the Transcendental is no boys' play or girls' play, but has an interest very near and dear to him; that it has a necessary place in history, is a Fact not to be overlooked, not possibly to be prevented, and, however discredited to the heedless and to the moderate and conservative persons by the foibles or inadequacy of those who partake the movement, yet is it the pledge and the herald of all that is dear to the human heart, grand and inspiring to human faith.

I think the genius of this age more philosophical than any other has been, righter in its aims, truer, with less fear, less fable, less mixture of any sort.

October 24.

Permanence is the nobility of human beings. We love that lover whose gayest love-song, whose fieriest engagement of romantic devotion is made good by all the days of all the years of strenuous

long-suffering, ever-renewing benefit. The old
Count said to the old Countess of Ilchester, " I
know that wherever thou goest, thou wilt both
trust and honor me, and thou knowest that wherever I am, I shall honor thee."

We read either for antagonism or for confir-
mation. It matters not which way the book works
on us, whether to contradict and enrage, or to
edify and inspire. " Bubb Dodington " is of the
first class, which I read to-day. A good indignation brings out all one's powers.

Everybody, old men, young women, boys, play
the doctor with me and prescribe for me. They
always did so.

*Life in Boston; A play in two acts. Youth and
Age.* Toys, dancing school, *sets*, parties, picture-
galleries, sleigh-rides, Nahant, Saratoga Springs,
lectures, concerts, — *sets* through them all; solitude and poetry, friendship, *ennui*, desolation, decline, meanness; plausibility, old age, death.

In the republic must always happen what happened here, that the steamboats and stages and
hotels vote one way and the nation votes the other:

and it seems to every meeting of readers and writers as if it were intolerable that Broad Street Paddies and bar-room politicians, the sots and loafers and all manner of ragged and unclean and foulmouthed persons without a dollar in their pocket should control the property of the country and make the lawgiver and the law. But is that any more than their share whilst you hold property selfishly? They are opposed to you: yes, but first you are opposed to them: they, to be sure, malevolently, menacingly, with songs and rowdies and mobs; you cunningly, plausibly, and wellbred; you cheat and they strike; you sleep and eat at their expense; they vote and threaten and sometimes throw stones, at yours.

Were you ever daguerrotyped, O immortal man? And did you look with all vigor at the lens of the camera, or rather, by the direction of the operator, at the brass peg a little below it, to give the picture the full benefit of your expanded and flashing eye? and in your zeal not to blur the image, did you keep every finger in its place with such energy that your hands became clenched as for fight or despair, and in your resolution to keep your face still, did you feel every muscle becoming every moment more rigid; the brows

contracted into a Tartarean frown, and the eyes
fixed as they are fixed in a fit, in madness, or in
death? And when, at last you are relieved of
your dismal duties, did you find the curtain
drawn perfectly, and the coat perfectly, and the
hands true, clenched for combat, and the shape
of the face and head? — but, unhappily, the total
expression escaped from the face and the portrait of a mask instead of a man? Could you not
by grasping it very tight hold the stream of a
river, or of a small brook, and prevent it from
flowing?

I told Garrison that I thought he must be a
very young man, or his time hang very heavy
on his hands, who can afford to think much and
talk much about the foibles of his neighbors, or
'*denounce*,' and play 'the son of thunder' as he
called it. I am one who believe all times to be
pretty much alike, and yet I sympathize so
keenly with this. We want to be expressed, yet
you take from us war, that great opportunity
which allowed the accumulations of electricity
to stream off from both poles, the positive and
the negative, — well, now you take from us our
cup of alcohol, as before you took our cup of
wrath. We had become canting moths of peace,

our helm was a skillet, and now we must become temperance water-sops. You take away, but what do you give? Mr. Jefts has been preached into tipping up his barrel of rum into the brook, but day after to-morrow when he wakes up cold and poor, will he feel that he has somewhat for somewhat! No, this is mere thieving. . . . If I could lift him by happy violence into a religious beatitude, or into a Socratic trance and imparadise him in ideas, or into the pursuit of human beauty, a divine lover, then should I have greatly more than indemnified him for what I have taken. I should not take; he would put away, or rather ascend out of this litter and sty, in which he had rolled, to go up clothed and in his right mind into the assembly and conversation of men. I fight in my fashion, but you, O Paddies and roarers, must not fight in yours. I drink my tea and coffee, but as for you and your cups, here is the pledge and the Temperance Society. I walk on Sundays, and read Aristophanes and Rabelais in church hours: but for you, Go to church. Good vent or bad we must have for our nature. . . . Make love a crime, and we shall have lust. If you cannot contrive to raise us up to the love of science and make brute matter our antagonist which we shall have joy in handling, mastering, penetrating, condensing to adamant, dissolving to light, then we must brawl, carouse, gamble, or go to bull-fights. If we can get no full demonstration of our heart and mind, we feel wronged and incarcerated: the philosophers and divines we shall hate most, as the upper turnkeys. We wish to take the gas which allows us to break through your wearisome proprieties, to plant the foot, to set the teeth, to fling abroad the arms, and dance and sing.

[Here follow many passages printed in "The Transcendentalist," and the "Lecture on the Times."]

Society ought to be forgiven if it do not love its rude unmaskers. The Council of Trent did not love Father Paul Sarpi. "But I show you," says the philosopher, "the leprosy which is covered by these gay coats." "Well, I had rather see the handsome mask than the unhandsome skin," replies Beacon Street. Do you not know that this is a masquerade? Did you suppose I took these harlequins for the kings and queens, the gods and goddesses they represent? I am not such a child. There is a terrific skepticism at the bottom of the determined conservers.

The Rhine of our Divinity School has strangely lost itself in the sands. A man enters the Divinity School, but knows not what shall befall him there, or where he shall come out of its tortuous track. Some reappear in trade, some in the navy, some in Swedenborg chapels, some in landscape painting.

Confide to the end in spiritual, and not in carnal weapons. It needs not to fight the battle of anti-slavery on the question of the seat in the cars: the doctrine advances every day among all people that a high chair, a platform, a strip of gold lace, a sword, a title, is not to protect an individual; but himself alone, his ability, his knowledge, his character. A clown, an idiot, may sit next him: he is begirt with an army of guards in the faculties and influences of his spirit: how can they contaminate him? Presently a man will commonly put his pride in sitting in low seats, in mean dress, in mean company, with mulattoes and blacks; and the legislature or the anti-slavery society will not need to interfere.

"What are you doing, Zeke?" said Judge Webster to his eldest boy.
"Nothing."

" What are you doing, Daniel ? "

" Helping Zeke."

A tolerably correct account of most of our activity to-day.

It seems to me sometimes that we get our education ended a little too quick in this country. As soon as we have learned to read and write and cipher, we are dismissed from school and we set up for ourselves. We are writers and leaders of opinion and we write away without check of any kind, play whatsoever mad prank, indulge whatever spleen, or oddity, or obstinacy, comes into our dear head, and even feed our complacency thereon, and thus fine wits come to nothing, as good horses spoil themselves by running away and straining themselves. I cannot help seeing that Doctor Channing would have been a much greater writer had he found a strict tribunal of writers, a graduated intellectual empire established in the land, and knew that bad logic would not pass, and that the most severe exaction was to be made on all who enter these lists. Now, if a man can write a paragraph for a newspaper, next year he writes what he calls a history, and reckons himself a classic incontinently, nor will his contemporaries in critical Journal or Review question his claims. It is

very easy to reach the degree of culture that
prevails around us; very hard to pass it, and
Doctor Channing, had he found Wordsworth,
Southey, Coleridge, and Lamb around him,
would as easily have been severe with himself
and risen a degree higher as he has stood where
he is. I mean, of course, a genuine intellectual
tribunal, not a literary junto of Edinburgh wits,
or dull conventions of Quarterly or Gentleman's
Reviews. Somebody offers to teach me mathematics. I would fain learn. The man is right. I
wish that the writers of this country would begin where they now end their culture.

Are the writers, then, to be reproached with
writing to the English public? No, but to be
congratulated. It shows they oversee their own,
and propose to themselves the best existing
standard.

Our Contemporaries. As Charles said, we have
one set. It takes time to learn their names and
allow for their humors so as to draw the most
advantage from them. We all know the same
stories, have read the same books, know the
same politics, churches, geniuses, felons, bores,
hoaxes, gossip, so that there is nothing to explain, but we can fall into conversation very

quickly and get and give such information by the road as we want without needing to collect lexicons and dragomans when we wish to ask the way to the next village.

October 28.

Good not to let the Conscience sleep, but to keep it irritated by the presence and reiterated action of reforms and ideas.

Ellen H. asks "whether Reform is not always in bad taste?" Oh no, the poet, the saint are not only elegant, but elegance. It is only the half poet, the half saint, who disgust. Thus now, the saint in us proposes, but the sinner in us executes so lamely. But who can be misled who trusts to a thought? That profound deep whereunto it leads is the Heaven of Heavens. On that pillow, softer than darkness, he that falls can never be bruised.

I told C. and M. that Aunt Mary was no easy flute, but a quite national and clanlike instrument; a bagpipe, for instance, from which none but a native Highlandman could draw music.

I sometimes fancy that the bitterness and prosaic side of our condition only obtrude in our conversation, or attempt to paint our portrait to another. Silent and alone, I have no such sad, unredeemed side.

Remove two miles, if you suffer from the influences of Fashion.[1] . . .

Why should I still postpone my existence and not take the ground to which I already feel that I am at last entitled? Why do I suffer a reference to others, and to *such* others, to keep me out of that which is most mine? Because, dear friend, it is as yet a thought, and not yet a spirit. You have not quite served up to it.

A foundation and cellar are good when one is going to build a house, but what is a foundation without a house but an offence to the eye and a stumbling-block to the feet?[2] Sensation is good as the organ, the servant, the body of the Soul, but a world of sensations is a world of men without heads. Once they dined, that they might pray and praise, and so dining the function itself was prayer and praise: now they

1 The rest of this paragraph is printed in "Manners" (*Essays*, Second Series, pp. 152, 153).

2 This passage is the conclusion of one printed in "Nature" (*Essays*, Second Series, pp. 191, 192).

dine that they may dine again, and pray and praise (as they call it) in order that they may dine. Hence the appearance — which everywhere strikes the eye of an aimless society, an aimless nation, an aimless world. The earth is sick with that sickness. The man was made for activity, and action to any end has some health and pleasure for him.

Calculation, if that would only go far enough, would go for enthusiasm too. We only ask arithmetic to go on, not to stop and bolt, and the conclusions of the broker and of the poet shall be one. We are not Manichæans, not believers in two hostile principles, but we think evil arises from disproportion, interruption, mistake of means for end. Is Transcendentalism so bad? And is there a Christian, or a civilian, a lawyer, a naturalist, or a physician so bold as not to rely at last on Transcendental truths? He dares not say it, the blind man.

We can well enough discuss this topic with any one because we believe we are all too deeply implicated for any man to give himself airs and talk down to the rest.[1] . . .

1 Here follow passages printed in the " Lecture on the Times " with regard to uncharitable philanthropy.

" *Donde hai tu pigliato tante coglionerie ?* " And
where did you pick up all this heap of frip-
peries, Messer Lodovico Ariosto? said the duke
to the poet. " Here in your court, your High-
ness," he replied. I own that all my universal
pictures are nothing but very private sketches ;
that I live in a small village, and am obliged to
guess at the composition of society from very
few and very obscure specimens, and to tell
Revolutions of France by anecdotes, etc., etc.
Yet I supposed myself borne out in my confidence that each individual stands for a class by
my own experience. Few as I have seen, I could
do with fewer, and I shrink from seeing thousands when in fifteen or twenty I have already
many duplicates.

We are very near to greatness : one step and
we are safe : can we not take the leap?

Daguerre. The strangeness of the discovery
is that Daguerre should have known that a picture was there when he could not see any. When
the plate is taken from the camera, it appears
just as when it was put there spotless silver : it
is then laid over steaming mercury and the picture comes out.

'T is certain that the Daguerreotype is the
true Republican style of painting. The artist

stands aside and lets you paint yourself. If you make an ill head, not he but yourself are responsible, and so people who go Daguerreotyping have a pretty solemn time. They come home confessing and lamenting their sins. A Daguerreotype Institute is as good as a national Fast.¹

False valuations are not in Nature; a pound of water in the ocean tempest or in the land-flood has no more momentum than in a mid-summer pond.² . . .

We are equal to something, if it is only silence, waiting, and dying. Let us do that. The piece must have shades too. When the musicians are learning their first scores, every one wishes to scream, and country orchestras usually have a reasonable volume of voice. Afterwards, they learn to be still and to sing underparts. Perhaps we may trust the Composer of our great music to give us voice when our aid is needed,

1 Though the beautiful sun-portraits of Daguerre's invention always appealed to Mr. Emerson's imagination, he hated to sit himself; said that his pictures showed that he was " no subject for art, but looked like a pirate."

2 The rest of the passage is in "Character" (*Essays,* Second Series, p. 101).

and to apply the bellows to other stops when we should mar the harmony. . . .

Do what you can, and the world will feel you: speak what you must, and only that, and the echoes will ring with music.

There is so much *ennui* that I am persuaded if any sign could appear in Nature of decay, imperfect chemistry, or the like, men are very ready to believe that the best age is gone. But the youth of Nature which astounds the imagination repudiates the thought.

There are three wants which can never be satisfied: that of the traveller, who says, "*Anywhere but here*"; that of the rich who wants *something more;* and that of the sick who wants *something different.*

The willing or acquiescent are certainly better candidates for that idea which is creating the new world than the recalcitrating.

Steam should be solid.

Every man somewhere solid.

Poor men at six hours, six weeks, six months, six years.

Scholars should not carry their memories to balls.

Do you not believe that advertisements are given you continually of that which most imports you to know; but you, in the din and buzz of the senses, do not regard the vision? Miracles are continually occurring in the privatest spiritual experience which the man heeds not in his headlong partisan fury to celebrate and assert the miracles of the Church. By attention and obedience to the heavenly vision he would bring his perception to a finer delicacy.

Why Cupid did not assault the Muses may be found in Rabelais, 3d vol., p. 25.

October 30.

On this wonderful day when Heaven and Earth seem to glow with magnificence, and all the wealth of all the elements is put under contribution to make the world fine, as if Nature would indulge her offspring, it seemed ungrateful to hide in the house. Are there not dull days enough in the year for you to write and read in, that you should waste this glittering season when Florida and Cuba seem to have left their seats and come to visit us, with all their shining Hours, and almost we expect to see the jasmine and the cactus burst from the ground instead of these last gentians and asters which have loitered to attend this latter glory of the year? All insects are out, all birds come forth, — the very cattle that lie on the ground seem to have great thoughts, and Egypt and India look from their eyes.[1]

"How dare I go to a person who will look at me only as a psychological fact?" said the thread-woman of G. R., and said well. But alas, that this awe which the writers inspire should prove at last to be so ill-founded! They ought to inspire most reverence when seen, and when they can thunder so loud at a distance not cheep so small in the chamber. "Ah! if they knew John as well as I!" said Mrs. M—— Good Paul whose letter was so mighty, and whose bodily presence mean and contemptible, has too many imitators.

The Age. Shelley is wholly unaffecting to me. I was born a little too soon: but his power is so

[1] This passage, although much of it appears in the opening page of the essay " Nature " (in the Second Series), is preserved because of the freshness and beauty of its expression on *the day of the experience.*

manifest over a large class of the best persons, that he is not to be overlooked.

There are tests enough of character if we really dare to apply them. Are you setting your expectation of happiness on any circumstance or event not within your control?

Vagueness of Character. I overheard Jove one day talking of destroying the Earth.[1] . . .

Soldier. Can one nowadays see a soldier without a slight feeling — the slightest possible — of the ridiculous?

The spiritual measure of inspiration is the depth of the thought: How deep? — how great its power to agitate and lift me? and never, *Who* said it? But the world answers, "Paul was inspired," and would crave a space and indulgence for him in my consciousness. I reply, I do not know the man. It makes then a claim for Jesus. But the great soul says, He shall not come in, no man shall come in, how amiable, how holy soever.

1 Here follows the fable with which " Manners " concludes (*Essays*, Second Series).

Skepticism esteems ignorance organic and irremovable, believes in the existence of pure malignity, believes in a poor decayed God who does what he can to keep down the nuisances, and to keep the world going for our day. It believes the actual to be necessary; it argues habitually from the exception instead of the rule; and, if it went to the legitimate extreme, the earth would smell with suicide.

To believe in luck, if it were not a solecism so to use the word *believe*, is skepticism.

Sickness also has its hero and brilliant vindication. Fontenelle, born feeble, a puny delicate creature, by care and nursing was preserved for a hundred years to be the delight of France and of Europe — laid up, they said, like a vase of porcelain in a cabinet and railed up and guarded to hold the softest and most volatile of perfumes. Mr. Pope also was born sick and a cripple, yet by care and study of these facts, and engaging, wherever he went, nursing and rubbing from the domestics, he lived long and enjoyed much and gave others much to enjoy.

Dandies of Moral Sentiment. Our contemporaries do not always contemporize us, but now one is continually surprised to find some stranger, who has been educated in the most different manner, dreaming the same dream.

We like all the better to see some graceful youth, free and beautiful as a palm or a pine tree, who hears with curiosity and intelligence our theory of the world and has his own, and does not hiss with our hiss, but only has the same mother-tongue.

Yet do not mistake a fine tulip for good timber. Do not fancy when you have vivacity and innocence and the charm of youthful manners, and have got for the time the ear of such an one to the gravest themes, do not rely on this polite and facile stripling as on a native and hereditary scholar. The newcomer for the moment casts all merits into eclipse, and the heart gives itself so gladly to the hope of indefinite and paradisaical times at hand. But none can adhere but the men that are born of that idea which they express.

But there are ways of anticipating Time. Always this cry of "Time, Time; give us time: men are not ready for it," means deficiency of spiritual force. Time is an inverse measure of the amount of spirit. If you are sure of your truth, if you are sure of yourself, you ascend now into eternity; you have already arrived at that, and that *takes place* with you which other men promise themselves.

In poetry we say we require the miracle. The bee flies among the flowers and gets mint and marjoram, and generates a new product which is not mint or marjoram but honey: and the chemist mixes hydrogen and oxygen to yield a new product which is not hydrogen or oxygen but water: and the poet listens to all conversations and receives all objects of Nature to give back, not them, but a new and perfect and radiant whole.

We concede, O Miss P.,[1] there is a difference between the spirit in which these poor men struggling to emancipate themselves from the yoke of a traditional worship, and crying out in their sorrow and hope, speak at the Chardon Street Convention, and the spirit in which he who is long already free from these fears turns

1 Miss Peabody? Apparently Miss Elizabeth Peabody had been troubled by Mr. Emerson's notice in the *Dial* of the Convention held in Boston the previous year, by the assembled friends of Universal Reform, as unsympathetic and holding of well-meaning people up to ridicule. (See *Lectures and Biographical Sketches*, pp. 371–377.

back and knowingly shoots sarcasms at the old
and venerated names.

"*That Influence which every Strong Mind has
over a Weak One.*" You believe in magnetism,
in new and preternatural powers, powers contrary to all experience, and do you not think
then that Cæsar in irons can shuffle off the
irons?[1] . . .

The new vegetable is always made out of the
materials of the decomposed vegetable, and the
triumph of thought to-day is over the ruin of
some old triumph of thought. I saw a man who
religiously burned his Bible and other books:
and yet the publication of the Bible and Milton
and the rest was the same act, namely, the burning of the then books of the world which had
also once been a cremation of more.

Our American geography is so large that the
noisy make no noise. Whoever hears of the
American army? or of the formidable Sopho-
mores who are said to rebel in our colleges? or
of the Law Students, or the Medical Students,
or of any other local village incendiaries who,

[1] Here follows the passage printed in "Character" (pp.
94, 95).

when we were young, filled whole neighbor-
hoods with alarm? The American Government
is fast becoming quite as innocent.

What can be affirmed of magnetisable subjects? To-day, seen unaffected, they are larvæ;
they are so low and earthy and bestial, they bark
and neigh, a good man or a poet is repelled who
goes near them, as if they would one day be
his executioners. But to-morrow, a great spirit
chances to approach them in a happy and un-
suspected way, and they receive his light and
influence into all the channels of their being and
are filled with him, enriched and ennobled by
this virtue, they are godlike, and he too is twice
himself. Straightway the earth seems to have
emerged from the primal curse and a new day
has dawned.

Great causes are never tried, assaulted, or defended on their merits : they need so long perspective, and the habits of the race are marked
with so strong a tendency to particulars. The
stake is Europe or Asia, and the battle is for
some contemptible village or dog-hutch. A man
shares the new light that irradiates the world and
promises the establishment of the Kingdom of

Heaven,—and ends with champing unleavened bread or devoting himself to the nourishment of a beard, or making a fool of himself about his hat or his shoes. A man is furnished with this superb case of instruments, the senses, and perceptive and executive faculties, and they betray him every day. He transfers his allegiance from Instinct and God to this adroit little committee. A man is an exaggerator. In every conversation see how the main end is still lost sight of by all but the best, and with slight apology or none, a digression made to a creaking door or a buzzing fly. What heavenly eloquence could hold the ear of an audience if a child cried! A man with a truth to express is caught by the beauty of his own words and ends with being a rhymester or critic. And Genius is sacrificed to talent every day.

[Here follows the passage about Osman, the ideal man, and the broad hospitality to persons half-crazed with poor reforms which is printed in the last pages of "Manners."]

November 10.

Genius is very well, but it is enveloped and undermined by Wonder. The last fact is still

Astonishment, — mute, bottomless, boundless, endless wonder. When we meet an intelligent soul, all that we wish to ask him — phrase it how we will — is, 'Brother have you wondered? Have you seen the Fact?' To come out from a forest in which we have always lived, unexpectedly on the ocean, startles us, for it is a symbol of this. . . .

Originality. All originality is relative.[1]

The young people complain that everything around them must be denied, and therefore, if feeble, it takes all their strength to deny, before they can begin to lead their own life. Aunt Betsey and Uncle Gulliver insist on their respect to this Sabbath and that Rollin's History or Fragment Society or some other school, or charity, or morning call, which, to preserve their integrity, they resist.[2]

Nature never troubles herself with the difficulty which Language finds in expressing her.

1 The passage beginning thus is printed in " Shakspeare " (*Representative Men*, pp. 198, 199).

2 The long passage beginning thus is, with slight variations, printed in "The Transcendentalist" (pp. 356, 357).

Man begets man who begets man, heedless of
the world of contradictions which the metaphysician finds in this cotemporaneous procession
of body, soul, and mind.

Is Character an educated will? "But bad
thoughts," said M., "Who could dare to uncover all the thoughts of a single hour?" Indeed!
is it so bad? I own that to a witness worse than
myself and less intelligent, I should not willingly
put a window into my breast, but to a witness
more intelligent and virtuous than I, or to one
precisely as intelligent and well intentioned, I
have no objection to uncover my heart.

Certainly the progress of character is in that
direction, namely, to introduce Beauty, the order of Beauty, into that invisible and private
world of my thoughts, and make them public
and heavenly in their discipline. It is a part of
friendship with me to carry its courtesies and
sacred boundaries into my silent solitude, and
not confound distinctions in my fancy which I
respect in my reason.

November 13.

Originality. The great majority of men are
not original, for they are not primary, have not
assumed their own vows, but are secondaries, —

grow up and grow old in seeming and following; and when they die they occupy themselves to the last with what others will think, and whether Mr. A and Mr. B will go to their funeral. The poet has pierced the shows and come out on the wonder which envelopes all: more, he has conspired with the high cause and felt the holy glee with which man detects the ultimate oneness of the Seer and the spectacle. . . .

As to the *Miracle*, too, of Poetry. There is truly but one miracle, the perpetual fact of Being and Becoming, the ceaseless saliency, the transit from the Vast to the particular, which miracle, one and the same, has for its most universal name the word *God*. Take one or two or three steps where you will, from any fact in Nature or Art, and you come out full on this fact; as you may penetrate the forest in any direction and go straight on, you will come to the sea. But all the particulars of the poet's merit, his sweetest rhythms, the subtlest thoughts, the richest images, if you could pass into his consciousness, or rather if you could exalt his consciousness, would class themselves in the common chemistry of thought, and obey the laws of the cheapest mental combinations.

In every moment and action and passion, you must be a man, must be a whole Olympus of gods. I surprised you, O Waldo Emerson, yesterday eve hurrying up one page and down another of a little book of some Menzel, panting and straining after the sense of some mob, better or worse, of German authors. I thought you had known better. Adhere, sit fast, lie low.

Anti-Transcendentalists. Yet we must not blame those who make the outcry against these refiners. It comes from one of two causes: either an instinctive fear that this philosophy threatens property and sensual comfort; or a distrust of the sincerity and virtue of persons who preach an impracticable elevation of life.

If from the first, it is a good sign, an eulogy of the innovators which should encourage them. And let them not be too anxious to show how their new world is to realize itself to men, but know that, as the Lord liveth, it shall be well with them who obey a spiritual law.

If from the second,—why, perhaps the world is in the right, and the reformer is not sound. There is an instinct about this too. It is in vain that you gild gold and whiten snow in your preaching, if, when I see you, I do not look through your pure eye into a society of angels and angelic thoughts within.

No man can write anything who does not think that what he writes is for the time the history of the world,[1] . . . or do anything well who does not suppose his work to be of greatest importance. My work may be of none, but I must not think it of none, or I shall not do it with impunity.

Whoso does what he thinks mean, is mean.

How finely we are told in the Hebrew story that the anger of the Lord was kindled against David because he had made a census of the people. Philosophy also takes an inventory of her possessions: and an inventory is of pride: it is the negative state. But Poetry is always affirmative, and Prayer is affirmative.

How much of life is affirmative? How many dare show their whole hand? For the most part we hide, and parry as we can the inquisition of each other.

I am for preserving all those religious writings which were in their origin poetic, ecstatic

[1] See "Nature" (*Essays*, Second Series, p. 189).

expressions which the first user of did not know what he said, but they were spoken through him and from above, not from his level; things which seemed a happy casualty, but which were no more random than the human race are a random formation. "It is necessary," says Iamblichus, "that ancient prayers, like sacred *asyla*, should be preserved invariably the same, neither taking anything from them nor adding anything to them which is elsewhere derived."

This is the reason, doubtless, why Homer declares that Jove loved the Ethiopians. And Iamblichus in answer to the query, "Why of significant names we prefer such as are barbaric to our own?" says, among other reasons: "Barbarous names have much emphasis, great conciseness, and less ambiguity, variety, and multitude"; and then afterwards: "But the Barbarians are stable in their manners, and firmly continue to employ the same words. Hence they are dear to the gods, and proffer words which are grateful to them." And the ancients spoke of the Egyptians and Chaldæans as "sacred nations."

Now the words "God," "Grace," "Prayer," "Heaven," "Hell," are these barbarous and sacred words, to which we must still return, whenever we would speak an ecstatic and universal sense? There are objections to them, no doubt, for academical use, but when the professor's gown is taken off, Man will come back to them.

The granite comes to the surface and towers into the highest mountains, and if we could dig down we should find it below all the superficial strata.[1] . . .

The question of Property wants seers. . . . The staunchest Whig and the poorest philosopher are all on the Property side, all abettors of the present abuse, all either owners or enviers: no man is on the other side, no man can give us any insight into the remedy, no man deserves to be heard against Property; only Love, only an Idea, is on the right side against Property as we hold it.

Good scholar, what are you for but for hospitality to every new thought of your time? Have you property, have you leisure, have you accomplishments and the eye of command, you

[1] The long passage thus beginning is found in the "Lecture on the Times" (Nature, Addresses, etc., pp. 289, 290).

shall be the Mæcenas of every new thought, every untried project that proceeds from good will and honest seeking. The newspapers, of course, will defame what is noble, and what are you for but to withstand the newspapers and all the other tongues of to-day? You do not hold of to-day, but of an age, as the rapt and truly great man holds of all ages or of Eternity. If you defer to the newspaper, where is the scholar?

Hints, fragments, scintillations of men enough and more than enough, but men valiant and who can execute the project they learned of no man, but which was born with them, there are none. Perfect and execute yourself an Orson, if Orson ; a Valentine, if Valentine. Let us see at least a good Orson, and know the best and worst of that.

(From H)

November 18.

Queenie's [1] dream of the statue so beautiful that the blooming child who was in the room looked pale and sallow beside it, and of the speech of the statue, which was not quite speech either, but something better, which seemed at

1 So Mr. Emerson often called his wife.

last identical with the thing itself spoken of. It described to the fair girl who sat by, and whose face became flushed with her earnest attention, —life and being;—and then, by a few slight movements of the head and body, it gave the most forcible picture of decay and death and corruption, and then became all radiant again with the signs of resurrection. I thought it a just description of that Eloquence to which we are all entitled — are we not?— which shall be no idle tale, but the suffering of the action, and the action it describes. That shall make intent and privileged hearers.

The blue vault silver-lined with hills of snow.

(From G)
November 22.

Edith.[1] There came into the house a young maiden, but she seemed to be more than a thousand years old. She came into the house naked and helpless, but she had for her defence more than the strength of millions. She brought into the day the manners of the Night.

[On the second day of December, Mr. Emerson began his course of lectures on "The

1 His second daughter.

Times," in the Masonic Temple in Boston:
I, The "Introductory," is printed in the first
volume of the Works as "Lecture on the Times";
II, "The Conservative"; III, "The Poet"
(much of the matter is in "Poetry and Imagination," in *Lectures and Biographical Sketches*);
IV, "The Transcendentalist"; V, "Manners"; VI, "Character"; VII, "Relation to
Nature"; VIII, "Prospects."]

(From J)

Robin Hood. Little John asks Robin "Where
shall we take? Where shall we leave? Where
shall we rob and beat and bind?" Robin says:—

"Look ye do no husband harm
That tilleth with his plough.

"These bishops and these archbishops
Ye shall them beat and bind;
The high sheriff of Nottingham,
Him holde in your mind."

When Jones Very was in Concord, he said
to me, "I always felt when I heard you speak
or read your writings that you saw the truth
better than others, yet I felt that your spirit
was not quite right. It was as if a vein of colder

air blew across me." He seemed to expect from me a full acknowledgment of his mission and a participation of the same. Seeing this, I asked him if he did not see that my thoughts and my position were constitutional, that it would be false and impossible for me to say his things or try to occupy his ground as for him to usurp mine? After some frank and full explanation, he conceded this. When I met him afterwards one evening at my lecture in Boston, I invited him to go home to Mr. Adams's with me and sleep, which he did. He slept in the chamber adjoining mine. Early the next day, in the grey dawn, he came into my room and talked whilst I dressed. He said, " When I was at Concord I tried to say you were also right; but the spirit said, you were not right. It is just as if I should say, It is not morning; but the morning says, It is the morning."

" Use what language you will," he said, " you can never say anything but what you are."

All writing is by the grace of God. People do not deserve to have good writing, they are so pleased with bad. In these sentences that you show me, I can find no beauty, for I see death in every clause and every word. There is a fossil or a mummy character which pervades this book. The best sepulchres, the vastest catacombs, Thebes and Cairo, Pyramids, are sepulchres to me. I like gardens and nurseries. Give me initiative, spermatic, prophesying, man-making words.

I am probably all the better spectator that I am so indifferent an actor. Some who hear or read my reports misjudged me as being a good actor in the scene which I could so well describe; but, when they came to talk with me, even those who fancied they strictly sympathized with me found I was dumb for them as well as for others. In this, both I and they must be passive and acquiescent, and take our fortune. And now that I have said it, I shall not suffer again from this misadventure.

It is never worth while to worry people with your contritions.¹ We shed our follies and absurdities as fast as the rosebugs drop off in July and leave the apple tree which they so threatened. Nothing dies so fast as a fault and the memory of a fault. I am awkward, sour, saturnine, lump-

---

1 This sentence occurs in " Character " (*Letters and Social Aims*, p. 98).

ish, pedantic, and thoroughly disagreeable and oppressive to the people around me. Yet if I am born to write a few good sentences or verses, these shall endure, and my disgraces utterly perish out of memory.

Woman should not be expected to write, or fight, or build, or compose scores; she does all by inspiring man to do all. The poet finds her eyes anticipating all his ode, the sculptor his god, the architect his house. She looks at it. She is the requiring genius.

We ask to be self-sustained, nothing less.[1]

The rude reformer rose from his bed of moss and dry leaves, gnawed his roots and drank water, and went to Boston. There he met fair maidens who smiled kindly on him, then gentle mothers with their babes at their breasts who told them how much love they bore them and how they were perplexed in their daily walk. What! he said, and this on rich, embroidered carpets, with fine marbles and costly woods![2]

1 The rest of the passage is in "Gifts" (*Essays*, Second Series, p. 162).

2 This long passage with some additions — the reformer appearing as Friar Bernard — is found in "The Conserva-

Who is up so high as to receive a gift well?
We are either glad or sorry at a gift.[1] . . .

(From J)

December 12.

We cannot forgive another for not being ourselves. Yet that is not all my dream just now;
but this also, that only the affirmative is good,
and methinks that is as much in what is called
Whiggery as in Protestantism, for the latter falls
into cold recusances, and love is the affirmative. Whigs love; Protestants have a good deal
of hating to do. Loyalty is affirming; Idleness is
denying. But out on your exhibitions! There
is somewhat a little scenic and showy in your lecturing. Those who take up thus much thought
into action, have nothing to say, no rhetoric to
please with, but it is elemental, strong. It is like
that great quantity of heat which ice absorbs in
becoming water without any indication on the
thermometer. . . .

tive" (*Nature, Addresses, etc.*, pp. 314–316). The relief
to Mr. Emerson of his occasional visits to the Wards and other
high-minded and refined friends in Boston, after persecution
by the unkempt or tedious "monotones" who sought him in
Concord, must have been great.

1 The passage beginning thus is found in "Gifts."

And yet Raphael's picture is bold and beautiful, affirming, and the *Midsummer Night's Dream*, and every thought of mine which I naturally and happily speak. Let me not be witty, but only faithful and bold and happy, and I put all Nature in the wrong.

We lose time in trying to be like others, accusing ourselves because we are not like others. If something surprises us from our propriety, we act well and strong, because we lose in our fright the recollection of others.

Those who defend the establishment are less than it. Those who speak from a thought must always be greater than any actual fact. I see behind the Whig no mighty matter, nothing but a very trite fact of his land titles and certificates of stock. But through the eyes of the theorist stares at me a formidable, gigantic spirit who will not undo if I bid him, who has much more to say and do than he has yet told, and who can do great things with the same facility as little.

In the feudal table the humblest retainer sat in the company of his lord, and so had some indemnity for his thraldom in the education he derived from the spectacle of the wit, the grace, and the valor of his superiors.

Mr. Frost [1] thought that there would not be many of these recusants who declared against the state, etc. I told him he was like the good man of Noah's neighbors who said, "Go to thunder with your old ark ! I don't think there'll be much of a shower."

Osman. Seemed to me that I had the keeping of a secret too great to be confided to one man ; that a divine man dwelt near me in a hollow tree.

A Dandy, *Godelureau* [2] in French, a favorite word with Napoleon. Napoleon was calm, serious, and well calculated to stand the gaze of millions : and d'Abrantès describes the splendor of his smile.

And cakes by female hands wrought artfully,
Well steep'd in the liquid of the gold-wing'd bee.
                                        PLUTARCH.

Atque ego peccati vellem modo conscius essem ;
Aequo animo poenam qui meruere ferunt.
                            OVID, *Amor* 2, VII, 11.

1 The Unitarian clergyman of Concord.
2 This word, of uncertain origin, means, according to Littré, Delight of the Ladies.

Historians of reform are not necessarily lovers of reform among their contemporaries.

Among the powers of circumstance none so striking as the provocation of thought in particular companies. Every art may be learned for itself, as, e.g., that of composure and good behavior in all companies; but a better way is to be inspired by a sentiment which shall ennoble the behaviour without intention.

The man is yet to arise who eats angels' food; who, working for universal aims, finds himself fed, he knows not how, and clothed he knows not how, and yet it is done by his own hands. The squirrel hoards nuts, and the bee gathers honey, each without knowing what he does, and thus they are provided, without any degradation or selfishness. In the man, I should look to see it adorned, beyond this innocency, with conscious efforts for the general good.

Trees draw nineteen twentieths of their nourishment from their aërial roots, the leaves.

The *pis aller* of Romanism for Tieck, Winckelmann, Schlegel, Schelling, Montaigne, Dana, Coleridge-men.

Midsummer Night entertainment can easily seem to me profane and I shall do penance for having delighted in such toys: and Dante must shrink before a great life, and appear a permitted greatness.

To those who have been accustomed to lead, it is not quite indifferent to find their word or deed for the first time unimportant to society. Yet a human being always has the indemnity of acting religiously, and then he exchanges an *éclat* with the society of his town, for a reputation and weight with the society of the Universe.

Every word we speak is million-faced, or convertible to an indefinite number of applications. If it were not so, we could read no book. Your remark would only fit your case, not mine. And Dante, who described his circumstance, would be unintelligible now. But a thousand readers in a thousand different years shall read his story and find it a picture of their story by making, of course, a new application of every word.

All Bernardo's wit and study did not enable him to answer M. de Gullivere's question. As it happened once, so it happened twenty times. M. de Gullivere asked pointedly of the scholar for information which he should certainly have supplied; but poor Bernardo always wondered that he should have failed to inform himself of just that particular fact. Afterwards he found that it was just the same with his actions: he was very able and very willing to do a thousand things: but the particular action which must now be done, he was not ready for: and so he played at cross-purposes with all men in this world. One thing more Bernardo remarked, and said as much to Xavier, — that he was convinced it was a chance and not a right that he had received the laurel of the Sorbonne: "For I," said he, "was not made by Nature for an original genius, but to take delight in the genius of others. I was made to read Virgil, and not to write Bucolics of my own; for always if I have anything to say, it clothes itself in the language of some poet or author I have been reading, or perhaps of one of my friends with whom I daily converse. The thought is not born sufficiently vigorous to clothe itself."

Credit, it seems, is to be abolished.[1] . . .

1 Most of what follows is printed in "Social Aims" (*Letters and Social Aims*, p. 84).

December 18.

We believe in the existence of matter, not because we can touch it or conceive of it, but because it agrees with ourselves, and the Universe does not jest with us, but is in earnest.

A man founding a reputation for benevolence on his expenditure! a great blunder.[1] . . .

How much one person sways us, we have so few. The presence or absence of Milton will very sensibly affect the result of human history: the presence or absence of Jesus, how greatly! Well, to-morrow a new man may be born, not indebted like Milton to the Old, and more entirely dedicated than he to the New, yet clothed like him with beauty.

As we take our stand on Necessity or on Ethics, shall we go for the Conservative or the Reformer?[2] . . . The view of Necessity is always good-tempered, permits wit and pleasantry. The view of Liberty is sour and dogmatical. Both

[1] Here follows much that is printed in "Character" (*Essays*, Second Series, p. 103).

[2] Several following sentences are omitted, as printed in "The Conservative" (*Nature, Addresses, and Lectures*, p. 301).

may be equally free of personal consideration. Wo unto me if I preach not the gospel.

I like the spontaneous persons of both classes: and those in the Conservative side have as much truth and progressive force as those on the Liberal.

Do not be so grand with your one objection. Do you think there is only one? If I should go out of church whenever I hear a false sentiment, I could never stay there five minutes.[1] . . .

According to Boehmen, the world was nothing else than the *relievo*, the print of a seal of an invisible world concealed in his own bosom. (See Penhoen, vol. i, p. 123.)

When, in our discontent with the pedantry of scholars, we prefer farmers, and when, suspecting their conservatism, we hearken after the hard words of drovers and Irishmen, this is only subjective or relative criticism, this is alkali to our acid, or shade to our too much sunshine; but abide with these, and you will presently find they are the same men you left. A coat has cheated you.

What a plague is this perplexity. We are so sharpsighted — that we are miserable and, as

[1] Here follow sentences printed in "New England Reformers" (*Essays*, Second Series, pp. 262, 263).

E. H. says, can neither read Homer, nor not read him.

"Kepler's science was a strange alliance of that sublime science of antiquity which proceeded by inspiration with that modern science which measures, compares, analyses." (Penhoen.)

Leibnitz predicted the Zoöphytes; Kant predicted the asteroids; Newton the decomposition of the diamond; Swedenborg, Uranus. (Penhoen, vol. i, p. 159.)

They say that the mathematics leave the mind where they found it. What if life or experience should do the same?

Writing, also, is a knack and leaves the man where it found him. And Literature and Nature and Life.

All that a man hath will he give for his erect demeanor, that he may never more be ashamed, — society the measure. I go to you and I expand, and I go to another and I contract.

Look out of the window and it is Eternal Now. Look in faces of men and it varies every minute.

Reading Herrick, I feel how rich is Nature. This art of poetry,—I see that here is work and beauty enough to justify a man for quitting all else and sitting down with the Muses. Did not Cæsar say to the Egyptian priest, Come, I will quit army, Empire, and all if you will show me the fountains of the Nile? Well, all topics are indifferent: you may reach the centre by boring a shaft from any point on the surface, with equal ease. And yet in this instance of poetry the provocation is not that the 'Law is there, but the means are alluring.

AUTHORS OR BOOKS QUOTED OR REFERRED TO IN THE JOURNAL FOR 1841

(including also books mentioned in letters)

Vishnu Sarna; Zoroaster; Confucius;

Hesiod; Heraclitus; Empedocles; Æschylus; Plato, *Banquet* and *Phædrus;*

Aristophanes; Aristotle;

Ovid, *Ars Amatoria;* Lucan, *Pharsalia;*

Hermes Trismegistus; Plotinus; Porphyry (Taylor's), *On Abstinence from Animal Food;* Iamblichus, *Life of Pythagoras;* Synesius; Proclus; Olympiadorus;

Robert Wace; Dante, *Paradiso;* Saadi; Hafiz;

Monstrelet; Froissart, *Chronicles;* Ariosto; Rabelais;

Fra Paolo Sarpi; Kepler; Burton; Boehme (Behmen), *The Aurora;* Herrick; Izaak Walton;

Waller; Dryden; Locke; Leibnitz, *apud* Penhoen; Fontenelle; Rollin, *History;* Bentley; Thomas Hearne;

Pitt (Lord Chatham); Winckelmann, *History of Ancient Art;* Merck, *Correspondence with Goethe;* Laplace; Fox; William Pitt; Goethe; Burns;

Saint-Simon; Dodington; Duchesse d'Abrantès, *Mémoires, ou Souvenirs sur Napoléon, la Révolution,* etc.;

Canning; Shelley; Southey;

Schleiermacher; Schlegel; Tieck; Schelling; Menzel, *apud* George Ripley's *Specimens of Foreign Literature;* Ritter;

Sir William Edward Parry, *Arctic Voyages;* Charles Lamb, *Essays;*

Manzoni, *I Promessi Sposi;* Dr. Channing, *Milton* and *Napoleon;*

Carlyle, *Heroes and Hero Worship, French Revolution;* Nichol, *Architecture of the Heavens;* Miss Edgeworth, *Novels;*

Béranger, *Chansons;* George Sand, *Letters;*

De Tocqueville; Barchon de Penhoen, *History of German Philosophy from Leibnitz to Hegel*;

Westland Martin, *The Patrician's Daughter*; Robert P. Ward, *De Clifford*;

Tennyson, *The Lotus-Eaters*, *Locksley Hall*;

Hawthorne; Frederic Henry Hedge; William Lloyd Garrison.

JOURNAL

WALDO'S DEATH

COURSES IN PROVIDENCE AND
NEW YORK

ALCOTT VISITS ENGLAND

HAWTHORNE COMES TO CON-
CORD

ALCOTT'S RETURN

JOURNAL XXXIII

1842

(From Journals E, J, K, and N)

Betrayed me to a book and wrapped me in a gown.
                                        HERBERT.

[THE year opened happily. A daughter (Edith)
had come safely into the family. Little Ellen,
the eldest, was thriving. Waldo, now five years
old, gave to his father and mother every promise
for the future, while

> " Gentlest guardians marked serene
> His early hope, his liberal mien,"

for every friend that came to the house, and
Henry Thoreau, who then formed one of the
family, delighted in the child. Mr. Emerson
was going once a week to Boston, by the stage
which passed his door, giving the last lectures
of the course on "The Times." Suddenly malignant scarlet fever struck the little boy and
he lived but a few days. Bowed down by the
blow, Mr. Emerson yet had to fulfil his engagements for lectures in Providence and also

for a short course in New York. These were a
fortunate distraction for him, away from associations that met him at home at every turn, and he
met at his lectures new and earnest young friends.
His brother William, with his good and refined
wife (Susan Haven of Portsmouth), received him
into their home at Staten Island. Of him Mr.
Emerson wrote to his wife, "William is not the
isolated man I used to find or fancy him, but,
under the name of 'the judge,' seems to be an
important part of the web of life here at the
island."]

(From J)

January 28, 1842.

Yesterday night, at fifteen minutes after eight,
my little Waldo ended his life.

January 30.

What he looked upon is better; what he
looked not upon is insignificant. The morning
of Friday, I woke at three o'clock, and every
cock in every barnyard was shrilling with the
most unnecessary noise. The sun went up the
morning sky with all his light, but the landscape was dishonored by this loss. For this
boy, in whose remembrance I have both slept
and awaked so oft, decorated for me the morn-

ing star, the evening cloud, how much more all
the particulars of daily economy; for he had
touched with his lively curiosity every trivial
fact and circumstance in the household, the hard
coal and the soft coal which I put into my stove;
the wood, of which he brought his little quota
for grandmother's fire; the hammer, the pincers
and file he was so eager to use; the microscope,
the magnet, the little globe, and every trinket
and instrument in the study; the loads of gravel
on the meadow, the nests in the hen-house, and
many and many a little visit to the dog-house
and to the barn. — For everything he had his
own name and way of thinking, his own pro-
nunciation and manner. And every word came
mended from that tongue. A boy of early wisdom, of a grave and even majestic deportment,
of a perfect gentleness.

Every tramper that ever tramped is abroad,
but the little feet are still.

He gave up his little innocent breath like a
bird.

He dictated a letter to his Cousin Willie on
Monday night, to thank him for the magic
lantern which he had sent him, and said, "I
wish you would tell Cousin Willie that I have
so many presents that I do not need that he

should send me any more unless he wishes to very much."

The boy had his full swing in this world; never, I think, did a child enjoy more; he had been thoroughly respected by his parents and those around him, and not interfered with; and he had been the most fortunate in respect to the influences near him, for his Aunt Elizabeth had adopted him from his infancy and treated him ever with that plain and wise love which belongs to her and, as she boasted, had never given him sugarplums. So he was won to her, and always signalized her arrival as a visit to him, and left playmates, playthings, and all to go to her. Then Mary Russell [1] had been his friend and teacher for two summers, with true love and wisdom. Then Henry Thoreau had been one of the family for the last year, and charmed Waldo by the variety of toys,—whistles, boats, popguns,—and all kinds of instruments which he could make and mend; and possessed his love and respect by the gentle firmness with

1 A much valued friend of Mr. and Mrs. Emerson, from Plymouth, who had a little infant school which Waldo and other children attended. Later, she married Mr. Benjamin Marston Watson, of Plymouth. In "Threnody," Mr. Emerson describes

"The school march, each day's festival."

which he always treated him. Margaret Fuller
and Caroline Sturgis had also marked the boy
and caressed and conversed with him whenever
they were here.

Meantime every day his grandmother gave
him his reading - lesson and had by patience
taught him to read and spell; by patience and
by love, for she loved him dearly.

Sorrow makes us all children again, — destroys all differences of intellect. The wisest
knows nothing.

It seems as if I ought to call upon the winds
to describe my boy, my fast receding boy, a child
of so large and generous a nature that I cannot
paint him by specialties, as I might another.

"Are there any other countries?" "Yes. I wish
you to name the other countries"; so I went on
to name London, Paris, Amsterdam, Cairo, etc.
But Henry Thoreau well said, in allusion to his
large way of speech, that "his questions did not
admit of an answer; they were the same which
you would ask yourself."

He named the parts of the toy house he was
always building by fancy names which had a good
sound, as "the interspeglium" and "the cori-
daga," which names, he told Margaret, "the children could not understand."

If I go down to the bottom of the garden it seems as if some one had fallen into the brook. Every place is handsome or tolerable where he has been. Once he sat in the pew.

His house he proposed to build in summer of burrs and in winter of snow.

"My music," he said, "makes the thunder dance," for it thundered when he was blowing his willow whistle.

"Mamma, may I have this bell which I have been making, to stand by the side of my bed?" "Yes, it may stand there." "But, Mamma, I am afraid it will alarm you. It may sound in the middle of the night, and it will be heard over the whole town; it will be louder than ten thousand hawks; it will be heard across the water, and in all the countries. It will be heard all over the world. It will sound like some great glass thing which falls down and breaks all to pieces." [1]

1 In the first part of "Threnody," in the *Poems*, several of the sentences written just after Waldo's death are found in poetic form. The latter part of the poem was written nearly two years later, when calm vision had returned.

Waldo's death was a blow to Thoreau, coming, too, soon after the heavier one, the sudden death of his beloved brother John, a bright and genial presence. Henry wrote to Mrs. Emerson's sister of this new death thus bravely, however:—

"As for Waldo, he died as the mist rises from the brook,

Masses; is the attraction of cohesion the same as the attraction of gravity? Is the law of masses one with the law of particles. And there is a certain momentum of mass which I recognize readily enough in literature. Chaucer affects me when I read many pages of *Romaunt of Love* or the *Canterbury Tales* by his mass, as much as by the merit of single passages. So does Shakspeare eminently: he adds architecture to costliness of material, and beauty of single chambers and chapels. So does Milton. Then, as I have remarked of Pythagoras, so I feel in reference to all great masters, that they are chiefly distinguished by the power of adding a second, a third, and perhaps a fourth step in a continuous line. Many a man had taken their first step. With every additional

which the sun will soon dart his rays through. Do not the flowers die every autumn? He had not even taken root here. I was not startled to hear that he was dead; it seemed the most natural death that could happen. His fine organization demanded it, and Nature gently yielded its request. It would have been strange if he had lived. Neither will Nature manifest any sorrow at his death, but soon the note of the lark will be heard down in the meadow, and fresh dandelions will spring from the old stocks where he plucked them last summer." (*Familiar Letters of Henry David Thoreau*. Edited by F. B. Sanborn, with introduction and notes. Houghton, Mifflin & Co., 1894.) For accounts of Waldo, see Mr. Cabot's *Memoir of Emerson*, vol. ii, pp. 481–483.

step you enhance immensely the value of your first. It is like the price which is sometimes set on a horse by jockeys; a price is agreed upon in the stall, and then he is turned into a pasture and allowed to roll, and for every time he shall roll himself over, ten dollars are added to the price.

Masses again. If you go near to the White Mountains, you cannot see them; you must go off thirty or forty miles to get a good view. Well, so is it with men, and with all that is high in our life, it is a total and distant effect, a *mass effect*, that instructs us, and not the first apprehension of them.

Then our relation to our friends is not only one of particular good offices, but one of the purest pleasures of life is the mutual consciousness of a long and uniform exchange of good offices between two persons; so that a good man seems to draw both simple and compound interest from his capital of love, both a particular and a mass benefit from his good deeds.

Will is a particular, Habit a massive force; Speech a particular, Manners a mass.

Take thy body away that I may see thee. Thou showest me this mask all the time.

I have seen the poor boy, when he came to a tuft of violets in the wood, kneel down on the ground, smell of them, kiss them, and depart without plucking them.

As if one needed eyes in order to see. Look at yonder tree which the sun has drawn out of the ground by its continual love and striving towards him, and which now spreads a hundred arms, a thousand boughs, in gratitude, basking in his presence. Does that not see? It sees all over, with every leaf and every blossom.

I am not a man to read books, but one receiving that which books are written to report, said the poet.

My thoughts run about vainly seeking to arrive at those distant persons. Then I see Facts or objects which serve me as horses. Each of my thoughts seizes one of these, and, being mounted, rides directly to men.

When Osman came to read a page of Proclus, he was impatient of reading, and wished to hear the horn sound from the farmhouse that he might put in practice what he had learned of the elegance of dancing in a temperate life, but the horn delaying to sound, he bethought himself that his temperance should begin now and he would establish tranquillity and order in his thoughts.

Bores are good, too. They may help you to a good indignation, if not to a sympathy; to a "mania better than temperance," as Proclus would say. Long Beard and Short Beard, who came hither the other day with intent as it seemed to make Artesian Wells of us, taught me something.

Ben Jonson is rude and Tennyson is fine, but Ben's beauty is worth more than Tennyson's.[1] . . .

My life is optical, not practical. I go out to walk for exercise and not to answer a necessity. I speculate on virtue, not burn with love. Is not this as if one should quiz Michael and Gabriel through an opera-glass?

It would be easy, would it not, to give your own color and character to any meeting, if your

1 Mr. Emerson was now editing the *Dial*. This sentence and what follows is printed in the *Dial* paper, "Europe and European Books" (*Natural History of Intellect*, p. 371).

spirit and insight was better than that of the speakers. Wait till the noisy man has done, and then speak and leave him out: he will feel that he is left out. What takes place in every parlor will take place there, that the less will yield to the greater and feel that his contribution is unnecessary.

Such a sense as dwells in these purple deeps of Proclus transforms every page into a slab of marble, and the book seems monumental. They suggest what magnificent dreams and projects. They show what literature should be. Rarely, rarely, does the Imagination awake; he alone knows Astronomy and Geology, the laws of Chemistry and Animation. He, the Imagination, knows why the plain or meadow of Space is strown with these flowers we call suns, moons, and stars: why the great Deep is adorned with animals, with men and Gods; for in every word he speaks he rides on them as the horses of thought.[1]

1 This passage, though printed in "The Poet," is given because here applied to Proclus, whose writings Mr. Emerson read, not continuously, nor necessarily always understandingly, but "for lustres," as he says in "Nominalist and Realist" (see *Essays*, Second Series, pp. 21 and 233).

I see, in reading this, that a man ought to renounce writing for his townsmen or his countrymen and express his spiritual history and motions in such images as have a private significance to him.

Hither came a lady with as much remoteness, fromness, or aversation expressed in her countenance as it could carry. All her speech was in the dialect of her church, and as unintelligible to others as a flash conversation. Such a person ceases to be a woman that she may be a churchmember, and is necessarily treated like the insane in all companies. Yet every one must respect her eminent truth.

Nature is very clear in her teachings on one point, that you shall not accept any man's person; for just as much as she distinguishes any man for wit or character, to the same extent she deforms him in some particular to the eye.

And see the mountainous greatness of Shakspeare is given to a man of a common life, and not himself, it would seem, aware of his possession.

(From K)

Friday evening, *February* 4.

I have heard that Sheridan made a good deal of *experimental writing* with a view to take what might fall, if any wit should transpire in all the waste pages. I, in my dark hours, may scratch the page, if perchance any hour of recent life may project a hand from the darkness and inscribe a record. Twice to-day it has seemed to me that truth is our only armor in all passages of life and death.[1] . . . I will speak the truth also in my secret heart, or, *think the truth* against what is called God. Born and bred as we are in traditions, we easily find ourselves denying what seems to us sacred. I must resist the tradition, however subtile and encroaching, and say, Truth against the universe. Truth has its holidays which seem to come but once in a century, when she absolves her children with triumph to all souls.

Saturday morn, *February 5.*

Character. There are many gross and obscure natures whose bodies seem impure as shambles or grocers' shops, but character makes flesh and blood comely and alive. A meek allegiance to the Supreme Law consecrates youth and age alike, refines the whole body, gives a charm to wrinkles and silver hairs.[2] . . . Character, in

1 Here occurs the passage beginning thus in "Worship" (*Conduct of Life*, p. 230).

2 Here follows a passage on Character as self-sufficingness ("Character," *Essays*, Second Series, p. 99).

short, is conquest, and if there is not *that*, there is not character.[1]

February 21.

Home again from Providence to the deserted house. Dear friends find I, but the wonderful Boy is gone. What a looking for miracles have I! As his walking into the room where we are would not surprise Ellen, so it would seem to me the most natural of all things.

In Providence I found Charles Newcomb,[2] who made me happy by his conversation and his reading of his tales.

1 The next entries in this Journal are printed in the essay "Experience," namely, those on the "middle region of life," and on the "opinion instilled into disaster" (*Essays,* Second Series, p. 62 and p. 48).

2 A young idealist and scholar, who had a great charm for Mr. Emerson; a man of great refinement and sensibility but strong originality, shy, and a bachelor all his life. Mr. Emerson valued his occasional visits and made him bring his Journal and read it to him. Much of this he transcribed, to make sure to keep a copy, should the author destroy the original. We believe that the only practical experience of Charles Newcomb was his service as a private in the Civil War. But at Brook Farm, where he was for a time a member or a boarder in the community, he probably had to do his share in house or field work, but he is said to have had a marked influence. He wrote "The Two Dolons" in the *Dial.*

March 18.

Home from New York, where I read six lectures on the Times, viz., Introductory; The Poet; The Conservative; The Transcendentalist; Manners; Prospects. They were read in the " Society Library," were attended by three or four hundred persons, and after all expenses were paid yielded me about two hundred dollars.

In New York I became acquainted with Henry James, John James, William Greene, Mrs. Rebecca Black, Thomas Truesdale, Horace Greeley, Albert Brisbane, J. L. H. McCracken, Mr. Field, Maxwell, Mason, Nathan, Delf, Eames, besides Bryant and Miss Sedgwick, whom I knew before.

Letters from beloved persons found me there. My lectures had about the same reception there as elsewhere : very fine and poetical, but a little puzzling. One thought it " as good as a kaleidoscope." Another, a good Staten Islander, would go hear, " for he had heard I was a rattler."

March 20.

The *Dial* is to be sustained or ended, and I must settle the question, it seems, of its life or death. I wish it to live, but do not wish to be

its life. Neither do I like to put it in the hands
of the Humanity and Reform Men, because
they trample on letters and poetry ; nor in the
hands of the Scholars, for they are dead and dry.
I do not like the *Plain Speaker* so well as the
Edinburgh Review. The spirit of the last may
be conventional and artificial, but that of the
first is coarse, sour, indigent, dwells in a cellar
kitchen, and goes to make suicides.

In New York, Thomas Delf modestly inquired, as if the question lay hard on his conscience, whether there could not be in every
number of the *Dial* at least one article which
should be a statement of principles, good for
doctrine, good for edification, so that there
should be somewhat solid and distinct for the
eye of the constant reader to rest upon, and an
advancing evolution of truth. A very reasonable question.

Life goes headlong.[1] . . .

When I read the "Lord of the Isles" last
week at Staten Island, and when I meet my
friend, I have the same feeling of shame at hav-

[1] The rest of the paragraph thus beginning is printed in
"Character" (*Essays*, Second Series, p. 113).

ing allowed myself to be a mere huntsman and follower. Why art thou disquieted, O Soul?

In New York lately, as in cities generally, one seems to lose all substance, and become surface in a world of surfaces. Everything is external, and I remember my hat and coat, and all my other surfaces, and nothing else. If suddenly a reasonable question is addressed to me, what refreshment and relief! I visited twice and parted with a most polite lady without giving her reason to believe that she had met any other in me than a worshipper of surfaces, like all Broadway. It stings me yet.

"What are brothers for?" said Charles G. Loring, when somebody praised a man who helped his brother. William Emerson is a faithful brother.

The least differences in intellect are immeasurable. This beloved and now departed Boy, this Image in every part beautiful, how he expands in his dimensions in this fond memory to the dimensions of Nature!

Ellen asks her grandmother "whether God can't stay alone with the angels a little while and let Waldo come down?"

The chrysalis which he brought in with care and tenderness and gave to his mother to keep is still alive, and he, most beautiful of the children of men, is not here.

I comprehend nothing of this fact but its bitterness. Explanation I have none, consolation none that rises out of the fact itself; only diversion; only oblivion of this, and pursuit of new objects.

March 23.

To-day Nelly thinks "the snow is on the ground and the trees so white as a tablecloth and so white as parched corn."

The scholar is a man of no more account in the street than another man; as the sound of a flute is not louder than the noise of a saw. But as the tone of the flute is heard at a greater distance than any noise, so the fame of the scholar reaches farther than the credit of the banker.

Osric was always great in the Present time.[1] . . .

Tecumseh: A Poem. A well-read, clerical person, with a skilful ear and with Scott and Camp-

1 This and what follows is in "Worship," *Benedict* being substituted for *Osric* (*Conduct of Life,* p. 234).

bell in full possession of his memory, has written this poem in the feeling that the delight he
has experienced from Scott's effective list of
names might be reproduced in America from
the enumeration of sweet or sonorous Indian
names. The costume, as is usual in all such essays, crowds the man out of nature. The most
Indian thing about the Indian is surely not his
moccasins or his calumet, his wampum or his
stone hatchet, but traits of character and sagacity, skill or passion which would be intelligible
to all men and which Scipio or Sidney or Colonel Worth or Lord Clive would be as likely
to exhibit as Osceola and Black Hawk. As
Johnson remarked that there was a middle style
in English above vulgarity and below pedantry,
which never became obsolete and in which the
plays of Shakspeare were written, so is there in
human language a middle style, proper to all
nations and spoken by Indians and by French-
men, so they be men of personal force.

Colonel Worth has lately declared Halleck
Tastenugge one of the best infantry officers,
and William Greene [1] said he found the spirit
among the Indians.

1 William B. Greene, who had been an officer in the
United States Army during the Seminole War, and later was

Hell is better than Heaven, if the man in Hell knows his place, and the man in Heaven does not. It is in vain you pretend that you are not responsible for the evil law because you are not a magistrate, or a party to a civil process, or do not vote. You eat the law in a crust of bread, you wear it in your hat and shoes. The Man — it is his attitude: the attitude makes the man.

Instead of wondering that there is a Bible, I wonder that there are not a thousand.

> Toiling in the naked fields
> Where no bush a shelter yields,
> Needy Labor dithering stands,
> Beats and blows his numbing hands,
> And upon the crumping snows
> Stamps in vain to warm his toes.
>
> Though all's in vain to keep him warm,
> Poverty must brave the storm;
> Friendship none its aid to lend —
> Constant health his only friend;
> Granting leave to live in pain,
> Giving strength to toil in vain.
>
> CLARE.

for a time a preacher. In the Civil War, Colonel Greene commanded the 14th Infantry, M. V.

Brisbane in New York pushed his Fourierism with all the force of memory, talent, honest faith, and impudence. It was the sublime of mechanics.[1] . . .

Here prepares now the good Alcott to go to England,[2] after so long and strict acquaintance

1 What follows is, in substance, printed in "Historic Notes of Life and Letters in New England" (*Lectures and Biographical Sketches*, pp. 348–354).

Albert Brisbane was an eager disciple of Fourier. Mr. Emerson published in the *Dial* of July of this year a paper by Brisbane called "Means of Effecting a Final Reconciliation between Religion and Science." After pointing out the principles by which this could be effected, he considered the practical means by which mankind can be elevated in this line, and said, "A Genius equal to the task has arisen, and in our age, and has accomplished it. That Genius is CHARLES FOURIER."

2 Mr. Alcott's high thoughts on life and on the education of the young had reached certain Englishmen, notably James Pierrepont Greaves, a retired merchant turned scholar and philanthropist, a friend of Pestalozzi and of Strauss, and of Mr. John A. Heraud, editor of a reform magazine. Mr. Alcott's "Records of a School" so interested these and others that a school was established at Ham, Surrey, on Alcott's principles and named for him. Letters from these friends urged Mr. Alcott to come where he would be warmly welcomed and eagerly heard. The voyage was made possible by the good offices of his friends here.

as I have had with him for seven years. I saw him for the first time in Boston in 1835.

What shall we say of him to the wise Englishman?[1]

He is a man of ideas, a man of faith. Expect contempt for all usages which are simply such. His social nature and his taste for beauty and magnificence will betray him into tolerance and indulgence, even, to men and to magnificence, but a statute or a practice he is con-

---

1 The subjoined letter, and not what follows in the succeeding pages of the Journal, is what Mr. Emerson did write to Carlyle of his friend, over and above some note of introduction, kindly and brief : —

CONCORD, March 21, 1842.

I write now to tell you of a piece of life. I wish you to know that there is shortly coming to you a man by the name of Bronson Alcott. If you have heard his name before, forget what you have heard. Especially if you have read anything to which his name was attached, be sure to forget that ; and, inasmuch as in you lies, permit this stranger, when he arrives at your gate, to make a new and primary impression. I do not wish to bespeak any courtesies, or good or bad opinion concerning him. You may love him or hate him, or apathetically pass by him, as your genius shall dictate ; only I entreat this, that you do not let him quite go out of your reach until you are sure you have seen him and know for certain the nature of the man. And so I leave contentedly my pilgrim to his fate.

demned to measure by its essential wisdom or folly.

He delights in speculation, in nothing so much, and is very well endowed and weaponed for that work with a copious, accurate and elegant vocabulary; I may say poetic; so that I know no man who speaks such good English as he, and is so inventive withal. He speaks truth truly; or the expression is adequate. Yet he knows only this one language. He hardly needs an antagonist, — he needs only an intelligent ear. Where he is greeted by loving and intelligent persons, his discourse soars to a wonderful height, so regular, so lucid, so playful, so new and disdainful of all boundaries of tradition and experience, that the hearers seem no longer to have bodies or material gravity, but almost they can mount into the air at pleasure, or leap at one bound out of this poor solar system. I say this of his speech exclusively, for when he attempts to write, he loses, in my judgment, all his power, and I derive more pain than pleasure from the perusal. The *Post* expresses the feeling of most readers in its rude joke, when it said of his *Orphic Sayings* that they "resembled a train of fifteen railroad cars with one passenger." He has moreover the greatest possession both of mind and of temper in his discourse, so that the mastery and moderation and foresight, and yet felicity, with which he unfolds his thought, are not to be surpassed. This is of importance to such a broacher of novelties as he is, and to one baited, as he is very apt to be, by the sticklers for old books or old institutions. He takes such delight in the exercise of this faculty that he will willingly talk the whole of a day, and most part of the night, and then again to-morrow, for days successively, and if I, who am impatient of much speaking, draw him out to walk in the woods or fields, he will stop at the first fence and very soon propose either to sit down or to return. He seems to think society exists for this function, and that all literature is good or bad as it approaches colloquy, which is its perfection. Poems and histories may be good, but only as adumbrations of this; and the only true manner of writing the literature of a nation would be to convene the best heads in the community, set them talking, and then introduce stenographers to record what they say. He so swiftly and naturally plants himself on the moral sentiment in any conversation that no man will ever get any advantage of him, unless he be a saint, as Jones Very was. Every one else Alcott will put in the wrong.

It must be conceded that it is speculation which he loves, and not action. Therefore he dissatisfies everybody and disgusts many. When the conversation is ended, all is over. He lives to-morrow, as he lived to-day, for further discourse, not to begin, as he seemed pledged to do, a new celestial life. The ladies fancied that he loved cake; very likely; most people do. Yet in the last two years he has changed his way of living, which was perhaps a little easy and self-indulgent for such a Zeno, so far as to become ascetically temperate. He has no vocation to labor, and, although he strenuously preached it for a time, and made some efforts to practise it, he soon found he had no genius for it, and that it was a cruel waste of his time. It depressed his spirits even to tears.

He is very noble in his carriage to all men, of a serene and lofty aspect and deportment in the street and in the house. Of simple but graceful and majestic manners, having a great sense of his own worth, so that not willingly will he give his hand to a merchant, though he be never so rich, — yet with a strong love of men, and an insatiable curiosity concerning all who were distinguished either by their intellect or by their character. He is the most generous and hospitable of men, so

that he has been as munificent in his long poverty as Mr. Perkins in his wealth, or I should say
much more munificent. And for his hospitality,
every thing in the form of man that entered his
door as a suppliant would be made master of all
the house contained. Moreover, every man who
converses with him is presently made sensible
that, although this person has no faculty or patience for our trivial hodiernal labors, yet if there
were a great courage, a great sacrifice, a self-im-
molation to be made, this and no other is the man
for a crisis,—and with such grandeur, yet with
such temperance in his mien.

Such a man, with no talent for household
uses, none for action, and whose taste is for precisely that which is most rare and unattainable,
could not be popular,— he could never be a doll,
nor a beau, nor a bestower of money or presents,
nor even a model of good daily life to propose to
virtuous young persons. His greatness consists
in his attitude merely; of course he found very
few to relish or appreciate him; and very many
to disparage him. Somebody called him a "moral
Sam Patch."

Another circumstance marks this extreme love
of speculation. He carries all his opinions and
all his condition and manner of life in his hand,

and, whilst you talk with him, it is plain he has
put out no roots, but is an air-plant, which can
readily and without any ill consequence be trans-
ported to any place. He is quite ready at any
moment to abandon his present residence and
employment, his country, nay, his wife and children, on very short notice, to put any new dream
into practice which has bubbled up in the effer-
vescence of discourse. If it is so with his way of
living, much more so is it with his opinions. He
never remembers. He never affirms anything
to-day because he has affirmed it before. You
are rather astonished, having left him in the morning with one set of opinions, to find him in the
evening totally escaped from all recollection
of them, as confident of a new line of conduct and heedless of his old advocacy. *Sauve
qui peut.*

Another effect of this speculation is that he is
preternaturally acute and ingenious to the extent
sometimes of a little jesuitry in his action. He
contemns the facts so far that his poetic repre-
sentations have the effect of a falsehood, and
those who are deceived by them ascribe the falsehood to him: and sometimes he plays with
actions unimportant to him in a manner not
justifiable to any observers but those who are

competent to do justice to his real magnanimity and conscience.

Like all virtuous persons he is destitute of the appearance of virtue, and so shocks all persons of decorum by the imprudence of his behavior and the enormity of his expressions. . . .

This man entertained in his spirit all vast and magnificent problems. None came to him so much recommended as the most universal. He delighted in the fable of Prometheus; in all the dim, gigantic pictures of the most ancient mythology; in the Indian and Egyptian traditions; in the history of magic, of palmistry, of temperaments, of astrology, of whatever showed any impatience of custom and limits, any impulse to dare the solution of the total problem of man's nature, finding in every such experiment an implied pledge and prophecy of worlds of science and power yet unknown to us. He seems often to realize the pictures of the old alchemists: for he stood brooding on the edge of discovery of the Absolute from month to month, ever and anon affirming that it was within his reach, and nowise discomfited by uniform shortcomings.

The other tendency of his mind was to realize a reform in the Life of Man. This was the steadily returning, the monotonous topic of years of conversation. This drew him to a constant intercourse with the projectors and saints of all shades, who preached or practised any part or particle of reform, and to a continual coldness, quarrel, and non-intercourse with the scholars and men of refinement who are usually found in the ranks of conservatism. Very soon the Reformers whom he had joined would disappoint him; they were pitiful persons, and, in their coarseness and ignorance, he began to pine again for literary society. In these oscillations from the Scholars to the Reformers, and back again, he spent his days.

His vice, an intellectual vice, grew out of this constitution, and was that to which almost all spiritualists have been liable, — a certain brooding on the private thought which produces monotony in the conversation, and egotism in the character. Steadily subjective himself, the variety of facts which seem necessary to the health of most minds, yielded him no variety of meaning, and he quickly quitted the play on objects, to come to *the Subject*, which was always the same, viz., *Alcott in reference to the World of To-day*.

From a stray leaf I copy this : —

Alcott sees the law of man truer and farther than any one ever did. Unhappily, his conversation never loses sight of his own personality. He never quotes ; he never refers ; his only illustration is his own biography. His topic yesterday is Alcott on the 17th October ; to-day, Alcott on the 18th October ; to-morrow, on the 19th. So will it be always. The poet, rapt into future times or into deeps of nature admired for themselves, lost in their law, cheers us with a lively charm ; but this noble genius discredits genius to me. I do not want any more such persons to exist.[1]

What for the visions of the night ? Our life is so safe and regular that we hardly know the emotion of terror. Neither public nor private

[1] It would seem that Mr. Emerson sat down to make a rough draft of a letter of introduction for Mr. Alcott and was led on by interest in the subject to write the above (never sent) resultant of seven years' experience of this strange Nineteenth-Century Apostle with his gifts and his gaps.

Twenty-five years later, Mr. Emerson said to his son, " It will be a thousand pities if I don't outlive Alcott and Ellery Channing, for nobody else knows them well enough to do them justice."

This long entry in the Journal is the fullest statement that Mr. Emerson left, and it was written at the time when Mr. Alcott's theories were at their highest flight, just before the tragic fall to earth in the winter of the following year when the Fruitlands community went to wreck.

violence, neither natural catastrophes, as earth-
quake, volcano, or deluge; nor the expectation
of supernatural agents in the form of ghosts, or
of purgatory and devils and hell fire, disturb the
sleepy circulations of our blood in these calm,
well-spoken days. And yet dreams acquaint us
with what the day ōmits. Eat a hearty supper,
tuck up your bed tightly, put an additional bed-
spread over your three blankets, and lie on your
back, and you may, in the course of an hour or
two, have this neglected part of your education
in some measure supplied. Let me consider:
I found myself in a garret disturbed by the
noise of some one sawing wood. On walking towards the sound, I saw lying in a crib an insane
person whom I very well knew, and the noise
instantly stopped: there was no saw, a mere
stirring among several trumpery matters, fur
muffs and empty baskets that lay on the floor.
As I tried to approach, the muffs swelled themselves a little, as with wind, and whirled off into
a corner of the garret, as if alive, and a kind of
animation appeared in all the objects in that corner. Seeing this, and instantly aware that here
was Witchcraft, that here was a devilish Will
which signified itself plainly enough in the stir
and the sound of the wind, I was unable to

move; my limbs were frozen with fear; I was bold and would go forward, but my limbs I could not move; I mowed the defiance I could not articulate, and woke with the ugly sound I made. After I woke and recalled the impressions, my brain tingled with repeated vibrations of terror; and yet was the sensation pleasing, as it was a sort of rehearsal of a Tragedy.

What room for Fourier phalanxes, for large and remote schemes of happiness, when I may be in any moment surprised by contentment?

Here was Edward Palmer, with somewhat ridiculous, yet much nobility, always combined in his person and conversation, truth, honesty, love, independence, yet this listening to men, and this credulity in days and conventions and Brisbane projects. His look has somewhat too priestly and ecclesiastic in its cut. He looks like an Universalist minister. But though his intellect is something low and limitary, prosaic, and a good roadster, yet he has great depth of character, and grows on your eye. Pathetic it was to hear of his little circle of six young men who met one evening long ago in a little chamber in Boston, and talked over his project of *No-Money* until all saw that it was true, and had new faith in the Omnipotence of love. In Alabama and Georgia, he seems to have stopped in every printing-house, and the only signs of hope and comfort he found were Newspapers, like Brisbane's "Future," which he found in these dusky universities. When shall we see a man whose image blends with nature? so that when he is gone, he shall not seem a little ridiculous, that same small man!

Edmund Hosmer [1] is a noble creature, so manly, so sweet-tempered, so faithful, so disdainful of all appearances, who always looks respectable and excellent to you in his old shabby cap and blue frock bedaubed with the slime of the marsh, and makes you respect and honor him through all. A man to deal with who always

1 Mr. Emerson's neighbor, half a mile away in the last house in Concord, on the Sandy Pond road to Lincoln. Mr. Hosmer, a hard-working farmer with a large family, was Mr. Emerson's adviser and helper in his family needs, ploughed and harrowed for him with his oxen, and carted sand from the hill opposite on to the too wet meadow to make grass-land.

He also liked to attend evening gatherings for conversation in Mr. Emerson's parlor when not too busy or tired. In the *Poems* he figures as Hassan the camel-driver ("Fragments on the Poet and the Poetic Gift," p. 323).

needs to be watched lest he should cheat himself;
with his admiration of his wife, harried by the care
of her poor household and ten children. Edmund says, the first time he saw her, he did not
observe that she was much different from other
women, but now he thinks her the handsomest
woman he ever saw ! And so you come to think
also when you see [her] . . . in her house at
her work, or hear her artless stories of her suf-
ferings and her works and opinions and tastes.

Friendship, five people; yes; Association
and grand phalanx of the best of the human
race.[1] . . .

Opus superabat materiem, said the Transcendentalist to the man who gave him money: or,
All my concern is with the expenditure.

"The Devil is the Lord's bulldog," said the
good Dow.[2]

April 3.

"The peculiarity of divine souls is shown by
Parmenides to consist in their being younger
and at the same time older both than themselves
and other things." — Proclus.

1 The rest of this passage occurs in "New England Reformers" (*Essays*, Second Series, pp. 264, 265).

2 Probably Lorenzo Dow, the vigorous Methodist apostle.

The population of the world is a conditional population. These are not the best, but the best that could live in the existing state of soils, gases, animals, and morals.

Shall the new thought make the magnificence of England rags?

An immense deduction is to be made from the doctrine of the wisest man to arrive at his truth. All his dogmatick is mere flourish and grammar. What a mass of nonsense in St. Paul, and again in Swedenborg, that has no relation to rain and sun and bird. Yet truth will resolve a magpie as well as a creed when once you get it pure.

He should not see poorest culinary stove but he saw its relation to the charity which is the fountain of nature.

Swedenborg a right poet. Everything protean to his eye.[1] . . . In his eye the eternal flux of things goes always on, there is no material kernel, only a spiritual centre.

1 The passage about his vision, printed in "The Poet" (*Essays*, Second Series, pp. 35, 36).

April 5.

Alcott brought here this day a manuscript paper written by his brother Junius, which had three good things in it, — first, that it was a Prayer, written in this prayerless age; second, that he thanks God for the continuance of their love, the one for the other; and third, he thanks him for the knowledge he has attained of him by his Sons.

Truth; Realism. Are you not scared by seeing that the Gypsies are more attractive to us than the Apostles? For though we love goodness and not stealing, yet also we love freedom and not preaching.[1]

The feeblest babe is a channel through which the tremendous energies stream which we call Life, Fate, Love, Conscience, Thought, Hope, Sensibility.

I began to write of Poetry and was driven at once to think of Swedenborg as the person who,

1 Mr. Emerson was reading George Borrow's *Gypsies in Spain*, which he reviewed in the *Dial* in July. From Borrow's books came the suggestions of the poem, "The Romany Girl."

of all the men in the recent ages, stands eminently for the translator of Nature into thought.
I do not know a man in history to whom things
stood so uniformly for words. Before him the
Metamorphosis continually plays. And if there
be in Heaven Museums of Psychology, the most
scientific angel could scarcely find a better example than the brain of Swedenborg, of the
tendency to interpret the moral by the material.[1] . . .

Swedenborg never indicates any emotion, —
a cold, passionless man.

What we admire is the majestic and beautiful
Necessity which necessitated him to see these
Heavens and Hells of his. The Heaven, which
overpowered his and every human mind in proportion to the apprehensiveness of each, is more
excellent than his picture; the Hell, which is its
negation, is more formidable than he had skill
to draw.

Very dangerous study will Swedenborg be to
any but a mind of great elasticity. Like Napoleon as a military leader, a master of such extraordinary extent of nature, and not to be acted

    1 One or two sentences in the above are printed in *Repre-
sentative Men*. The omitted sentences which follow are found
in that volume on pages 36 and 37.

on by any other, that he must needs be a god
to the young and enthusiastic.

April 6.

Having once learned that in some one thing,
although externally small, greatness might be
contained, so that in doing that, it was all one as
if I had builded a world; I was thereby taught,
that every thing in nature should represent total
nature; and that whatsoever thing did not represent to me the sea and sky, day and night,
was something forbidden or wrong.

Heroes.

> Heaven's exiles straying from the orb of light.
>
> EMPEDOCLES.

Pericles, the father of these youths, has beau-
tifully and well instructed them in those things
which are taught by masters; but in those things
in which he is wise he has neither instructed
them himself, nor has he sent them to another
to be instructed; but they, feeding, as it were,
without restraint, wander about, to see if they
can casually meet with virtue. — PLATO, in *Pro-
tagoras.*

You should never ask me what I can do. If
you do not find my gift without asking, I have
none for you. Would you ask a woman wherein

her loveliness consists? Those to whom she is
lovely will not discover it so. Such questions
are but curiosity and gossip. Besides, I cannot
tell you what my gift is unless you can find it
without my description.

THE POET [1]

On that night the poet went
From the lighted halls
Beneath the darkling firmament
To the seashore, to the old sea walls.

Dark was night upon the seas,
Darker was the poet's mind;
For his shallow suppleness
Black abyss of penitence.

The wind blew keen, the poet threw
His cloak apart, to feel the cold;
The wind, he said, is free and true,
But I am mean and sold.

---

1 Perhaps as early as 1838, and onward for years, Mr.
Emerson was writing fragmentary verses on this theme, at
first uneven in quality in a period of unrest, later improving.
They began with "The Discontented Poet, A Masque."
A large part of them are gathered in the Riverside and Centenary editions of the *Poems* in the Appendix. The portion
occurring here in this Journal may be there found in a smoother
form. At this period Mr. Emerson used to walk out under the
stars the last thing before going to rest.

Out shone a star between the clouds,
The constellation glittered soon, —
You have no lapse : so have ye glowed
But once in your dominion.
And I to whom your light has spoken,
I pining to be one of you,
I fall, my faith is broken;
Ye scorn me from your deeps of Blue —
And yet, dear stars, I know ye shine
Only by needs and loves of mine;
Light-loving, light-asking life in me
Feeds those eternal lamps I see.

The history of Christ is the best document of the power of Character which we have. A youth who owed nothing to fortune and who was "hanged at Tyburn," — by the pure quality of his nature has shed this epic splendor around the facts of his death which has transfigured every particular into a grand universal symbol for the eyes of all mankind ever since.[1]

He did well. This great Defeat is hitherto the highest fact we have. But he that shall come shall do better. The mind requires a far higher

1 Although this passage, in substance, is given in " Char-acter" (*Essays*, Second Series, p. 114), the original form, full and more daring, is preserved here.

exhibition of character, one which shall make itself good to the senses as well as to the soul; a success to the senses as well as to the soul. This was a great Defeat; we demand Victory. More character will convert judge and jury, soldier and king; will rule human and animal and mineral nature; will command irresistibly and blend with the course of Universal Nature.

In short, there ought to be no such thing as Fate. As long as we use this word, it is a sign of our impotence and that we are not yet ourselves. . . . Whilst I adore this ineffable life which is at my heart, it will not condescend to gossip with me, it will not announce to me any particulars of science, it will not enter into the details of my biography, and say to me why I have a son and daughters born to me, or why my son dies in his sixth year of joy. Herein, then, I have this latent omniscience coexistent with omnignorance. Moreover, whilst this Deity glows at the heart, and by his unlimited presentiments gives me all Power, I know that to-morrow will be as this day, I am a dwarf, and I remain a dwarf. That is to say, I believe in Fate. As long as I am weak, I shall talk of Fate; whenever the God fills me with his fulness, I shall see the disappearance of Fate.

I am *Defeated* all the time; yet to Victory I am born.[1]

But the objection to idolatry of which all Christendom is guilty, why do you not feel? viz., that it is retrospective, whilst all the health and power of man consists in the prospective eye. A saint, an angel, a chorus of saints, a myriad of Christs, are alike worthless and forgotten by the soul, as the leaves that fall, or the fruit that was gathered in the garden of Eden in the golden age. A new day, a new harvest, new duties, new men, new fields of thought, new powers call you, and an eye fastened on the past unsuns nature, bereaves me of hope, and ruins me with a squalid indigence which nothing but death can adequately symbolize.

The Poet should not only be able to use nature as his hieroglyphic, but he should have a still higher power, namely, an adequate message to communicate; a vision fit for such a

1 The archangel Hope
   Looks to the azure cope,
      Waits through dark ages for the morn,
      Defeated day by day, but unto victory born.
                                 Poems, Appendix, p. 354.

faculty. Therefore, when we speak of Poet in the great sense, we seem to be driven to such examples as Ezekiel and Saint John and Menu with their moral burdens; and all those we commonly call Poets become rhymesters and poetasters by their side.

All our works which we do not understand are symbolical. If I appear to myself to carry rails into the shed under my barn, if I appear to myself to dig parsnips with a dung-fork, there is reason, no doubt, in these special appearances as much as in the study of metaphysics or mythology, in which I do not see meaning.

We are greatly more poetic than we know; poets in our drudgery, poets in our eyes, and ears, and skin.

The schoolboys went on with their game of baseball without regard to the passenger, and the ball struck him smartly in the back. He was angry. Little cared the boys. If you had learned how to play when you was at school, they said, you would have known better than to be hit. If you did not learn then, you had better stop short where you are, and learn now. Hit him again, Dick!

Sunday eve.

I say that he will render the greatest service
to criticism which has been known for ages who
shall draw the line of relation that subsists between Shakspeare and Swedenborg.[1] . . .

Always there is this Woman as well as this
Man in the mind; Affection as well as Intellect.

You might know beforehand that your
friends will not succeed, since you have never
been able to find the Institution in the Insti-
tutor.[2]

" If he who brings corn to sale be entitled to
a remunerating price for it by law, by what just
law is he disentitled to a remunerating price
who likewise brings his property to sale — his
labour ? " — Lord Nugent.

If I go into the churches in these days, I
usually find the preacher in proportion to his
intelligence to be cunning, so that the whole

1 For the rest of the passage, see " Swedenborg " (Representative Men, p. 94).

2 The rest of this passage is in " Character" (Essays, Second Series, pp. 101, 102).

institution sounds hollow. X, the ablest of all the Unitarian clergy, spread popular traps all over the lecture which I heard in the Odeon. But in the days of the Pilgrims and the Puritans, the preachers were the victims of the same faith with which they whipped and persecuted other men, and their sermons are strong, imaginative, fervid, and every word a cube of stone.

As soon as my guests are gone, they show like dreams.

Mr. Clapp, of Dorchester, to whom I described the Fourier project, thought it must not only succeed, but that agricultural association must presently fix the price of bread, and drive single farmers into association in self-defence, as the great commercial and manufacturing companies had done.

Last night I read many pages in Chester Dewey's *Report of Herbaceous Plants in Massachusetts*. With what delight we always come to these images! The mere names of reeds and grasses, of the milkweeds, of the mint tribe and the gentians, of mallows and trefoils, are a lively pleasure. The odorous waving of these children of .

beauty soothes and heals us. The names are poems often. *Erigeron*, because it grows old early, is thus named the Old Man of the Spring. The *Pyrola umbellata* is called *Chimaphila*, Lover of Winter, because of its bright green leaves in the snow; called also Prince's Pine. The Plantain (*Plantago major*), which follows man wherever he builds a hut, is called by the Indians "White Man's Foot." And it is always affecting to see Lidian or one of her girls stepping outside the door with a lamp at night to gather a few plantain leaves to dress some slight wound or inflamed hand or foot. What acres of Houstonia whiten and ripple before the eye with innumerable pretty florets at the mention of May. My beloved Liatris in the end of August and September acquires some added interest from being an approved remedy for the bite of serpents, and so called "Rattlesnake's Master." The naming of the localities comforts us — "ponds," "shady roads," "sandy woods," "wet pastures," etc. I begin to see the sun and moon, and to share the life of Nature, as under the spell of the sweetest pastoral Poet.

Fireweed, a *Hieracium* which springs up abundantly on newly cleared land. The aromatic fields of dry *Gnaphalium;* the sweet flags live in

my memory this April day. But this dull country professor insults some of my favorites, as
the well beloved *Lespedeza*,[1] for instance. The
beautiful *Epigæa*, pride of Plymouth woods, he
utterly omits. He who loves a flower, though
he knows nothing of its botany or medicine,
is nearer to it than one of these catalogue-
makers.[2] . . .

These are our Poetry. What, I pray thee,
O Emanuel Swedenborg, have I to do with jas-
per, sardonyx, beryl, and chalcedony?[3] . . .

One would think that God made fig trees and
dates, grapes and olives, but the Devil made
Baldwin apples and pound-pears, cherries and
whortleberries, Indian corn and Irish potatoes.
I tell you, I love the peeping of a Hyla in a pond
in April, or the evening cry of a whip-poor-will,
better than all the bellowing of all the Bulls of
Bashan or all the turtles of whole Palestina. The

---

1 In his poem, the "Dirge," commemorating his lost
brothers, Mr. Emerson speaks of it as

> This flower of silken leaf
> Which once our childhood knew.

2 Here follows the passage about the flowers jilting us, in
"Nature" (*Essays*, Second Series, p. 182).

3 The rest of the passage is printed in "Swedenborg"
(*Representative Men*, pp. 135, 136).

County of Berkshire is worth all Moab, Gog, and Kadesh, put together.

When Swedenborg described the roads leading up from the " world of spirit " into Heaven as not visible at first to any Spirit, but after some time visible to such as are pure, he figuratively reports a familiar truth in relation to the history of thought. The gates of thought, — how slow and late they discover themselves! Yet when they appear, we see that they were always there, always open.

April 13.

Read last night Mr. Colman's *Fourth Report of the Agriculture of Massachusetts*. The account he gives of the fat cattle raised on Connecticut River and sold at Brighton is pathetic almost. The sale sometimes will not pay the note the farmer gave for the money with which he bought his stock in the fall. The miseries of Brighton would make a new chapter in Porphyry on "Abstinence from Animal Food." The Maple Sugar business is far more agreeable to read of. One tree may be tapped for eighty or ninety years and not injured. One man can tap three hundred in a day. I read with less pleasure that a principal crop of Franklin County is broomcorn.

The babe is not disconcerted. I delight in her eyes: they receive good-humoredly everything that appears before them, but give way to nothing. Scrap as she is, she is never displaced, as older children are.

I like a meeting of gentlemen; for they also bring each one a certain cumulative result. From every company they have visited, from every business they have transacted, they have brought away something which they wear as a certain complexion or permanent coat, and their manners are a certificate, a trophy of their culture. What we want when you come to see us is country culture. We have town culture enough and to spare. Show us your own, inimitable and charming to us, O Countryman!

At New York I saw Mrs. Black, a devout woman bred in the Presbyterian Church, but who had left it and come out into the light, as she said, " in a moment of time." She was spiritual and serene. The contemplation of the presence and perfection of the Moral Law contented her. She had read Madame Guion and Jacob Behmen, and now, lately, the Book of Esdras, the author of which she said was an impatient

spirit, but yet wise. She quoted Scripture a good
deal, but in the poetic and original way of Jones
Very. I was greatly contented with her, at my
first interview; but at the second I asked her,
"Had she no temptations?" No. "Had she no
wish to serve some creature who could only be
served by her involving herself in affairs?" No.
For herself she satisfied me pretty well, but I
soon felt that she had no answers to give the In-
quirers whom I usually meet. She only said, they
must be willing to be fools. "Yes," I said, "but
they already are fools and have been so a long
time, and now they begin to whimper, How
long, O Lord!"

Goodness is not good enough, unless it has
insight, universal insights, results that are of
universal application.

Men whom we see are whipped through the
world;[1] . . . The most private is the most public energy. We shall see that quality atones for
quantity; that creative action in one outvalues
feeble exhibition and philanthropic declamation
to crowds; and that grandeur of character acts
in the dark, and succors them who never saw it.

1 The part omitted of this passage is printed in "Domestic Life" (*Society and Solitude*, p. 125).

I ought to be obeyed. The reason I am not is because I am not real. Let me be a lover, and no man can resist me. I am not united, I am not friendly to myself, I bite and tear myself. I am ashamed of myself. When will the day dawn, of peace and reconcilement, when, self-united and friendly, I shall display one heart and energy to the world?

"Every intellect," says Proclus, "is an impartible essence." Very likely and very unimportant; but that every intellect is an impart*a*ble essence, or is communicable in the same proportion with its amount or depth, — is a theme for the song of angels.

Quotation. It is a great advantage to come first in time. He that comes second must needs quote him that came first. You say that Square never quotes: you say something absurd. Let him speak a word, only to say " chair," "table," " fire," " bread,"—what are these but quotations from some ancient savage?

I have sometimes fancied my friend's wisdom rather corrective than initiative, an excellent element in conversation to counteract the common exaggerations and preserve the sanity, but chiefly valuable so, and not for its adventure and exploration or for its satisfying peace.

(From E)

April 14.

If I should write an honest diary, what should I say? Alas, that life has halfness, shallowness. I have almost completed thirty-nine years, and I have not yet adjusted my relation to my fellows on the planet, or to my own work. Always too young or too old, I do not justify myself; how can I satisfy others?

Christianity. I do not wonder that there was a Christ; I wonder that there were not a thousand.

Dull, cheerless business this of playing lion and talking down to people. Rather let me be scourged and humiliated; then the exaltation is sure and speedy.

(From K)

April 19.

My daily life is miscellaneous enough, but when I read Plato or Proclus, or, without Plato, when I ascend to thought, I do not at once arrive at satisfactions, as when I drink being thirsty, or go to the fire being cold; no; I am only apprized at first of my vicinity to a new and most bright region of life.[1] . . .

Life. Where do we find ourselves?[2] . . .

April 22.

This afternoon I found Edmund Hosmer in his field, after traversing his orchard where two of his boys were grafting trees; Mr. Hosmer was ploughing and Andrew driving the oxen. I could not help feeling the highest respect as I approached this brave laborer. Here is the Napoleon, the Alexander of the soil, conquering and to conquer, after how many and many a hard-fought summer's day and winter's day, not like Napoleon of sixty battles only, but of six thousand, and out of every one he has come victor. . . . I am ashamed of these slight and useless limbs of mine before this strong soldier.[3] . . .

[1] The rest of this long passage is in "Experience" (*Essays,* Second Series, pp. 71, 72).

[2] Here follows the opening passage, on stairs, in "Experience."

[3] The episode, of which the above is the first paragraph, Mr. Emerson published in the *Dial,* July, 1842, and the

True it is, I thought, as he talked, that Necessity farms it, that Necessity finds out when to go to Brighton, and when to feed in stall, better than Mr. Colman.

Elizabeth gives me two Proverbs to-day, which are both bucolic poetry : —

> " When the oaks are in the grey,
> Then, Farmers, plant away."

And the other : —

> " The Mistress makes the morning,
> But the Lord makes the afternoon."

Strange that what I have not is always more excellent than what I have, and that Beauty, no, not Beauty, but *a* beauty instantly deserts possession, and flies to an object in the horizon.

If I could put my hand on the Evening Star, would it be as beautiful ?

In the fields, this lovely day, I was ashamed of the inhospitality of disputing. Very hoarsely

whole is printed under the title "Agriculture in Massachusetts" (see *Natural History of Intellect*, pp. 358–363). In the Appendix to the *Poems* (p. 322) Mr. Hosmer, in the guise of Hassan the camel-driver, receives the poet's homage.

sounds the parlor debate on theology from the lonely, sunny hill, or the meadow where the children play.

> As sings the pine tree in the wind,
> So sings in the wind a sprig of the pine.

As Proclus ascribes to the Deity the property of being in contact, and of not being in contact at the same moment of time, so we demand of men that they should exhibit a conduct which is at once continence and abandonment; "a wanton heed, and giddy cunning."

We look wishfully to emergencies, to eventful revolutionary times from the desart of our ennui, and think how easy to have taken our part when the drum was rolling and the house was burning over our heads. But is not Peace greater than War, and has it not greater wars and victories? Is there no progress? To wish for war is atheism.

When I saw the sylvan youth, I said, "Very good promise, but I cannot now watch any more buds: like the good Grandfather when they brought him the twentieth babe, he declined the dandling, he had said 'Kitty, Kitty' long enough."

Queenie says, "Save me from magnificent souls. I like a small common-sized one."

As they say that when your razor is dull, lay it away in your drawer and use another until that becomes dull, then take the old one and you shall find it sharp again, so I have heard scholars remark of their skill in languages, that by putting away the Greek or German book for a time, when they resumed it afterwards, they were surprised at their own facility.

(From J)

April 28.

Q. Why not great and good?

Ans. Because I am not what I ought to be.

Q. But why not what you ought?

Ans. The Deity still solicits me, but this self, this individuality, this will resists.

Q. Well for you that it does: if it did yield, you would die, as it is called. But why does it resist?

Ans. I can only reply, God is great: it is the will of God. When he wills, he enters: when he does not will, he enters not.

(From K)

May 1.

" And the most difficult of tasks to keep
　Heights which the soul is competent to gain."

These lines of Wordsworth are a sort of elegy on these times. When I read Proclus, I am astonished with the vigor and breadth of his performance. Here is no epileptic modern muse, with short breath and short flight, but an Atlantic strength which is everywhere equal to itself and dares great attempts, because of the life with which it feels itself filled.

There will come a day when a man shall appear who will so draw men to him as a mistress or a friend draws a lover or a friend, making it the happiness and honor of the other party to serve him. In that way character will inspire the kindness it requires, and will not need to provide in the direct way for its bodily wants. Then every man will " live by his strength and not by his weakness," as A said. God hates inquisitiveness, said Euclides.

Boldness we wish to see, — boldness in any kind, whether in behavior and action, or in thought or poetry or music or building. But whence is boldness? What is it but the badge and sign of Life, of Spirit? And sometimes that wind bloweth here, and sometimes there, none can tell why, or how, or when, it listeth. Am I master of any of the conditions of its presence, or must I fold my hands and wait until I be bold?

Now is our salvation nearer than when we believed.

Doctor James Jackson said it always took some time to learn the scale of patients and nurses; what they meant by "*violent pain*," "feeling that they should die," etc., etc. Almost all persons delight in the superlative, and for this reason seize upon an exaggeration, as on sugar, in all their actual observations of each character. It proceeds from the want of skill to detect quality that they hope to move your admiration by quantity: for they feel that here in this or that person is somewhat remarkable.

A reading man, or a child self-entertained, is the serpent with its tail in the mouth.[1] Let Saadi sit alone.

The Surfaces threaten to carry it in Nature. The fox and musquash, the hawk and snipe and

1 The symbol of Continuity, hence Eternity.

bittern, when near by seen, are found to have
no more root than man, to be just such superficial tenants in the globe. Then this new mo-
lecular philosophy goes to show that there are
astronomical interspaces betwixt atom and atom;
the world is all outside; it has no inside.

> Atom from atom yawns as far
> As moon from earth, as star from star.

Elizabeth Hoar says, when we spoke of the
beauty of morning and the beauty of evening,
—" I go a beggar to the sunset, but in the morning I am equal to Nature."

(From J)

May 6.

Here is a proposition for the formation of a
good neighborhood: Hedge shall live at Concord, and Mr. Hawthorne; George Bradford
shall come then; and Mrs. Ripley afterward.
Who knows but Margaret Fuller and Charles
Newcomb would presently be added? These, if
added to our present kings and queens, would
make a rare, an unrivalled company. If these all
had their hearth and home here, we might have
a solid social satisfaction, instead of the disgust
and depression of visitation. We might find that

each of us was more completely isolated and
sacred than before. You may come — no matter
how near in place, so that you have metes and
bounds, instead of the confounding and chaos of
visiting.

May 15.

The instruction at church seemed very infan-
tile. Calvinism seems complexional merely; . . .

In general, I recognize, in stagecoach and elsewhere, the constitutional Calvinist, the inconvertible. And in all companies we find those
who are self-accused, who live in their memories
and charge themselves with the seven deadly sins
daily, like my Queen without guile;[1] and the
other class, who cumber themselves never with
contrition, but appeal from their experience
always hopefully to their faith.

Our poetry reminds me of the catbird, who
sings so affectedly and vaingloriously to me near
Walden. Very sweet and musical! very various!
fine execution! but so conscious, and *such a per-*

1 Mr. Emerson does not class his wife with Calvinists, but
refers to her saintly, oversensitive conscience. She abhorred
the doctrines representing the Father as foreordaining most of
his children for eternal fires, and all for his own glory..

former! not a note is his own, except at last,
Miou, miou.

Of recent men, one may say that Milton's
opinion might be adduced on Marriage, and
Swedenborg's and even Shelley's. Goethe gave
none that I remember, and no others occur to me.

"Abou ben Adhem" seems to promise its
own immortality beyond all the contemporary
poems. And how long will one search books to
find as good a story as that of the woman of
Alexandria with her torch and bucket of water
to burn Heaven and extinguish Hell?[1]

Stick to thy affirming, how faint and feeble
soever. A poet is an affirmer. Such loud and
manifold denial as certain chemists, astronomers,
and geologists make, imposing on me and all,
and we think they will do wonders. Years pass
and they are still exposing errors, and some quiet
body has done in a corner the deed which they
must worship.

It seems a mark of rarest genius to be able to
distinguish the affirmative talent. Such geniuses

[1] She said that she would do this that men might practise
goodness for itself alone.

as we know are deceived every day, as grossly almost as common society.

June 14.

Talent makes comfort. I propose to set an Athenæum on foot in this village; but to what end? We know very well what is its utmost, to make, namely, such agreeable and adorned men as we ourselves, but not to open doors into Heaven, as genius does in every deed of genius. This goes rather to fix and to content with fixedness; the comfort of talent. London is the kingdom of Talent. Every paper and book and journal comes from that tree. Civilization is Talent's version of human life.

A highly endowed man with good intellect and good conscience is a Man-woman and does not so much need the complement of woman to his being as another. Hence his relations to the sex are somewhat dislocated and unsatisfactory. He asks in woman sometimes the woman, sometimes the man.

As when I have walked long in one direction, and then, if I turn around, discover that a large fair star has long risen and shined on me, I feel a kind of wonder that I should be so long in such a presence without knowing it, so feel I when a fine genius, which has been born and growing to full age in my neighborhood, now first turns its full deep light on my eyes.

June 15.

To-day. The ascetic of every day is how to keep me at the top of my condition ; because a good day of work is too important a possession to be risked for any chance of good days to come.

Shut your eyes and hear a military band play on the field at night and you shall have kings and queens and all regal behavior and beautiful society, all chivalry walking visibly before you.[1] . . .

Doctor Bradford said it was a misfortune to be born when children were nothing and live until men were nothing.

June 16.

Literary criticism, how beautiful to me, and I am shocked lately to detect such omnipresent egotism in my things. My prayer is that I may

1 The above lines and a long passage about the magic of a horn, and the romantic imagination concerning the rich, are printed in "Nature" (*Essays*, Second Series).

be never deprived of a fact, but be always so rich in objects of study as never to feel this impoverishment of remembering myself.

That the Intellect grows by moral obedience seems to me the Judgment Day.[1] Let that fact once obtain credence, and all wrongs are righted; sorrow and pity are no more, nor fear nor hatred; but a justice as shining and palpable as the best we know of kings and caliphs and ordeals, and what we call "poetical justice," — that is, thorough justice, justice to the eye and justice to the mind — takes place.

Friendship.

For Gods are to each other not unknown.

Odyssey, v, 79.

The same depth which dew gives to the morning meadow, the fireflies give to the evening meadow. Fire, though a spark on the chimneyback, is always a deep.

---

1 Compare the verses beginning —

> Power that by obedience grows,
> Knowledge which its source not knows, —

in the Appendix to the *Poems*, to which the editor gave the title "Insight."

I read the *Timæus* in these days, but am never sufficiently in a sacred and holiday health for the task. The man must be equal to the book. A man does not know how fine a morning he wants until he goes to read Plato and Proclus.

Elizabeth Hoar says that Shelley is like shining sand; it always looks attractive and valuable, but, try never so many times, you cannot get anything good. And yet the mica-glitter will still remain after all.

I admire the unerring instinct with which, like an arrow to its mark, the newborn fine genius always flies to the geniuses. Here is this young stripling darting upon Shakspeare, Dante, Spenser, Coleridge, and can see nothing intervening.

Charles King Newcomb took us all captive. He had grown so fast that I told him I should not show him the many things I had bribed him with. Why teaze him with multitude? Multitude is for children. I should let him alone. His criticism in his "Book-Journal" was captivating and in its devotion to the author, whether Æschylus, Dante, Shakspeare, Austin, or Scott, as feeling that he had a stake in that book, — "who touches that, touches me"; — and in the total solitude of the critic, the Patmos of thought from which he writes, in total unconsciousness of any eyes that shall ever read this writing, he reminds me of Aunt Mary. Charles is a Religious Intellect. Let it be his praise that when I carried his manuscript story to the woods, and read it in the armchair of the upturned root of a pine tree, I felt for the first time since Waldo's death some efficient faith again in the repairs of the Universe, some independency of natural relations whilst spiritual affinities can be so perfect and compensating.

Robert Bartlett defined the church as " the organic medium of life from the Lord to the Divine Humanity." He and Weiss gave an amusing account of the truckman who came with the square-cap mob [1] to the college yard and bullied for an hour. It was the richest swearing, the most æsthetic, fertilizing, — and they took notes.

Nelly waked and fretted at night and put all sleep of her seniors to rout. Seniors grew very

[1] This refers, not to the "mortarboard" cap of English Universities, not introduced here until the latter part of the nineteenth century, but probably to the square brown-paper cap often then worn by mechanics.

cross, but Nell conquered soon by the pathos
and eloquence of childhood and its words of
fate. Thus, after wishing it would be morning,
she broke out into sublimity: "Mother, it must
be morning." Presently after, in her sleep, she
rolled out of bed; I heard the little feet running round on the floor, and then, "O dear!
Where's my bed?"

She slept again, and then woke: "Mother,
I am afraid; I wish I could sleep in the bed
beside of you. I am afraid I shall tumble into
the waters — it is all water!" What else could
papa do? He jumped out of bed and laid himself down by the little mischief, and soothed
her the best he might.

I think that language should aim to describe
the fact, and not merely suggest it. If you, with
these sketchers and *dilettanti*, give me some
conscious, indeterminate compound word, it is
like a daub of color to hide the defects of your
drawing. Sharper sight would see and indicate
the true line. The poet both draws well, and
colors at the same time.

When C. says, "If I were a Transcendentalist I should not seal my letters," what does

he truly say but that he sees he ought not to seal his letters?

" When I shall be deserted," said the scholar. And he told his thoughts and read his favorite pieces to many visitors, and when he saw the club-moss, or when he saw the night heaven, and when he saw his dead mistress, he knew that this, though fair and sorrowful, was good for his song; and it seemed then as if what had been a sphere of polished steel became a surface, or a convex mirror. Then he defended copyright until the Muse left him, and Apollo said, He may die. Yet before this befel, he had been a lover of things which he did not know how to praise, nor suspected they were loved by others. Again the scholar will come to scorn this putting his gods at *vendue*. The loosestrife waved over him its pagoda of yellow bells.

None longs for a church so much as he who stays at home.

But my increasing value of the present moment, to which I gladly abandon myself when I can, is destroying my Sunday respects, which always, no doubt, have some regard to the state and conservatism. But when to-day is great I fling all the world's future into the sea.

In June, about the time when Alcott sailed for England, Manlius C. Clarke, a lawyer, came to Elizabeth Peabody and told her that he was going to sell seven hundred and fifty copies of Alcott's *Conversations on the Gospels* in sheets, for the sum of fifty dollars to trunkmakers for waste paper. There are nine hundred pounds and they are sold at five cents a pound.[1]

I hear with pleasure that a young girl in the midst of rich, decorous Unitarian friends in Boston is well-nigh persuaded to join the Roman Catholic Church. Her friends, who are also my friends, lamented to me the growth of this inclination. But I told them that I think she is to be greatly congratulated on the event. She has lived in great poverty of events. In form and years a woman, she is still a child, having had no experiences, and although of a fine, liberal, susceptible, expanding nature, has never yet found any worthy object of attention ; has not been in love, nor been called out by any taste, except lately by music, and sadly wants adequate objects. In this church, perhaps, she shall find what she needs, in a power to call out the slum-

1 On May 8, Mr. Alcott sailed for England in response to the cordial invitations of friends, whom his books, especially the *Record of a School,* had made for him there.

bering religious sentiment. It is unfortunate that the guide who has led her into this path is a young girl of a lively, forcible, but quite external character, who teaches her the historical argument for the Catholic faith. I told A. that I hoped she would not be misled by attaching any importance to that. If the offices of the church attracted her, if its beautiful forms and humane spirit draw her, if St. Augustine and St. Bernard, Jesus and Madonna, cathedral music and masses, then go, for thy dear heart's sake, but do not go out of this icehouse of Unitarianism, all external, into an icehouse again of external. At all events, I charged her to pay no regard to dissenters, but to suck that orange thoroughly.

In Boston I saw the new second volume of Tennyson's *Poems*. It had many merits, but the question might remain whether it has *the* merit. One would say it was the poetry of an exquisite; that it was prettiness carried out to the infinite, but with no one great heroic stroke; a too vigorous exclusion of all mere natural influences.

In reading aloud, you soon become sensible of a monotony of elegance. It wants a little northwest wind, or a northeast storm; it is a

lady's bower — garden-spot ; or a lord's con-
servatory, aviary, apiary, and musky greenhouse. And yet, tried by one of my tests, it
was not found wholly wanting — I mean that
it was liberating; it slipped or caused to slide
a little "this mortal coil." The poem of
"Locksley," and "The Talking Oak," — I
bear cheerful witness both gave me to feel a
momentary sense of freedom and power.

In town I also talked with Sampson Reed,
of Swedenborg, and the rest. " It is not so in
your experience, but is so in the other world."
— Other world ? I reply, there is no other
world ; here or nowhere is the whole fact,[1] all
the universe over, there is but one thing, —
this old double, Creator-creature, mind-matter,
right-wrong. He would have devils, objective
devils. I replied, That pure malignity exists, is
an absurd proposition.[2] . . . In regard to Swedenborg, I commended him as a grand poet.
Reed wished that if I admired the poetry, I
should feel it as a fact. I told him, All my concern is with the subjective truth of Jesus's or
Swedenborg's or Homer's remark, not at all

[1] This sentence is printed in "Sovereignty of Ethics"
(*Lectures and Biographical Sketches*, p. 199).

[2] See "Swedenborg" (*Representative Men*, p. 138).

with the object. To care too much for the object were low and gossiping. He may and must speak to his circumstance and the way of events and of belief around him; he may speak of angels, or Jews, or gods, or Lutherans, or gypsies, or whatsoever figures come next to his hand; I can readily enough translate his rhetoric into mine.

Every consciousness repeats mine and is a sliding scale from Deity to Dust. Sometimes the man conspires with the Universe, and sometimes he is at the other extreme and abides there, a criminal confessing sin. The moment he begins to speak I apprehend his whole relations and fix him at his point in the scale.

One seems in debate to play a foolish game for mastery, so inconvertible men are. . . .

There is a formula well known to children, " Did," " Did n't," " Did," " Did n't," etc.

Three Classes. I had occasion to say the other day to Elizabeth Hoar that I like best the strong and worthy persons like her father, who support the social order without hesitation or misgiving. I like these: they never incommode us by exciting grief, pity, or perturbation of any sort.

But my conscience, my unhappy conscience, respects that hapless class who see the faults and stains of our social order and who pray and strive incessantly to right the wrong. This annoying class of men and women commonly find the work altogether beyond their faculty, and though their honesty is commendable, their results are for this present distressing. But there is a third class who are born into a new heaven and earth with organs for the new element, and who from that Better behold this bad world in which the million gropes and suffers. By their life and happiness in the new, I am assured of the doom of the old, and these, therefore, I love and worship.

July 12.

Looking in the wrong directions for light.

Obedience is the only ladder to the throne.

It is sad to outgrow our preachers, our friends, and our books, and find them no longer potent. Proclus and Plato last me still, yet I do not read them in a manner to honor the writer.[1] . . .

I read these English tracts with interest. Goodwyn Barmby is another Ebenezer Elliot, but more practical. Revolution is no longer formid-

---

1 Here follows the passage about "reading for lustres" in "Nominalist and Realist" (*Essays*, Second Series, p. 233).

able when the Radicals are amiable. If Jack Cade loves poetry, and goes for " Love Marriage " with Milton and Shelley, for community, phalanxes, dietetics, and so forth, I no longer smell fagots. Strange it is that Carlyle should skip this remarkable class of Dissenters and Radicals so near him, Lane, Owen, Wright, Fry, etc., etc.

It probably arises from that necessity of isolation which genius so often feels. He must stand on his glass tripod if he would keep his electricity. Keep them off, then, my brave Carlyle, thou worshipper of Beauty, and publisher of beauty to the world. Every sentence of thine is joyful proclamation that Beauty the Creator, Venus Creatrix, yet exists; the sentences are written for no utility, to no moral, but for the joy of writing.

Yes, Carlyle represents very well the literary man, makes good the place of and function of Erasmus and Johnson, of Dryden and Swift, to our generation. He is thoroughly a gentleman and deserves well of the whole fraternity of scholars, for sustaining the dignity of his profession of Author in England. Yet I always feel his limitation, and praise him as one who plays his part well according to his light, as I praise the Clays and Websters. For Carlyle is worldly, and speaks not out of the celestial region of Milton and Angels.

July 16.

Chaucer is such a poet as I have described Saadi, possessing that advantage of being the most cultivated man of the times. So he speaks always sovereignly and cheerfully. For the most part, the poet nature, being very susceptible, is overacted on by others. The most affecting experience, that of the religious sentiment, goes to teach the immensity of every moment, the indifference of magnitudes. The present moment is all that the soul is God; — a great, ineffable lesson whose particulars are innumerable.

Yet experience shows that, great as is this lesson, great and greatest, yet this discipline also has its limits. One must not seek to dwell always in contemplation of the Spirit. So should the man decline into an indolent and unskilful person and stop short of his possible enlargement into a gloomy person; under churches are tombs, but Intellect is cheerful.

As bookbinders separate each sheet or each set of sheets in a large pile, by interposing a small block of pasteboard, so it seemed as if some genius had laid a ray of light underneath every

thought and fact in nature to this man's eye, so
that all things separated themselves according to
their laws before him and he never confounded
the similar with the same.

July 21.

Profound meaning of "Good will makes insight." It is as when one finds his way to the
sea by embarking on a river; or finds a passage
for the mind through a lump of matter by following the path of electricity, or magnetism, or
heat, or light, through it; anyhow, knows the
nature by sharing the nature; is at once victim
and victor.

All our days are so unprofitable whilst they
pass.[1]

Very often there seems so little affinity between the man and his works that it seems as if
the wind wrote the book and not he.

Put dittany in your greenhouse, asphodel,
nepenthe, moly, poppy, rue, self-heal.[2]

1 Here follows the passage in "Experience" thus beginning, about Hermes playing at dice with the moon (*Essays*,
Second Series, p. 46).

2 Compare, in "Concord Walks," a similar passage as to
plants that by their romantic or classic association stir the imagination (*Natural History of Intellect*, p. 174).

Rosebugs of splendid fate living on apple trees and roses and dying by an apoplexy of sweet sensations in the golden days, middle days of July.

He hoed the desart, his potatoes were poled, his asparagus grew to trees, his melons and gourds ran for miles, and had roots like oak trees.

The Telescope. The greatest genius adds nothing; he only detaches from the mass of life a particle not before detached, so that I see it separated.

Fate takes in the holidays and the work-minutes; it was writ on your brow before you were born; the watch was wound up to go seventy years, and here to stop, and there to hasten. Just this neuralgia and that typhus fever, this good October and that most auspicious friendship were all rolled in. The little barrel of the music-box revolves until all its ditties are played.

Wright, Lane, Barmby, Harwood, Heraud, Doherty, Barham, Greaves, Marston, Owen.[1]

1 These are the names of the persons in England especially interested in the new movement of thought and reform in New

August 2.

Zanoni. We must not rail if we read the book. Of all the ministers to luxury these novelwrights are the best. It is a trick, a juggle. We are cheated into laughter or wonder by feats which only oddly combine acts that we do every day.

England. Many of them gave hospitable reception to Mr. Alcott and his ideas. H. G. Wright was the head of the Alcott House School in Surrey; he, with Charles Lane and his son, came to America with Mr. Alcott on his return; Goodwyn Barmby was editor of the *Promethean, or Communitarian Apostle;* Harwood wrote for some of the reform journals; John A. Heraud was the editor of the London *Monthly Magazine,* to which journal Mr. Emerson gave some praise in vol. iii of the *Dial.* In the editorial Record of the Months of this magazine of January, 1843, a *Life of Charles Fourier,* by Hugh Doherty, is mentioned ; also the *London Phalanx* as from him. Francis Barham wrote dramatic poetry, *The Death of Socrates,* etc. He was editor of *The Alist,* a *monthly magazine of Divinity and Universal Literature.* John Pierrepont Greaves has been already mentioned in these notes as a retired merchant who became the friend of Pestalozzi and of Strauss and devoted himself, on returning to England, to improvement of English schools, especially the establishment of Infant Schools : he died in 1842. J. Westland Marston has been praised in this Journal for his dramatic poem *The Patrician's Daughter.* Robert Owen, brother of the great anatomist, was the promoter of community life in England and America.

In the *Dial* of October, 1842, in a paper called " English Reformers " Mr. Emerson tells of most of these men.

There is no new element, no power, no furtherance. It is only confectionery, not the raising of
new corn; and being such, there is no limit to
its extension and multiplication. Mr. Babbage
will presently invent a Novel-writing machine.
The old machinery cannot be disguised, however gaily vamped. Money and killing and the
Wandering Jew, these are the mainsprings still;
new names, but no new qualities in the *dramatis
personæ*. Italics and capitals are the stale substi-
tutes for natural epigram and the revelations of
loving speech. Therefore the vain endeavor to
keep any bit of this fairy gold which has rolled
like a brook through our hands. A thousand
thoughts awoke, great rainbows seemed to span
the sky. A morning among the mountains; but
as we close the book, we end the remembrance,
nothing survives, not a ray.

The power to excite which the page for moments possessed is derived from you. You read
it as you read words in a dictionary, or hear a
sonorous name of some foreigner and invest the
stranger with some eminent gifts. But because
there was not wisdom in the book, nothing fixes
itself; all floats, hovers, and is dissipated forever.

The young men are the readers and victims

of *Vivian Grey*.[1] . . . One would say of *Vivian
Grey* that it was written by a person of lively
talent who had rare opportunities of society and
access to the best anecdotes of Europe. Beck-
endorf is a sketch after nature, and whoever
was the model was a strong head, a strong hu-
morist, who deserved his empire for a day
over these college boys.

Bulwer evidently is the dissolute Alcibiades,
who has been the pupil once of Socrates, and
now and then recites a lesson which his master
taught him. But the worst of Bulwer is that he
has no style of his own; he is always a collector,
and neither contributes flash, nor low life, nor
learning, nor poetry, nor religion, nor description, from his own stores.

August 3.

Our eagerness for anecdotes of the face, form,
manners, dress, dwelling, etc., of any remarkable
mind should teach us that the man should make
all these anew, and not borrow them from Custom.

A noble brain, a searching eye, but alas! he
hath no hands.

1 The rest of the paragraph is printed in the *Dial* paper,
"Europe and European Books" (*Natural History of Intellect*, p. 377).

Work in every hour; paid or unpaid, see only that thou work;[1] . . .

Some play at chess, some at cards, some at the Stock Exchange. I prefer to play at Cause and Effect.

Bettine is more real, more witty than George Sand or Mme. de Staël; as profound and greatly more readable.

Gold represents labor and rightly opens all doors, but labor is higher and opens secreter doors, opens man, and finds new place in the kingdom of intelligence.

We read *Zanoni* with pleasure because magic is natural;[2] . . .

A mean, obscure weed by the doorstep, trodden by every foot that entered the house, was the plantain, yet, when the master's foot was wounded and lame, they went out at night with a lamp to seek its leaves, and it brought re-

1 The rest of the paragraph occurs in " New England Reformers " (*Essays*, Second Series, p. 283).

2 The rest of this long paragraph is found in " Europe and European Books," a *Dial* paper (*Natural History of Intellect*, p. 374).

freshment and healing. Temperance is the poor plantain, a mean virtue in its daily details, but what an interest — compound on compound interest — it yields at last.

Our Concord Athenæum ought to be celebrated in the town's newspaper. What shall we say but that it is good for us to club our newspapers and journals, that it will liberalize the village to make readers here, that it will give a new and handsome hospitality to our guests : and that we shall value small subscriptions more than large ones, for they always look sincere and affectionate.

(From E)

August.

The only poetic fact in the life of thousands and thousands is their death. No wonder they specify all the circumstances of the death of another person.

To give eminency to facts : to select facts, requires genius. Indigence of egotists.

Phi Beta Kappa. Nine cold hurrahs at Cambridge to Lord Ashburton. Pity they should

lie so about their keen sensibility to cold hurrahs. Men of the world value truth in proportion to their ability. Of such, and especially of
diplomatists, one has a right to [expect] wit and
ingenuity to avoid the lie, if they must comply
with the form. Elizabeth Hoar repeats Colonel
Shattuck's [1] toast to poor K——: "The orator
of the day. His *subject* deserves the attention
of every agriculturist." It does honor to Colonel
Shattuck. I wish the great lords and diplomatists at Cambridge had only as much ingenuity
and respect for truth.[2] The speeches froze me
to my place. At last Bancroft thawed the ice,
and released us, and I inwardly thanked him.

Balzac has two merits, talent and Paris. The
doctrine in which the world has acquiesced (has
it not?) on this much agitated question of the
Classic and Romantic is, that it is not a question of times, nor of forms, but of methods;
that the Classic is creative and the Romantic is
aggregative; that the Greek in the Christian

1 Colonel Shattuck kept a large country store on the common in Concord, where now the Colonial Hotel stands. He
presided at the "Cattle Show Dinner" in 1842.

2 This incident is introduced without local color in "The
Superlative" (*Lectures and Biographical Sketches*, pp. 170,
171).

Germany would have built a Cathedral; and that the Romantic in our time builds a Parthenon Custom House.

We stopped at a farmhouse at Lincoln, and asked for milk, and when we came away I offered money, but this was wrong. We injure everybody with this money, both ourselves and the receivers. We owe men a great behavior, and knowing that we have half a dollar in our pocket, we skulk and idle and misbehave, and do not put ourselves on our courtesy and sentiment.

Never look at my book and perhaps it will be better worth looking at. My thought to-day was how rightly Swedenborg pictured each man with a sphere, for we use for moral qualities the word *great*, and really conceive of Socrates, Milton, or Goethe, as a large personality.

But this also occurred as the security of the institution of marriage against the Shelleys of the time, that we need in these twilights of the gods all the conventions of the most regulated life to crutch our lame and indigent loves. The least departure from the usage of marriage would bring too strong a tide against us for so weak a reed as modern love to withstand. Its frigidities, its ebbs already need all the protection and humoring they can get from the forms and manners.

(From J)

August 11.

Yes, they are all children, and when we speak of actual parties, that must be borne in mind.

Queenie says that, according to Edmund Hosmer, it was a piece of weak indulgence in the good God to make plums and peaches.

August 20.

Last night a walk to the river with Margaret, and saw the moon broken in the water, interrogating, interrogating. Thence followed the history of the surrounding minds. Margaret said she felt herself amidst Tendencies : did not regret life, nor accuse the imperfections of her own or their performance whilst these strong native Tendencies so appeared, and in the children of all of us will be ripened. I told her that I could not discern the least difference between the first experience and the latest in my own case. I had never been otherwise than indolent, never strained a muscle, and only saw a difference in the circumstance, not in the man ; at first a circle of boys — my brothers at home, with aunt and cousins, or the schoolroom; all agreed that my verses were obscure nonsense ; and now a larger public say the same thing, " obscure nonsense," and yet both conceded that the boy had wit. A little more excitement now, but the fact identical, both in my consciousness and in my relations.

Margaret would beat with the beating heart of Nature; I feel that underneath the greatest life, though it were Jove's or Jehovah's, must lie an astonishment that embosoms both action and thought.

In talking with W. Ellery Channing on Greek mythology as it was believed at Athens, I could not help feeling how fast the key to such possibilities is lost, the key to the faith of men perishes with the faith. A thousand years hence it will seem less monstrous that those acute Greeks believed in the fables of Mercury and Pan, than that these learned and practical nations of modern Europe and America, these physicians, metaphysicians, mathematicians, critics, and merchants, believed this Jewish apologue of the poor Jewish boy, and how they contrived to attach that accidental history to the religious idea, and this famous dogma of the Triune God, etc., etc.

Nothing more facile, so long as the detachment is not made; nothing so wild and incredible the moment after that shall happen.

Lecturers. Bancroft, Giles, Mann, Rantoul, Longfellow, Theodore Parker, Doctor [S. G.] Howe, Doctor [Charles T.] Jackson, George B. Emerson.[1]

(From E)

September 1.

A walk in the most wonderful sunset this afternoon with W. E. Channing. The sunset is very unlike anything that is underneath it. But it must always seem unreal, until it has figures that are equal to it. The sunset wanted men. But unutterable is all we know of Nature.[2] How well we know certain winds, certain lights, certain aspects of the soil and the grove. Yet no words can begin to convey that which they express to us monthly and daily.

The reason why lunatics swear is because

1 Suggestions or engagements for the Concord Lyceum.

2 One or two sentences printed in "Nature" (*Essays,* Second Series, p. 178).

their exaggerated sensation requires an exaggerated speech. But Nature never swears, loves temperate expressions and sober colors, green grass, fawns and drabs, greys and blues and dark mixed; now and then a grim Acherontian fungus. Yet the sunset was vows of love of the angels. Swearing has gone out of vogue on the earth, because society, which means discriminating persons, rejects unmeasured speech. Oaths never go out of fashion, but are always beautiful and thrilling; but the sham of them, which is called profane swearing, is rightly voted a bore. Sham damns we do not like.

Results. Report of a Committee of One on the Subject of Nature. If this is the age of Criticism, let it be written greatly from a point of view that is at least Olympian or super-Olympian, and treats gods and men alike.[1] . . . It must be roundly told the upper power that, though there is a landscape, it is not yet peopled; that Nature is not enjoyed or enjoyable until man finds his completion; that we have examined very carefully both sides of the Thing, and have ascertained and do here declare that there is no Re-

1 Here follow sentences used in "The Superlative" (*Lectures and Biographical Sketches*, pp. 174, 175).

concilement; Want is always larger than Have, Idea than Fact. Consider also that our practical pyrrhonism is increased by our observation that the most lamented circumstance is the source of new power, and that we owe our wisdom to our folly.

It is much to know that poetry has been written this very day, under this very roof, by your side.[1] . . .

We may well be slow of belief concerning Genius, since we give up all to it as soon as we know it. I pardon everything to it: everything is trifling before it; I will wait for it for years, and sit in contempt before the doors of that inexhaustible blessing.

You say, perhaps Nature will yet give me the joy of friendship. But our pleasures are in some proportion to our forces. I have so little vital force that I could not stand the dissipation of a flowing and friendly life; I should die of consumption in three months. But now I husband all my strength in this bachelor life I lead; no doubt shall be a well-preserved old gentleman.

1 The rest of the passage is in " The Poet " (*Essays*, Second Series, pp. 10, 11).

September 4.

A few noble victims life shows us who do and suffer with temper and proportion; the rest are slight people, and shirk work, to use the common phrase. But every deed deepens the literture and exalts the art of the doer, and the soul doubles, trebles, quadruples, and infinitely multiplies itself.

Marston's Tragedy, *The Patrician's Daughter*. When we have such a gift, let us read it and thank God. Undoubtedly it may have faults, but what a benefit to speak to my imagination and paint with electric pencil a new form, new forms on my vacant sky. This is refreshing to read, — written with so much simplicity and spirit; the character of Mordaunt very natural and familiar to English experience in the Cannings, Pulteneys, Burkes, Foxes: the Lady Mabel also well and easily conceived. Pity that the catastrophe should be wrought by a wholesale lie on the part of the Lady Lydia, which lovers can so easily pierce. It is a weak way of making a play whose crises ought, as in life, to grow out of the faults and the conditions of the parties, as in Goethe's *Tasso*. The play seems on all accounts but one, namely, the lapse of five years between two acts, to be eminently fit for representation. The "No" of Mordaunt is wonderful for the stage.

[Passages from "Experience," on Nature and Books, and on optical illusion about persons, followed (*Essays*, Second Series, pp. 50 and 52).]

I remember that Mr. [Samuel] Ripley said to the young coxcomb from the South, "Fiddle, faddle," in reply to all his brag. Pity that we do not know how to say Fiddle faddle to people who take our time and do not exercise our wit. Most men are dupes of the hour, dupes of the nearest object: they cannot put things in perspective; but the nearest is still the largest. They talk with inferiors and do not know it, do not know that they are talking down. As on a mountain, you must level your gun at another mountain and see if the shot run out of the barrel, to know that the summit is lower than yours. The eye cannot measure it.

The poor Irish Mary Corbet, whose five weeks' infant died here three months ago, sends word to Lidian that "she cannot send back her bandbox (in which the child's body was carried to Boston): she must please give it to her; and she cannot send back the little handkerchief (with which its head was bound up): she must please give it to her."

Nathaniel Hawthorne's reputation as a writer is a very pleasing fact, because his writing is not good for anything, and this is a tribute to the man.

Sam Ward says, "I like women, they are so finished."

Edmund Hosmer's suffrage on Sunday evening to Alcott was good, so qualified and so strong. I said to him, what is really Alcott's distinction, that, rejoicing or desponding, this man always trusts his principle, never deserts it, never mistakes the convenient, customary way of doing the thing for the right and might, whilst all vulgar reformers, like these Community people, after sounding their sentimental trumpet, rely on the arm of money and the law. It is the effect of his nature, of his natural clearness of spiritual sight, which makes this confusion of thought impossible to him. I have a company who travel with me in the world, and one or other of whom I must still meet, whose office none can supply to me: Edward Stubler;[1] my Methodist Tarbox;[2] Wordsworth's Pedlar; Mary Rotch;[3] Alcott; Manzoni's Fra Cristoforo; Swedenborg; Mrs. Black;[4] and now Greaves, and his disciple Lane;[5] supreme people who represent, with whatever defects, the Ethical Idea. Elizabeth Hoar, the true Elizabeth Hoar, that is, felt the element of self in her intellectual and in her devout friends; the former loved truth, but loved self in the truth; the latter would make sacrifices, but never forgot their claims. Strange, all is strange. O Edith small,[6] thyself strange, life is strange, and God the greatest strange and stranger in his universe.

The lady said that S—— never forgot himself, he was affected, but his affectation was natural

1 The Quaker chance acquaintance met by Mr. Emerson in his youth.

2 This was the man who, working in the hayfield at Uncle Ladd's in Newton, suggested to Mr. Emerson the idea of his first sermon.

3 The New Bedford friend, whose doctrine of Acquiescence so interested him.

4 Mrs. Rebecca Black, a lady in New York of liberal ideas.

5 Mr. Alcott's English friends and admirers.

6 His second daughter, then not quite ten months old.

to him; also that the only thing she was afraid of was of being frightened. Mr. C—— sold his Boston house, and went to live in the country, because he found he could not make a bow. It was a very sensible reason, and yet Charles's criticism on it was, that he should have raised his ceiling and made his rooms larger; because an awkward man in the area of the State House, or on the Common, is no longer awkward. Large space, high rooms, have the same exhilarating and liberating quality as great light. A dance in a half-lighted ballroom would be a sad affair, but make the light intense, and the spirits of the party all rise instantly. There are two choices for one who is unhappy in an evening party: one, to go no more into such companies, which is flight; the other, to frequent them until their law is wholly learned and they become indifferent, which is conquest. O fine victim, martyr-child! clowns and scullions are content with themselves, and thou art not.

Intellect always puts an interval between the subject and the object. Affection would blend the two. For weal or for woe, I clear myself from the thing I contemplate: I grieve, but am not a grief. I love, but am not a love.

Marriage in what is called the spiritual world is impossible, because of the inequality between every subject and every object.[1] . . .

Young S—— went out tutor in the family travelling through Italy. It would have been so easy to have made his life joyful, — one human creature made happy; yet they contrived to make him feel that he was a servant, and poisoned every day, and he has come back with a fixed disgust at aristocracy. Too happy if he has. Too cheap the price he paid, if he has really attained to despise or to pity their joyless joys. But I doubt, I doubt.

I hate this sudden crystallization in my poets. A pleasing poem, but here is a rude expression, a feeble line, a wrong word. "I am sorry," returns the poet, "but it stands so written." "But you can alter it," I say. "Not one letter," replies the hardened bard.[2]

I question when I read Tennyson's *Ulysses*, whether there is taste in England to do justice

1 The rest of this long paragraph is found in "Experience" (*Essays*, Second Series, p. 77).

2 Mr. Emerson always found his friend Mr. Channing hopelessly obdurate about the faults in his verses, interrupting admirable lines.

to the poet; whether the riches of Dante's greatness would find an equal apprehension. Yet it seems feeble to deny it. The poet and the lover of poetry are born at one instant twins; and when Wordsworth wrote *Laodamia*, Landor found it out and celebrated it, and so did an Edinboro' critic. . . .

We are dissipated with our fine reading, we have too many fine books, and as those who have had too much cake and candy long for a brown crust, so we like the *Albany Cultivator*.

(From N)

September.

There is reality, however, in our relations to our friend, is there not?

Yes, and I hail the grander lights and hints that proceed from these, as the worthiest fruits of our being, thus far.

But do not these show that the existence you so loved is not closed?

I have no presentiment of that.

Alas, my friend, you have no generosity; you cannot give yourself away. I see the law of all your friendships. It is a bargain. You tell your things, your friend tells his things, and as soon as the inventory is complete, you take your hats.

Do you see that kitten chasing so prettily her own tail? If you could see with her eyes, you would see her surrounded with hundreds of figures performing complex dramas.[1] . . .

How slowly, how slowly we learn that witchcraft and ghostcraft, palmistry and magic, and all the other so-called superstitions, which, with so much police, boastful skepticism, and scientific committees, we had finally dismissed to the moon as nonsense, are really no nonsense at all, but subtle and valid influences, always starting up, mowing, muttering in our path, and shading our day. The things are real, only they have shed their skin which with much insult we have gibbeted and buried. One person fastens an eye on us, and the very graves of the memory render up their dead.[2] . . .

It is with Literature as it is with the Faculty of Medicine. The poor man catches the disease and dies, nobody knows how; the rich man takes the same disease and dies also, but has the honor and the satisfaction of having the disease named by his physician and a council of physi-

1 For the rest of the passage, see " Experience " (*Essays,* Second Series, p. 80).

2 See " Character " (*Essays,* Second Series, p. 110).

cians. It is a great matter to have the thing named.

Chemistry, Entomology, Conic Sections, Medicine, each science, each province of science, will come to satisfy all demands: the whole of poetry, of mythology, of ethics, of demonology, will be expressed by it: a new rhetoric, new methods of philosophy, perhaps new political parties, will celebrate the culmination of each one.

Just to fill the hour, that is happiness.[1] . . . It pains me never that I cannot give you an accurate answer to the question, What is God? What is the operation we call Providence? and the like. There lies the answer: there it exists, present, omnipresent to you, to me. . . .

I woke up and found the dear old world, wife, babe and mother, Concord and Boston, the dear old spiritual world, and even the dear old Devil not far off.[2]

"Blind Love," yes, Love lives in the stratum of the Relative and is blind to the Abso-

1 The rest of the passage is printed in "Works and Days" (*Society and Solitude*, p. 181).
2 Used in "Experience."

lute. But Self is blind too, and not lovelily but
odiously. As far as that element comes in, we
run on about ourselves and never perceive that
we have long lost the ear of our companion.

Transcendental Criticism. With this eternal demand for *more*, which belongs to our modest
constitutions, how can we be helped? The gods
themselves could not help us, they are just as
badly off themselves.

T. P.[1] has beautiful fangs, and the whole am-
phitheatre delights to see him worry and tear his
victim.

Rings and jewels are not gifts, but apologies for
gifts. The only gift is a portion of thyself.[2] . . .

That were a right problem for a dramatist to
solve; *given* a bandit, the strongest temptation
and opportunity for violence or plunder, — how
to bring off the man of wit by his wit only,
exercised not immediately, but directly through
speech. It is a problem perfectly easy to solve

1 Theodore Parker?

2 Here follows much of the matter of the opening pages of
"Gifts" but differently arranged (*Essays*, Second Series).

in action whenever the right Cæsar comes. He
does not exert courage but wit. The Corsair has
caught a Captain.[1]

Sterling writes well of sculpture, and if I were
rich, I would have my reception-room for my
friends filled with statues or casts of all the gods,
to preach serenity to me, and my friends.[2] But
it is vain to make a matter of conscience of calm-
ness ; a man will not become grand by accusing
himself, but grandeur will come in where God
wills, like a fine day.

T. sells me peat or wood or apples for more
money than he sells the same to Hosmer, who
can use certain test questions or examinations

1 This subject is treated in more concrete form in " Character " (p. 96).

2 Mr. Emerson probably refers to John Sterling's beautiful lament for Greek art, the poem " Dædalus." Mr. Emerson included it in his *Parnassus*. The following two verses
are here suggested : —

> Ever thy phantoms arise before us,
> Our loftier brothers, but one in blood ;
> By bed and table they lord it o'er us
> With looks of beauty and words of good.

> Calmly they show us mankind victorious
> O'er all that is aimless, blind and base ;
> Their presence has made our nature glorious,
> Unveiling our night's illumined face.

which I cannot apply. Well, do I not exclude T. also from the use of certain test questions and examinations in reference to other matters more important to his honor and standing as a man than are his peat and apples to me?

The highest criticism should be written in poetry.

Goethe received four, Fichte five, and Richter seven louis d'ors a sheet for their best works. A louis = $4.00.

I have a kind of promise to write, one of these days, a verse or two to the praise of my native city, which in common days we often rail at, yet which has great merits to usward.[1] That, too, like every city, has certain virtues, as a museum of the arts. The parlors of private collectors; the Athenæum Gallery; and the College; become the city of the City. Then a city has this praise, that, as the bell or band of music

1 A score of years later were published "Boston," which, begun in the sad days preceding the War, was finished in happier times; and the "Boston Hymn," which Mr. Emerson read in the Music Hall in his native city on the celebration of the emancipation of the slaves, January 1, 1863.

is heard outside, beyond the din of carts, so
the beautiful in architecture, or in political and
social institutions, endures: all else comes to
nought. So that the antiquities and permanent
things in each city are good and fine.

In London, Alcott saw Carlyle, Lane, O'Connell; Robert Owen, Heraud, Marston, Wright,
Barham, Browning, Milnes, W. J. Fox, Harwood, Doctor Bowring, Doctor Elliotson, Morgan, Doherty, Barmby, George Thompson.

All persons are puzzles until at last we find
in some word or act the key to the man, to
the woman; straightway all their past words and
actions lie in light before us.

Men are so gregarious that they have no solitary merits. They all — the reputed leaders and
all — lean on some other, — and this supersti-
tiously, and not from insight of his merit. They
follow a fact, they follow success, and not skill.
Therefore, as soon as the success stops, fails,
and Mr. Jackson blunders in building Pemberton
Square, they quit him; already they remember that long ago they suspected Mr. Jackson's judgment, and they transfer the repute

of judgment to the next succeeder who has not yet blundered.

Vegetables, Plants, are the young of the Universe, the future men, but not yet ripe for that rank in Nature. Yet they are all handsome, and men, let them once be fifteen years old, are for the most part unsightly. The reason is that the men, though young, are already dissipated, but the maples and ferns are not. Yet, no doubt, when they come to it, they, too, will curse and swear.[1] In the wood I heard the laughter of the crows.

Milnes brought Carlyle to the railway, and showed him the departing train. Carlyle looked at it and then said, "These are our poems, Milnes." Milnes ought to have answered, "Aye, and our histories, Carlyle."

But it is worth noticing how fast the poet can dispose of these formidable facts. One sees the Factory village and the Railway, and thinks of Wordsworth and what will be his dismay. Wordsworth has the sense to see that this also

1 The foregoing passage in a less entertaining form is printed in "Nature" (*Essays*, Second Series, pp. 181, 182).

falls in, *un bête de plus*, with the known multitude of mechanical facts and that all Mechanics
have not gained a grain's weight from the addi-
tion. The spiritual Fact alike remains Unalter-
able by many or by few particulars, as no mountain is of any appreciable height to break the
curve of the sphere.[1]

Men are great in their own despite. They
achieve a certain greatness, but it was while they
were toiling to achieve another conventional
one. The boy at college apologizes for not
learning the tutor's task, and tries to learn it,
but stronger Nature gives him Otway and Massinger to read, or betrays him into a stroll to
Mount Auburn in study hours. The poor boy,
instead of thanking the gods and slighting the
mathematical tutor, ducks before the functionary, and poisons his own fine pleasures by a perpetual penitence. Well, at least let that one
never brag of the choice he made; as he might
have well done, if he had known what he did
when he was doing it.[2]

1 Sentences to the same purpose without mention of Wordsworth occur in " The Poet " (*Essays*, Second Series).

2 Compare the above bit of autobiography with similar passages in " Spiritual Laws " and in " Heroism " (*Essays*, First
Series, pp. 133 and 237).

Alcott, when he went to England, wished to carry with him miniatures of Elizabeth Peabody, of Margaret Fuller, and of me. — I remember once that A. thought that the head would soon put off from it the trunk, which would perish, whilst the brain would unfold a new and higher organization.

(From a loose sheet)

I am most of the time a very young child who does not pretend to oversee Nature and dictate its law. I play with it, like other infants, as my toy. I see sun and moon and river without asking their causes. I am pleased by the mysterious music of falling water or the rippling and washing against the shores, without knowing why. Yet, child as I am, I know that I may in any moment wake up to the sense of authority and deity herein. A seer, a prophet, passing by, will bring me to it; poetry will; nay, I shall think it in the austere woods and they will tremble and turn to dreams.

(From N)

Richter said, " In the great world I despise the men and their joyless joys, but I esteem the women ; in them alone can one investigate the spirit of the times."

I think that in my house where there are no ears, no fine person should be so much wronged as to be asked to sing.

White Lies. It shall be the law of this Society that no member shall be reckoned a liar who is a sportsman, and indicates the wrong place when asked where he shot his partridge; or who is an angler, and misremembers where he took his trout; or who is an engineer, and misdirects his inquiring friends as to the best mill privilege; or who is a merchant, and forgets in what stock he proposes to invest; or who is an author, and being asked if he wrote an anonymous book, replies in the negative.

Ghost (under the floor). It shall not be the law.

[The account of Edward Everett, which occupies the following nine pages of the Journal, seems to have been written at this time. Mr. Emerson introduced almost all of it into a lecture delivered in the later years of his active life (perhaps 1867 and later) after Everett's death. This, called "Historic Notes of Life and Letters in New England," Mr. Cabot first published in the Riverside Edition of the Works, in the volume *Lectures and Biographical Sketches*, a year or two after Mr. Emerson died.

The opening passage of the journal entry, and one or two others that showed his young enthusiasm for Everett, also one or two not printed in the posthumous volume, are here given.]

Edward Everett. There was an influence on the young people from Everett's genius which was almost comparable to that of Pericles in Athens. That man had an inspiration that did not go beyond his head, but which made him the genius of elegance. He had a radiant beauty of person, of a classic style, a heavy, large eye, marble lids, which gave the impression of mass which the slightness of his form needed, sculptured lips, a voice of such rich tones, such precise and perfect utterance that, although slightly nasal, it was the most mellow and beautiful and correct of all the instruments of the time. The word that he spoke, in the manner in which he spoke it, became current and classical in New England.

Especially beautiful were his poetic quotations. He quoted Milton; more rarely Byron; and sometimes a verse from Watts, and with such sweet and perfect modulation that he seemed to give as much beauty as he borrowed, and whatever he had quoted will seldom be remembered by any who heard him without inseparable association with his voice and genius. This eminently beautiful person was followed like an Apollo from church to church, wherever the fame that he would preach led, by all the most cultivated and intelligent youths with grateful admiration. His appearance in any pulpit lighted up all countenances with delight. The smallest anecdote of his behavior or conversation was eagerly caught and repeated, and every young scholar could repeat brilliant sentences from his sermons with mimicry; good or bad, of his voice. . . . The church was dismissed, but the bright image of that eloquent form followed the boy home to his bedchamber, and not a sentence was written in a theme, not a declamation attempted in the College Chapel, but showed the omnipresence of his genius to youthful heads. He thus raised the standard of taste in writing and speaking in New England.

Meantime all this was a pure triumph of Rhetoric. This man had neither intellectual nor moral principles to teach. He had no thoughts. It was early asked, when Massachusetts was full of his fame, what truths he had thrown into circulation, and how he had enriched the general mind, and agreed that only in graces of manner, only in a new perception of Grecian beauty, had he opened our eyes. It was early observed that he had no warm personal friends. Yet his genius made every youth his defender and boys filled their mouths with arguments to prove that the orator had a heart. . . .

Everett's fame had the effect of giving a new lustre to the University — which it greatly needed. Students flocked thither from the South and the West, from the remote points of Georgia, Tennessee, Alabama, and Louisiana.

Well, this bright morning had a short continuance. Mr. Everett was soon attracted by the vulgar prizes of politics, and quit coldly the splendid career which opened before him (and which, not circumstances, but his own genius had made) for the road to Washington, where it is said he has had the usual fortune of flattery and mortification, but is wholly lost to any real and manly usefulness.

Everett had as lief his manuscript was in your pocket, he read so well.

In every conversation, even the highest, there is a certain trick, one may say, which may be soon learned by an acute person, and then that particular style be continued indefinitely. This is true of Very's, Alcott's, Lane's, and all such specialists or mystics; more true of these than of other classes.

Sam Ward said that men died to break up their styles; but Nature had no objection to Goethe's living, for he did not form one.

September 27 was a fine day, and Hawthorne and I set forth on a walk. We went first to the Factory where Mr. Damon makes Domett cloths, but his mills were standing still, his houses empty. Nothing so small but comes to honor and has its shining moment somewhere; and so was it here with our little Assabet or North Branch; it was falling over the rocks into silver, and above was expanded into this tranquil lake. After looking about us a few moments, we took the road to Stow. The day was full of sunshine, and it was a luxury to walk in the midst of all this warm and colored light. The days of September are so rich that it seems natural to walk to the end of one's strength, and then fall prostrate, saturated with the fine floods, and cry, *Nunc dimittis me.* Fringed gentians, a thornbush with red fruit, wild apple trees whose fruit hung like berries, and grapevines were the decorations of the path. We scarcely encountered man or boy in our road nor saw any in the fields. This depopulation lasted all day. But the outlines of the landscape were so gentle that it seemed as if we were in a very cultivated country, and elegant persons must be living just over yonder hills. Three or four times, or oftener, we saw the entrance to their lordly park. But nothing in the farms or in the houses made this good. And it is to be considered that when any large brain is born in these towns, it is sent, at sixteen or twenty years, to Boston or New York, and the country is tilled only by the inferior class of the people, by the second crop or *rowan* of the Men. Hence all these shiftless poverty-struck pig-farms. In Europe, where society has an aristocratic structure, the land is full of men of the best stock, and the best culture, whose interest and pride it is to remain half of the year at least on their estates and to fill these with every convenience and ornament. Of course these make model-farms and model-architecture, and are a constant education to the eye and hand of the surrounding population.

Our walk had no incidents. It needed none, for we were in excellent spirits, had much conversation, for we were both old collectors who had never had opportunity before to show each

other our cabinets, so that we could have filled
with matter much longer days. We agreed that
it needed a little dash of humor or extravagance
in the traveller to give occasion to incident in his
journey. Here we sober men, easily pleased,
kept on the outside of the land and did not by
so much as a request for a cup of milk creep into
any farmhouse. If want of pence in our pocket
or some vagary in our brain drove us into these
" huts where poor men lie," to crave dinner or
night's lodging, it would be so easy to break
into some mesh of domestic romance, learn so
much pathetic private history, perchance see the
first blush mantle on the cheeks of the young
girl when the mail stage came or did not come,
or even get entangled ourselves in some thread
of gold or grey. Then again the opportunities
which the taverns once offered the traveller, of
witnessing and even sharing in the joke and the
politics of the teamster and farmers on the road,
are now no more. The Temperance Society
emptied the bar-room. It is a cold place. Hawthorne tried to smoke a cigar, but I observed he
was soon out on the piazza. After noon we
reached Stow, and dined, and then continued
our journey towards Harvard, making our day's
walk, according to our best computation, about

twenty miles. The last miles, however, we rode in a wagon, having been challenged by a friendly, fatherly gentleman, who knew my name, and my father's name and history, and who insisted on doing the honors of his town to us, and of us to his townsmen; for he fairly installed us at the tavern, introduced us to the Doctor, and to General ——, and bespoke the landlord's best attention to our wants. We get the view of the Nashua River Valley from the top of Oak Hill, as we enter Harvard village. Next morning we began our walk at 6.30 o'clock for the Shaker Village, distant three and a half miles. Whilst the good Sisters were getting ready our breakfast, we had a conversation with Seth Blanchard and Cloutman of the Brethren, who gave an honest account, by yea and by nay, of their faith and practice. They were not stupid, like some whom I have seen of their Society, and not worldly like others. The conversation on both parts was frank enough; with the downright I will be downright, thought I, and Seth showed some humor. I doubt not we should have had our own way with them to a good extent (not quite after the manner of Hayraddin Maugrabin with the Monks of Liège) if we could have stayed twenty-four hours; although my powers of persuasion were crippled by a disgraceful barking cold, and Hawthorne inclined to play Jove more than Mercurius. After breakfast Cloutman showed us the farm, vineyard, orchard, barn, pressing-room, etc. The vineyard contained two noble arcades of grapes, both white and Isabella, full of fruit; the orchard, fine varieties of pears and peaches and apples.

They have fifteen hundred acres here, a tract of woodland in Ashburnham, and a sheep pasture somewhere else, enough to supply the wants of the two hundred souls in this family. They are in many ways an interesting Society, but at present have an additional importance as an experiment of Socialism which so falls in with the temper of the times. What improvement is made is made forever; this Capitalist is old and never dies, his subsistence was long ago secured, and he has gone on now for long scores of years in adding easily compound interests to his stock. Moreover, this settlement is of great value in the heart of the country as a model-farm, in the absence of that rural nobility we talked of yesterday. Here are improvements invented, or adopted from the other Shaker communities, which the neighboring farmers see and copy. From the Shaker Village we

came to Littleton and thence to Acton, still in
the same redundance of splendor. It was like
a day of July, and from Acton we sauntered
leisurely homeward, to finish the nineteen miles
of our second day before four in the afternoon.

In a town which you enter for the first time
at late sunset, the trees and houses look pictorial in the twilight, but you can never play tricks
with old acquaintances.

There is something very agreeable in fatigue.
I am willinger to die, having had my swing of
the fair day; and seven times in his life, I suppose, every man sings, Now, Lord, let thy servant depart.

Landor, though like other poets he has not
been happy in love, has written admirable
sentences on the passion. Perhaps, said Hawthorne, their disappointment taught them to
write these things. Well, it is probable. One
of Landor's sentences was worth a divorce;
"Those to whom love is a secondary thing
love more than those to whom it is a primary."

This thought appeared in all the Shakers
said about admission of members to their Society,
that people came and proved themselves; they
soon showed what they were, and remained or
departed, as the Spirit made manifest, alike *to*

themselves and to the Society. No man should join them for a living: and no man should be turned off because he was poor or bedridden, but only for not being of them.

Cloutman told us their hospitality was costly, for they entertain without price all the friends of any member who visit them.

We talked of Scott. There is some greatness in defying posterity and writing for the hour, and so being a harper.

Piety, like chivalry, has no stationary exemplar, but is evanescent and receding like rainbows. You cannot find any specimen of a religious man now in your society; you hear the fame of one; you go far and find him; and he begins, "I had a friend in my youth," etc. Yet it seems as if nothing would make such good picture in national sketches as genuine Connecticut, if you could lay your hand on it.

At night the frogs were loud, but the eagle was silent in his cliff.

If in this last book of Wordsworth there be dulness, it is yet the dulness of a great and cultivated mind.

We have our culture, like Allston, from Europe, and are Europeans. Perhaps we must be content with this and thank God for Europe for a while yet, and there shall be no great Yankee, until, in the unfolding of our population and power, England kicks the beam, and English authors write to America; which must happen ere long.

I have not yet begun to regret much the omission to see any particular part of nature or art, but perhaps, as we live longer, we begin to compare more narrowly the chances of life with the things to be seen in it, and count the Niagaras we have not visited. For me, not only Niagara, but the Prairie, and the Ohio and the Mississippi rivers are still only names. And yet, better see nothing beyond your village than to go coldly and hardly to work to see the Meccas of the mind. It were indeed an enlargement, a duplication of life, if, in fit company and with good reason, I can go to Italy; but Florence is not Florence if the visit is forced.

Avarice, ambition, almost all talents, are restless and vagrant; they go up to the cities; but Religion is a good rooter.

October 8.

The commercial relations of the world are so intimately drawn to London, that it seems as if every dollar in the world contributed to strengthen the English government.

It is ridiculous to quote solemnly what the young W. said in his sermon as decisive of his faith in this or that. These young preachers are but chipping birds, who chirp now on the bushes, now on the ground, but do not mean anything by their chirping. He must be very green who would go to infer anything in respect to their character from what they say.

What does the extraordinary taste for Indian names which now appear on every Hotel and every Omnibus, betoken?

Edward Washburn told me that at Andover they sell shelvesful of Coleridge's *Aids to Reflection* in a year.

Queenie says that Edie spends half her time in looking innocent, and the other half in looking dignified. Nelly, asleep in her bed, had the air and attitude of one who rides a horse of Night.

Edmund Hosmer thinks there is a good deal of unnecessary labor spent to feed the ani-

mals, — especially the pig and horse. Many a
farmer is but a horse's horse or a pig's pig.[1]

At the Shakers' house in Harvard I found a
spirit-level on the window-seat, a very good em-
blem for the Society ; but, unfortunately, neither
the table nor the shelf nor the window-seat
were plumb.

It appears that there are people, both men
and women, who transgress every rule of prudence, and yet have unexceptional health and
bring much to pass ; and it seems just as well,
if one can get on a good exception, to live off
the road as to keep the highway.

The sons of great men should be great ; if
they are little, it is because they eat too much
pound cake, which is an accident ; or, because
their fathers married dolls.

" The spring of her economy fed the fountain of her bounty."

October 12.

The merit of a poem or tragedy is a matter

[1] This entry might be the origin of the lines in the " Ode,"
inscribed to W. H. Channing, in the *Poems* : —

The horseman serves the horse, the neatherd serves the neat.

of experience. An intelligent youth can find little wonderful in the Greeks or Romans. These tragedies, these poems, are cold and tame. Nature and all the events passing in the street are more to him, he says, than the stark, unchangeable crisis of the *Iliad* or the *Antigone;* and as for thoughts, his own thoughts are better and are more numerous. So says one, so say all. Presently, each of them tries his hand at expressing his thought; — but there is a certain stiffness, or a certain extravagance in it. All try, and all fail, each from some peculiar and different defect. The whole age of authors tries; many ages try; and in the millions and millions of experiments these confessedly tame and stark-poems of the Ancient are still the best. It seems to be certain that they will go on discontenting yet excelling the intelligent youths of the generations to come.

But always they will find their admirers, not in the creative and enthusiastic few, who will always feel their ideal inferiority, but in the elegant, cultivated and conservative class.

You praise Homer and disesteem the art that makes the tragedy. To me it seems higher — the unpopular and austere muse that casts human life into a high tragedy, *Prometheus, Œdi-*

pus, *Hamlet* (midway between the Epic and the Ode) — than the art of the epic poet, which condescends more to common humanity, and approaches the ballad. Man is nine parts fool for one part wise, and therefore Homer and Chaucer more read than *Antigone*, *Hamlet*, or *Comus*.

Making Money.[1] Men think there is some magic about this. . . .

The worst times that ever fell were good times to somebody. There is always some one in the gap.

He is shallow who rails at men and their contrivances and does not see Divinity behind all their institutions and all their fetiches, even behind such as are odious and paltry ; they are documents of beauty also. The practice of Prayer is not philosophical, — there is somewhat of absurd and ridiculous in it to the eye of science ; it is juvenile, and, like plays of children, though nonsense, yet very useful and educative nonsense. Well, so with all our things. . . .

The prosperity of Boston is an unexpected

1 See the passage beginning thus in " Wealth " (*Conduct of Life*, p. 100).

consequence of Steam - communication. The
frightful expenses of steam make the greater
neighborhood of Boston to Europe a circumstance of commanding importance, — and the
ports of Havre and Liverpool are two days
nearer to Boston than to New York. This
superiority for the steam-post added to the con-
temporaneous opening of its great lines of railroad, like iron rivers, which already are making
it the dépôt for flour from Western New York,
Michigan, Illinois, promise a great prosperity
to that city.

I woke with a regret that I had made a bargain
at B. and had not rather thrown myself wholly
on their sense of justice. The Olympian must
be Olympian in carriage and deeds wherever
he can be symmetrically, not rudely, — and he
must dare a little, and try Olympian experiments. Well, courage, and do better again.

A man cannot free himself by any self-deny-
ing ordinances, neither by water nor potatoes
nor by violent passivities, by refusing to swear,
refusing to pay taxes, by going to jail, or by
taking another man's crop or squatting on his
land, — by none of these ways can he free him-

self ; no, nor by paying his debts with money ;
only by obedience to his own genius ; only by
the freest activity in the way constitutional to
him, does an angel seem to arise and lead him
by the hand out of all wards of the prison.[1]

Pecunia est alter Sanguis.

> The seamstress' wax,
> The woodman's axe, —
> These pay the tax.

I think Doctor Channing was intellectual by
dint of his fine moral sentiment, and not pri-
marily.[2] . . . His paper on Milton contained
the true doctrine of Inspiration ; " Milton observes higher laws than he transgresses."

When the friend has newly died, the survivor
has not yet grief, but the expectation of grief.
He has not long enough been deprived of his
society to feel yet the want of it. He is surprised, and is now under a certain intellectual

1 The last part of the sentence, in a similar connection,
occurs in the last pages of "New England Reformers"
(*Essays*, Second Series).

2 More is said of Doctor Channing in "Historic Notes of
Life and Letters in New England" (*Lectures and Biographical Sketches*, pp. 339, 340).

excitement, being occupied and in a manner amused by the novelty of the event, and is exploring his changed condition. This defends him from sorrow. It is not until the funeral procession has departed from his doors, and the mourners have all returned to their ordinary pursuits, and forgotten the deceased, that the grief of the friend begins. In the midst of his work, in the midst of his leisure, in his thoughts which are now uncommunicated, in his successes which are now in vain, in his hopes which now are quickly checked and run low, he sees with bitterness how poor he is. As it is with the mourner, so it is with the man of Virtue in respect to the practice of virtue. The evil practice of the country and the time is exposed by some preacher of righteousness, and after some time the land is filled with the noise of the reform. Men congratulate themselves on the great evil they have escaped and on the signal progress of society. But it is not until after this tumult is over, and all have, one after another, come in to the new practice, and the reaction has occurred, and great numbers are disgusted and have gone back again, not until then does the true reformer, the noble man, begin to find his virtue and advantage. Through the clamor he has said nothing,

— he embraced the right which was shown, at once and forever. Now society is back again where it was before, but he has added this beauty to his life.

Le Peau d'Ane. You *can* do two things at a time; and when you have got your pockets full of chestnuts, and say I have lost my half-hour, behold you have got something besides, for the tops of the Silver Mountains of the White Island loomed up whilst you stood under the tree, and glittered for an instant; therefore there is no *peau de chagrin*.

Life. Everything good, we say, is on the highway. A *virtuoso* hunts up with great pains a landscape of Guercino, a crayon sketch of Salvator, but the Transfiguration, The Last Judgment, The Communion, are on the walls of the Vatican where every footman may see them without price. You have got for five hundred pounds an autograph receipt of Shakspeare; but for nothing a schoolboy can read *Hamlet*, and, if he has eyes, can detect secrets yet unpublished and of highest concernment therein. I think I will never read any but the commonest of all books: the Bible, Shakspeare, Milton, Dante, Homer.

Somebody cried to him out of the walnut woods, "Ho! Ho! Be sure not to get imposed upon. Ho! Ho!" And Arthur rubbed his eyes, looked round him, and bethought him that he would not again. But at night he found the whole journey was a blunder, and he was a dupe. The next morning when he woke, he heard his old neighbor calling to the cattle in the yard under his window, and when Arthur looked out, the man said, "Ho! Ho! Be sure you don't get imposed upon. Ho! Ho!" Forewarned, thought Arthur once more.

The sannup and the squaw do not get drunk at the same time. They take turns in keeping sober, and husband and wife should never be low-spirited at the same time, but each should be able to cheer the other.

We learn with joy and wonder this new and flattering art of language, deceived by the exhilaration which accompanies the attainment of each new word. We fancy we gain somewhat. We gain nothing. It seemed to men that words come nearer to the thing; described the fact; were the fact. They learn later that they only suggest it. It is an operose, circuitous way of putting us in mind of the thing, — of flagellating our attention. But this was slowly discovered. With what good faith these old books of barbarous men record the genesis of the world. Their best attempts to narrate how it is that star and earth and man exist, run out into some gigantic mythology, which, when it is ended, leaves the beautiful principal facts where they were, and the stupid gazing fabulist just as far from them as at first. Garrulity is our religion and philosophy. They wonder and are angry that some persons slight their books and prefer the thing itself. But with all progress this happens, that speech becomes less, and finally ceases in a noble silence.

I, oh, I am only here to see. Droll privilege of Spectatorship that we all feel; I have an unquestioning presumption, on hearing that a good man is coming by, that this man is true, consistent, and his conscience greatly more faithful and effective than mine. And unluckily he has the same feeling respecting me and others, that not he, but I and they, are the responsible persons.

In our parties there is no great difference: the Democratic Party is not more human than the

Whig. I think the leaders, in my little experience, to be worse men than the Whig leaders. I think their democracy no more principled than the conservatism; that it is only a little worse Whiggism. They have no higher objects. To vote at all for either party is Whiggism, and it is only a little more to vote for those whose bias is conservatism. I have many points of sympathy with the Whigs in these "dregs of Romulus," and I cannot for a moment permit these profligate Tammany Hall and *Morning Post* adventurers to represent the cause of humanity and love.

It is odious that our fine geniuses should all have this imperfection, that they cannot do anything useful.[1] . . .

Cheerfulness is so much the order of nature that the superabundant glee of a child lying on its back and not yet strong enough to get up or to sit up, yet cooing, warbling, laughing, screaming with joy, is an image of independence which makes power no part of independence. Queenie looks at Edie kicking up both feet into the air, and thinks that Edie says "the world was made

1 The rest of this paragraph is printed in *Society and Solitude* (pp. 6, 7).

on purpose to carry round the little baby; and the world goes round the sun only to bring titty-time and creeping - on - the - floor - time to the Baby."

Ogden respected nothing in —— so much as this tenacious trick of asking at breakfast and on 'Change, at work and at bedtime, between glasses of wine or drops taken for fever, questions touching God and duty, the salvation of the soul. The Devil take you and your soul! said Ogden; but on second thought nothing seemed to him that he had met within Marseilles more respectable than this determined curiosity and thoughtfulness in a being in so many ways inferior, in one so superior.

And really and truly, — so ought a person to end, — we cannot spare any the coarsest muniment of virtue, and the purest sense of justice that lives in any human breast needs a law founded on force as index and remembrancer.[1]

Margaret [Fuller] described E. as hobgoblin nature and full of indirections. But he is a good

---

1 Compare "Grace," beginning —

> How much, preventing God, to thee I owe
> For the defences thou hast round me set.

Poems, Appendix.

vagabond and knows how to take a walk. The
gipsy talent is inestimable in the country, and
so rare. In a woman it would be bewitching.
Margaret Fuller has not a particle, and only the
possibility. And yet this is a relative talent, and
to each there doubtless exists a gipsy-maker. I
told Hawthorne yesterday that I think every
young man at some time inclines to make the
experiment of a dare-God and dare-devil originality like that of Rabelais. He would jump on
the top of the nearest fence and crow. He makes
the experiment, but it proves like the flight of
pig-lead into the air, which cannot cope with the
poorest hen. Irresistible custom brings him
plump down, and he finds himself, instead of
odes, writing gazettes and leases. Yet there is
imitation and model, or suggestion, to the very
archangels, if we knew their history, and if we
knew Rabelais's reading we should see the rill
of the Rabelais river. Yet his hold of his place
in Parnassus is as firm as Homer's. A jester, but
his is the jest of the world, and not of Touch-
stone or Clown or Harlequin. His wit is universal, not accidental, and the anecdotes of the
time, which made the first butt of the satire and
which are lost, are of no importance, as the wit
transcends any particular mark, and pierces to

permanent relations and interests. His joke will fit any town or community of men.

The style at once decides the high quality of the man. It flows like the river Amazon, so rich, so plentiful, so transparent, and with such long reaches, that longanimity or longsightedness which belongs to the Platos. No sand without lime, no short, chippy, indigent epigrammatist or proverbialist with docked sentences, but an exhaustless affluence.

It is only a young man who supposes there is anything new in Wall Street. The merchant who figures there, so much to his own satisfaction and to the admiration or fear or hatred of the younger or weaker competitors, is a very old business. You shall find him, his way, that is, of thinking concerning the world and men and property and eating and drinking and marriage and education and religion and government, — the whole concatenation of his opinions, the very shade of their color, the same laughter, the same knowingness, the same unbelief, and the same ability and taste, in Rabelais and Aristophanes. Panurge was good Wall Street. Pyrrhonism and Transcendentalism are just as old; and I am persuaded that by and by we shall find them in the chemical element, that excess of oxygen makes the sinner, and of hydrogen the saint.

"My evening visitors," said that excellent Professor Fortinbras, "if they cannot see the clock should find the time in my face. As soon as it is nine, I begin to curse them with internal execrations that are minute-guns." And yet, he added, "The devil take half-hospitalities, this self-protecting civility whose invitations to dinner are determined exclusions from the heart of the inviter, as if he said, 'I invite you to eat, because I will not converse with you.' If he dared only say it, that exception would be hospitality of angels, an admission to the thought of his heart."

Mary Rotch inclined to speak of the spirit negatively and instead of calling it a light, "an oracle," a "leading," she said, "When she would do that she should not, she found an objection."

Sad the swiftness with which life culminates and the humility of the expectations of the greatest part of men.[1] . . .

---

1 The long passage following, about the event which seems to each a crisis of life and from which he dates his

In the Indian summers, of which we have eight or ten every year, you can almost see the Indians under the trees in the wood. These are the reconciling days which come to graduate the autumn into winter, and to comfort us after the first attacks of the cold. Soothsayers, prediction as well as memory, they look over December and January into the crepuscular light of March and April.

This feeling I have respecting Homer and Greek, that in this great, empty continent of ours, stretching enormous almost from pole to pole, with thousands of long rivers and thousands of ranges of mountains, the rare scholar, who, under a farmhouse roof, reads Homer and the Tragedies, adorns the land. He begins to fill it with wit, to counterbalance the enormous disproportion of the unquickened earth. He who first reads Homer in America is its Cadmus and Numa, and a subtle but unlimited benefactor.

Rabelais is not to be skipped in literary history, as he is the source of so much proverb,

later experience, is printed in "Domestic Life," *Society and Solitude* (pp. 123–125).

story, and joke which are derived from him into all modern books in all languages. He is the Joe Miller of modern literature.

Thou shalt read Homer, Æschylus, Sophocles, Euripides, Aristophanes, Plato, Proclus, Plotinus, Jamblichus, Porphyry, Aristotle, Virgil, Plutarch, Apuleius, Chaucer, Dante, Rabelais, Montaigne, Cervantes, Shakspeare, Jonson, Ford, Chapman, Beaumont and Fletcher, Bacon, Marvell, More, Milton, Molière, Swedenborg, Goethe.

Every spinner is not a spider. Society — what a delicate result! No matter how good the associates, the society is sure to spoil, if the least overdone,[1] . . . Do not let us meet to argue; let us meet to rest. Let us dispose quite unceremoniously of these obstreperous selves and of their vain talents, and dwell, for a little, in the great Peace. Self-respect and brotherly love seem equally to demand silence.

You shall have joy, or you shall have power, said God; you shall not have both.

1 What is omitted is printed in "Character" (p. 112).

Books. Theophrastus said " that the most il-
literate were able to speak in the presence of
the most elegant persons, while they spake
nothing but truth and reason."

Every man writes after a trick, and you need
not read many sentences to learn his whole
trick. Richter is a perpetual exaggeration and
I get nervous.

October is come, and the harvest home, and
the need that the journalist should make his in-
dexes for the winter's prælections. Let us consider.[1] . . .

Our fine cousin reminded us of a fierce terrier
who conceives it a duty for a dog of honor to
bark at every passer - by, whether poet or reformer, and do the honors of the house by barking him out of sight.

Men are delicate ware to bring across the sea,
more delicate than Sèvres porcelain and glass,
or than tropical fruit, for the least non-reception
of them in the thought and heart of those to
whom they come makes cruelty, futility, and

[1] Here Mr. Emerson takes account of material available
for the New York course on New England in February.

confusion.[1] The thought that at once occurred
when the strangers came was, Have you been
victimized in being brought hither? Yea or nay?
Or, prior to that, answer me this, Are you vic-
timizable? Then, Will you waste my time? Or,
Are you afraid I shall waste yours? If so, we
shall agree like lovers.

(From E)

October 19.

To his Aunt Mary. Nothing has occurred to
interest us so much as Doctor Channing's departure, and perhaps it is saddest that this should
interest us no more. Our broad country has few
men; none that one would die for; worse, none
that one could live for. If the great God shined
so near in the breast that we could not look aside
to other manifestations, such defamation of our
Channings and Websters would be joy and
praise; but if we are neither pious nor admirers
of men — I wish you would write me what you
think, after so long a perspective as his good
days have afforded, of your old preacher. For

1 Apropos of "Alcott's victims," as Mr. Emerson called
the Englishmen whom his friend had encouraged to come, and
who weighed sorely upon him. (Compare "Character,"
p. 107.)

a sick man, he has managed to shame many sound ones, and seems to have made the most of his time, and was bright to the last month and week. A most respectable life; and deserves the more praise that there is so much merely external, and a sort of creature of society, in it; — that sort of merit of which praise is the legitimate fee. He seems sometimes as the sublime of calculation, as the nearest that mechanism could get to the flowing of genius. His later years — perhaps his earlier — have been adorned by a series of sacrifices. . . . He has been, whilst he lived, the Star of the American Church, and has left no successor in the pulpit.[1] . . . The sternest Judges of the Dead, who shall consider our wants and his austere self-application to them, and his fidelity to his lights, will absolve this Soul as it passes, and say, This man has done well. Perhaps I think much better things of him too. His *Milton* and *Napoleon* were excellent for the time (the want of drill and thorough breeding as a writer from which he suffered, being considered), and will be great ornaments of his biography.

1 A large part of what follows is found in "Life and Letters in New England" (*Lectures and Biographical Sketches*).

We are very ungrateful, but we do not willingly give the name of poet to any the rarest
talents, or industry and skill in metre.[1] Here is
Tennyson, a man of subtle and progressive mind,
a perfect music-box for all manner of delicate
tones and rhythms, to whom the language seems
plastic, so superior and forceful in his thought.
— But is he a poet? We read Burns and said,
He is a poet. We read Tennyson and do him
the indignity of asking the question, Is he poet?
I feel in him the misfortune of the time. He is
a strict contemporary, not Eternal Man. He
does not stand out of our low limitations like
a Chimborazo under the line, running up from
the torrid base through all the climates of the
globe on its high and mottled sides with rings
of the herbage of every latitude, but in him
as in the authors of *Paracelsus*, and *Festus*,
I hear through all the varied music the native
tones of an ordinary, to make my meaning
plainer, say, of a vulgar man. They are men of
talents who sing, but they are not the children

1 A large part of this entry was used in " The Poet" (*Essays*, Second Series), but as Tennyson and Burns are not there
named, nor the *Paracelsus* of Browning nor the *Festus* of
Bailey spoken of, the passage is printed here entire. In his
later years Mr. Emerson valued Tennyson more.

of music. The particular which under this gen-
erality deserves most notice is this (and it is a
black ingratitude to receive it so), that the argument of the poem is secondary, the finish of the
verses primary. It is the splendor of the versi-
fication that draws me to the sense, and not the
reverse. Who that has read the " Ode to Memory," the " Poet," the " Confessions of a Sensitive Mind," the " Two Voices," remembers the
scope of the poem when it is named, and does
not rather call to mind some beautiful lines; or,
when reading it, does not need some effort of
attention to find the thought of the writer, which
is also rather poor and mean? Even in " Locksley Hall," which is in a prouder tone, I have
to keep a sharp lookout for the thought, or it
will desert me. It is the merit of a poet to be
unanalyzable. We cannot sever his word and
thought. We listen because we must, and become aware of a crowd of particular merits, after
we have been thoroughly commanded and elevated. I should not go to these books for a
total diversion, and the stimulus of thought, as
I should go to the Catskills or the Sea, or to
Homer, Chaucer, or Shakspeare.

To the makers of artificial flowers, we say

" the better, the worse." The best verse-maker, not inspired, is accountable for the sentiment and spirit of his piece; it never exceeds his own dimensions. But the inspired writer, let his verse be never so frivolous in its subject, or treatment, — a mere catch or street verse, — is yet not accountable for the piece, but it came as if out of a spiracle of the great animal world. Therefore, these little pieces about owls and autumn gardens and the sea are not tinged with London philosophy, which makes all the best pieces " disconsolate preachers," but are quite independent of Mr. Alfred Tennyson, and are natural.

A poor man had an insufficient stove which it took him a great part of the winter to tend : he was up early to make the fire and very careful to keep it from going out. He interrupted his work at all hours of the day to feed it : he kept it late into the night, that the chamber walls need not get hopelessly cold. But it never warmed the room, he shivered over it, hoping it would be better, but he lost a great deal of time and comfort.[1]

1 This is a bit of autobiography. Mr. Emerson's study, a northwest room with four large windows, was, before the days

Once Latin and Greek had a strict relation to all the science and culture there was in Europe, and the mathematics had a momentary importance at some era of activity in physical science. These things became stereotyped as *Education*.[1]

Life is so much greater than thought, that when we talk on an affair of grave personal interest with one with whom hitherto we have had only intellectual discourse, we use lower tones, much less oratory, but we come much nearer and are quickly acquainted.

of furnaces (about 1852), very hard to heat, without a sufficiently large air-tight stove, which it seems for a time he lacked. He was sensitive to cold, and Mrs. Emerson made him a large, dark-purple study-gown, with a broad velvet collar. This he enjoyed, and called his "gaberlunzie." He always insisted on bringing in his wood by the armful himself from the great woodpile in the yard, which interruptions gave him air and exercise in the forenoons.

1 The long passage thus beginning is printed in "New England Reformers" (*Essays*, Second Series, pp. 258–260). Mr. Emerson "liked people who were able to do things," and would have liked to see much that is now being done towards Vocational Instruction. At the same time it should be remembered in spite of what he says in that essay, that he valued the classics greatly, and would have deplored the effect of their neglect on the spoken and written English of to-day.

(From N)

October 26.

Boston is not quite a mean place, since in walking yesterday in the street I met George Bancroft, Horatio Greenough, Sampson Reed, Sam Ward, Theodore Parker, George Bradford, and had a little talk with each of them.

I doubt if I recorded what pleased me so well, when Jones Very related it, years ago, that at the McLean Asylum the patients severally thanked him when he came away, and told him that he had been of great service to them.

The strangers have brought with them a complete library of the mystical writers, and the first feeling I have in looking at them is, I am too old for so many books.¹ These are for younger

1 Mr. James Pierrepont Greaves, who died in England early in the year, has been already mentioned as a man of virtues and learning. The library here referred to, which the philosophers brought with them from England, was a remarkable one, containing many rare volumes. Among Mr. Emerson's papers is a list of these books, more than three hundred titles, of works often in several volumes. They are the books of the Neoplatonists (in translation) and works of philosophy, religion, or of reform. One Oriental book, the *Desatir*, appears among them. They were, probably, sold to various persons after the breaking-up of the Fruitlands community.

men, and what fuel, what food for an open
youth is here! Then comes the suggestion of our
old plan of the University, but these men, though
excellent, are none of them gifted for leaders.
They are admirable instruments for a master's
hand, if some instituting Pythagoras, some mar-
shalling Mirabeau, some royal Alfred were here;
he could not have better professors than Alcott
and Lane and Wright. But they are too des-
ultory, ignorant, imperfect, and whimsical to be
trusted for any progress, — excellent springs,
worthless regulators. Alcott is a singular person,
a natural Levite, a priest forever after the order
of Melchizedek, whom all good persons would
readily combine, one would say, to maintain as
a priest by voluntary contribution to live in his
own cottage, literary, spiritual, and choosing his
own methods of teaching and action. But for
a founder of a family or institution, I would as
soon exert myself to collect money for a madman.

Read Cornelius Agrippa this morning on the
Vanity of Arts and Sciences; another specimen
of that scribaciousness which distinguishes the
immense readers of his time. Robert Burton
is the head of the class.[1] . . . One cannot

[1] The rest of the passage is found in " Books " (*Society and
Solitude*, p. 211).

afford to read for a few sentences. He will learn more by praying. They are good to read . . . for suggestion, I use them much for that. Plato or Shakspeare are not suggestive. Their method is so high and fine, that they take too much possession of us.

The communities will never have men in them, but only halves and quarters. They require a sacrifice of what cannot be sacrificed without detriment. The Community must always be ideal. . . .

Men talk about ideas all the time, not persons; they name persons, but it is only illustratively, they are really pursuing thoughts — the men they speak of are like metaphors which will not bear to be too hard driven — will not go on all fours, as we say. Thus they praise the farmer's life, but it is only to express their sense of some wrong in the merchants: praise the farmers a little more, you shall find they do not like it. A man is a partiality.

To-day I think the common people very right, and literary justice to be certain. These London Newspapers are sure to be just to each new book. Books full of matter they accept;

for the matter is like the atmosphere or bread, and small thanks to the author of the book. But other books of thought, of poetry, of taste, in which the author mainly appears, they read-ily damn, if they are not admirable; and if they are not admirable, such books are damnable. But the people — no thanks to them — are al-ways nearly right, have a low sort of right, that of common sense and instinct; and the man of talent and transcendent ingenuity is wrong.

> " Waste not thy gifts
> In profitless waiting for the gods' descent."

> " Would God translate me to his throne, believe
> That I should only listen to his words
> To further my own aims."

Paracelsus is written for a natural history of a scholar, who, following his ambition through great successes, at last finds himself arrived at being a quack. He is too proud for this, very impatient of quackery, and tells his friend that he cannot afford to spare the luxury of being sincere to one friend, so unbosoms himself to him and in all scorn and bitterness depicts the quackery and the barrenness of his results and the despair into which he seems sinking. And here the Poet leaves him, a disease without a remedy. The laws of disease are as beautiful as the laws of health, say the physicians, and the poet is of that mind, and so contents himself with painting with great accuracy and eloquence the symptoms. But the poem is withering, the wolfish hunger for knowledge for its own sake.

Lane and Wright, our friends, have brought with them a thousand volumes, making, no doubt, one of the best mystical libraries in the world, and twelve manuscript volumes of J. P. Greaves, and his head in a plaster cast; and with these professions they think they have brought England with them; that the England they have left behind is a congregation of no-things, spiritless, and therefore not to be taxed or starved or whipped into revolution.

Could they not die? or succeed? or help themselves? or draw others? in any manner, I care not how, could they not be disposed of, and cease to hang there in the horizon an un-settled appearance, too great to be neglected, and not great enough to be of any aid or com-fort to this great craving humanity?[1]

1 Mr. Emerson was human, and though he showed all kindness and hospitality to the worthy Englishmen, and re-

Few strokes and much color: they draw a lion, and then a lion, and then a small red lion![1] there is a fact in the mind of the writer, but so near to the known facts in other minds that he does not venture to say it quite simply lest it should not prove worth saying, but partly conceals it in rich dress and figures.

Yet each near fact, like these which Paracelsus celebrates and which George Bradford bemoans, the wolfish hunger for knowledge which still leaves us hungry, and the defaced and degraded condition of the scholar, as if his heart and bowels had been drawn out, deserves nearest study, for this way of seeing it in men, in

ferred to them with great respect in the *Dial*, they were not of his kind, and his journal had to be his safety-valve now and then.

1 This was a favorite story of Mrs. Emerson's of a decorator employed by the owner of a baronial mansion. Lions were all he could execute well. "What shall we have at the gate?" "Two lions *couchant* would be admirable." "And what over the door?" "Lions *rampant* would produce a fine effect, sir." "What can you have for a frieze?" "Don't you think, sir, that a fine processional effect could be produced of lions?" "Well, perhaps. But now here is a beautiful dark panel in a fine light. Think of something very effective there." "*A small red lion*," said the little man with a persuasive smile.

Carlyle, or whatever dried and so-called dead
scholar, is only the announcement of the shortcomings of the Universe. Nature itself has not
been able, up to this moment, to drive her tendencies farther: and the Bulletin or Gazette in
which always she announces her news is a man.
So Carlyle, Browning, Bradford, must represent
the Court of God up to the latest dates.

We do not care for the topic, but for the
speaker. Mr. Webster, or Mr. Allston, may
give me his opinions on what he will, I shall
learn his philosophy; for really every point is
equidistant from the centre, whether it be beets,
rutabaga, or the Gnostic sect.

The material is nothing; proportion is all.

Fourier our Paracelsus.

Oh, if they could take a second step, and a
third! The reformer is so confident, that all
are erect whilst he puts the finger on your
special abuse, and tells you your great want in
America. I tell him, yea, but not in America only,
but in the Universe ever since it was known,
just this defect has appeared. But when he has
anatomized the evil, he will be called out of

the room, or have got something else in his head. Remedied it never will be. But Charles Lane gives a very good account of his conversation with Brownson,[1] who would drive him to an argument. He took his paper and pencil out of his pocket, and asked Brownson to give him the names of the profoundest men in America. Brownson stopped, and gave him one, and then another, and then his own for a third. Brownson never will stop and listen, neither in conversation, but what is more, not in solitude.

Men of aim must always rule the aimless. And yet there will always be singing-birds.

Union. Many voices call for it, Fourier, Owen, Alcott, Channing. And its effect will be magical. That is it which shall renovate institutions and destroy drudgery. But not in the way these

1 Orestes A. Brownson, a Vermonter, vigorous in body and mind, but unstable. He passed from Presbyterianism, through Universalism and Unitarianism, into the Catholic Church at last. For years he was the pastor of the Society for Christian Union and Progress in Boston, where he edited and mainly wrote the *Boston Quarterly Magazine,* later merged in the *Democratic Quarterly Magazine.* He wrote also for the *Dial.*

men think, in none of their ways. But only in a method that combines union with isolation : silent union, actual separateness; ideal union, actual independence.

If a man will kick a fact out of the window, when he comes back he finds it again in the chimney corner.

Time respects only what he has himself made.

The Englishmen remarked that the greatest interior advantage which they observed in our Community over theirs was in the Women. In England the women were quite obtuse to any liberal thought; whilst here they are intelligent and ready.

Henry Thoreau made, last night, the fine remark that, as long as a man stands in his own way, everything seems to be in his way, governments, society, and even the sun and moon and stars, as astrology may testify.

'T is a pity that we should fail in our ambition to live well, since, I suppose, all considerate persons must agree that, although there is selfishness and frivolity, yet the general purpose in the

HENRY DAVID THOREAU

great number of people is fidelity. . . Each of us,
too, has at home in the shape of woman (who
is naturally good) a directing conscience to hold
him in the right. And yet we do no better; yet
we get on so little way; it seems as if there must
be mountains of difficulty to lift.

November 11.

The selfish man suffers more from his selfishness than he from whom that selfishness
withholds some important benefit.[1] . . .

To-day I have the feeling, to a degree not
experienced by me before, that discussions, like
that of yesterday and many the like in which I
have participated, invade and injure me. I often
have felt emptiness and restlessness to a sort of
hatred of the human race after such prating by
me and my fellows, but, never so seriously as
now, that absence from them is better for me
than the taking an active part in them.

You may associate on what grounds you like,
for economy, or for good neighborhood, for a
school, or for whatever reason, only do not say

1 The long passage thus beginning is found in " New England Reformers " (pp. 277, 278).

that the Divine Spirit enjoins it. The Spirit detaches you from all associations, and makes you, to your own astonishment, secretly a member of the Universal Association, but it descends to no specialties, draws up no Articles of a Society, but leaves you just as you were for that matter, to be guided by your particular convenience and circumstance whether to join with others, or whether to go alone.

It seems to be true that our New England population was settled by the most religious and ideal of the Puritans of England. It is natural enough that we should be more ideal than old England.

It is taking a great liberty with a man to offer to lend him a book, as if he also had not access to that truth to which the bookmaker had access. Each of the books, if I read, invades me, displaces me; the law of it is, that it should be first, that I should give way to it; I, who have no right to give way, and, if I would be tranquil and divine again, I must dismiss the book.

And yet I expect a great man to be a good reader, or in proportion to the spontaneous power should be the assimilating power.

Every book serves us at last only by adding some one word to our vocabulary, or perhaps two or three. And perhaps that word shall not be in the volume, or shall only be the author's name. And yet there are books of no vulgar origin, but the work and the proof of faculties so comprehensive, so nearly equal to the universe which they paint, that although one shuts them also with meaner ones, yet he says with a sigh the while, This were to be read in long thousands of years by some stream in Paradise.

Do not gloze 'and prate and mystify. Here is our dear, grand Alcott says, You shall dig in my field for a day and I will give you a dollar when it is done, and it shall not be a business transaction! It makes me sick. Whilst money is the measure *really* adopted by us all as the most convenient measure of all material values, let us not affectedly disuse the name, and mystify ourselves and others ; let us not "say no, and take it." We may very well and honestly have theoretical and practical objections to it ; if they are fatal to the use of money and barter, let us disuse them ; if they are less grave than the inconvenience of abolishing traffic, let us not pretend to have done with it, whilst we eat and drink and wear and breathe it.

Do not be too timid and squeamish about your actions. All life is an experiment. The more experiments you make the better. What if they are a little coarse, and you may get your coat soiled or torn? What if you do fail, and get fairly rolled in the dirt once or twice? Up again, you shall never be so afraid of a tumble. This matter of the lectures, for instance. The engagement drives your thoughts and studies to a head, and enables you to do somewhat not otherwise practicable; that is the action. Then there is the reaction; for when you bring your discourse to your auditory, it shows differently. You have more power than you had thought of, or less. The thing fits, or does not fit; is good or detestable.

It is a peculiar feature of New England that young farmers and mechanics who work all summer on the soil, or in a shop, take a school in the winter months. Mr. Fay, the pump-maker in this town, goes to Marlborough this winter for that purpose; young Wheeler and Wood do the same thing.

Edmund Hosmer was willing to sell his farm five years ago for $3800 and go to the West. He found and still finds that the Irish, of which there are two hundred in this town, are underselling him in labor, and he does not see how he and his boys can do those things which only he is willing to do; for, go to market he will not, nor shall his boys with his consent do any of those things for which high wages are paid, as, for example, take any shop, or the office of foreman or agent in any corporation wherein there seems to be a premium paid for faculty, as if it were paid for the faculty of cheating. He does not see how he and his children are to prosper here, and the only way for them is to run, the Caucasian before the Irishman.

I call the terror of starving, Skepticism, and say that I do not believe that I can be put in any condition in which I cannot honestly maintain myself, and honestly be rich, that is, not be poor. It is in vain that you put to me any case of misfortune or calamity — the extremest, the Manchester weaver, the Carolina slave; I doubt not that in the history of the individual is always an account of his condition, and he knows himself to be party to his present estate. Put me in his condition, and I should see its outlets and reliefs, though now I see them not. The main and capital remedy of the religious sentiment and all the abundance of its counsels for his special distresses, it were atheism to doubt. But do not require of me, sitting out here, to say what he, within there, ought to do. I can never meddle with other people's facts, I have enough of my own. But this one thing I know, that, if I do not clear myself, I am in fault, and that my condition is matched, point for point, with every other man's. I can only dispose of my own facts.

Last night Henry Thoreau read me verses which pleased, if not by beauty of particular lines, yet by the honest truth, and by the length of flight and strength of wing; for most of our poets are only writers of lines or of epigrams. These of Henry's at least have rude strength, and we do not come to the bottom of the mine. Their fault is, that the gold does not yet flow pure, but is drossy and crude. The thyme and marjoram are not yet made into honey; the assimilation is imperfect. It seems as if the poetry was all written before time was.[1] . . . But it is a

1 The rest of the passage, slightly varied, is found in "The Poet" (*Essays*, Second Series, p. 8).

great pleasure to have poetry of the second degree also, and mass here, as in other instances, is some compensation for superior quality, for I find myself stimulated and rejoiced like one who should see a cargo of sea-shells discharged on the wharf, whole boxes and crates of conchs, *cypræas,* cones, *neritas, cardiums, murexes,* though there should be no pearl-oyster nor one shell of great rarity and value among them.

Time is the little grey man who takes out of his breast-pocket first a pocketbook, then a Dollond telescope, then a Turkey carpet, then four saddled and bridled nags and a sumptuous canvas tent. We are accustomed to chemistry and it does not surprise us. But chemistry is but a name for changes and developments as wonderful as those of this Breast-Pocket.

I was a little chubby boy trundling a hoop in Chauncy Place, and spouting poetry from Scott and Campbell at the Latin School. But Time, the little grey man, has taken out of his vest-pocket a great, awkward house (in a corner of which I sit down and write of him), some acres of land, several full-grown and several very young persons, and seated them close beside me; then he has taken that chubbiness and that hoop quite away (to be sure he has left the declamation and the poetry), and here left a long, lean person threatening to be a little grey man, like himself.

Religion has failed ! Yes, the religion of another man has failed to save me. But it has saved him. We speak of the Past with pity and reprobation, but through the enormities, evils, and temptations of the past, saints and heroes slipped into heaven. There is no spot in Europe but has been a battle-field ; there is no religion, no church, no sect, no year of history, but has served men to rise by, to scale the walls of heaven, and enter into the banquets of angels. Our fathers are saved. The same, precisely the same conflicts have always stood as now, with slight shiftings of scene and costume.

(From Z)

November 19.

I should willingly give you an account of one of these conversations. For example, we had one yesterday afternoon. I begged Alcott to paint out his project, and he proceeded to say that there should be found a farm of a hundred acres in excellent condition, with good buildings, a good orchard, and grounds which admitted of being laid out with great beauty; and this should be purchased and given to them, in the first place. I replied, You ask too much. This is not solving the problem; there are hundreds of innocent young persons, whom, if you will thus stablish and endow and protect, will find it no hard matter to keep their innocency. And to see their tranquil household, after all this has been done for them, will in no wise instruct or strengthen me. But he will instruct and strengthen me, who, there where he is, unaided, in the midst of poverty, toil, and traffic, extricates himself from the corruptions of the same and builds on his land a house of peace and benefit, good customs, and free thoughts. But, replied Alcott, how is this to be done? How can I do it who have a wife and family to maintain? I answered that he was not the person to do it, or he would not ask the question. When he that shall come is born, he will not only see the thing to be done, but invent the life, invent the ways and means of doing it. The way you would show me does not commend itself to me as the way of greatness.

The Spirit does not stipulate for land and exemption from taxes, but, in great straits and want, or even on no land, nowhere to lay its head, it manages, without asking for land, to occupy and enjoy all land, for it is the law by which land exists; it classifies and distributes the whole creation anew. If you ask for application to particulars of this *Way of the Spirit*, I shall say that the coöperation you look for is such coöperation as colleges and all secular institutions look for, — money. True coöperation comes in another manner. A man quite unexpectedly shows me that which I and all souls looked for, and I cry, " That is it; Take me and mine; I count it my chief good, to do in my way that very thing." — That is real coöperation, unlimited, uncalculating, infinite coöperation.

The Spirit is not half so slow or mediate, or needful of conditions or organs, as you suppose. A few persons in the course of my life have at certain moments appeared to me, not measured men of five feet, five or ten inches, but large, enormous, indefinite; but these were not great proprietors, nor heads of communities, nor men in office, or in any action which affected large numbers of men, but, on the contrary, nothing could be more private, they were in some want, or affliction, or other relation which called out the emanation of the Spirit, which dignified and transfigured them to my eye. And the good Spirit will burn and blaze in the cinders of your condition, in the drudgeries of your endeavor, — in the very process of extricating us from the evils of want and of a bad society.

This fatal fault in the logic of our friends still appears : Their whole doctrine is spiritual, but they always end with saying, Give us much land and money. If I should give them anything, it would be facility and not beneficence. Unless one should say after the maxims of the world, Let them drink their own error to saturation, and this will be the best hellebore.[1] I know the Spirit *by its victorious tone.*

An immense force has that man whose part is taken, and who does not wait for society in any part of his conduct of life. Now it is plain, of our three adventurers, that this gives them the most of their importance with us, and the deductions to be made from each are the hesitations at the plunge, the reserves which they still make and the reliances and expectations they still cherish on the arm of flesh, the aid of others.

1 And this remedy worked most effectually in the coming winter, — the pitiful breaking up of Fruitlands.

A reformer must be born; he can never be made such by reasons. All reform, like all form, is by the grace of God, and not otherwise.

You ask, O Theanor, said Amphitryon, that I should go forth from this palace with my wife and my children and that you and your family may enter and possess it. The same request in substance has been often made to me before by numbers of persons. Now I also think that I and my wife ought to go forth from this house, and work all day in the fields, and lie at night under some thicket, but I am waiting where I am, only until some god shall point out to me which among all these applicants, yourself or some other, is the rightful claimant.

Transcendentalism is the Saturnalia of faith. It is faith run mad. Nature is transcendental [1] ...

Lethe. It seemed strange to men that they should thus forget so fast, that they became suspicious, that there was some treachery, and began to suspect their food that perhaps the bread they eat, or 'the flesh, was narcotic. Hence rose Graham societies.

[1] The rest of this paragraph is in "The Transcendentalist" (*Nature, Addresses, etc.,* pp. 338, 339).

Government should find its perfectness in its obedience and good conduction of the elemental fluids. Because persons will have their effect, and things theirs — we are safe anyhow.

I think the power of things such that property's will is done whether by law, or against law, openly or underhand. It was obviously the feeling and the right of a ruder age to say persons must make law for persons, property for property. But now we begin to feel that persons are the only interest, and that property will follow them; that a special care need not be given to the farm. Let us be wise, and the culture of men being the end of government, love will write the law, and the law which has been so given will be gentle.[1]

Since I have been here in New York I have grown less diffident of my political opinions. I supposed once the Democracy must be right. I see that they are aimless. Whigs have the best men, Democrats the best cause. But the last are destructive, not constructive. What hope, what end have they?

1 Compare "Politics" (*Essays*, Second Series, p. 202).

(From K)

November 25.

Yesterday I read Dickens's *American Notes.*
It answers its end very well, which plainly was
to make a readable book, nothing more. Truth
is not his object for a single instant, but merely
to make good points in a lively sequence, and
he proceeds very well. As an account of America
it is not to be considered for a moment: it is too
short, and too narrow, too superficial, and too
ignorant, too slight, and too fabulous, and the
man totally unequal to the work. A very lively
rattle on that nuisance, a sea voyage, is the first
chapter; and a pretty fair example of the historical truth of the whole book. We can hear throughout every page the dialogue between the author
and his publisher, — "Mr. Dickens, the book
must be entertaining — that is the essential point.
Truth? Damn truth! I tell you, it must be entertaining." As a picture of American manners
nothing can be falser. No such conversations
ever occur in this country in real life, as he re-
lates. He has picked up and noted with eagerness each odd local phrase that he met with, and,
when he had a story to relate, has joined them
together, so that the result is the broadest caricature; and the scene might as truly have been

laid in Wales or in England as in the States.
Monstrous exaggeration is an easy secret of romance. But Americans who, like some of us
Massachusetts people, are not fond of spitting,
will go from Maine to New Orleans, and meet
no more annoyance than we should in Britain or
France. So with "yes," so with "fixings," so with
soap and towels; and all the other trivialities
which this trifler detected in travelling over half
the world.[1] The book makes but a poor apology
for its author, who certainly appears in no dignified or enviable position. . . .

(From N)

November 26.

The young people, like Brownson, Channing,
Greene,[2] Elizabeth P. Peabody, and possibly

1 It is not unlikely that Mr. Emerson would have modified
these last sentences after his experiences a few years later as a
Lyceum lecturer in the pioneer West.

2 Brownson has been already spoken of in these notes.

William Henry Channing, nephew and biographer of Rev.
Dr. Channing, and cousin of William Ellery Channing, the
Concord poet, was a minister, lovable and eager in all good
causes. He was pastor of various Unitarian churches, among
others, at Cincinnati, at Washington during the War, and in
London.

William B. Greene was a West Point graduate, served in

Bancroft, think that the vice of the age is to exaggerate individualism, and they adopt the word *l'humanité* from Le Roux, and go for "*the race.*" Hence the Phalanx, Owenism, Simonism, the Communities. The same spirit in theology has produced the Puseyism, which endeavors to rear "the Church" as a balance and overpoise to the conscience.

London, New York, Boston, are phalanxes ready-made, where you shall find concerts, books, balls, medical lectures, prayers, or Punch and Judy, according to your fancy, on any night or day.

It is indifferent whether you show a new object to the child, or a new relation in an old object. You may give him another toy, or you may show him the iron block among his blocks is a magnet. The avaricious man seeks to add to the number of his toys, the scientific man to find new relations.

You never can hurt us by new ideas. God speed you, gentlemen reformers.

the Seminole War, then became a clergyman, and in the Civil War was colonel of the 14th Infantry, Massachusetts Volunteers (later, the 1st Massachusetts Heavy Artillery).

Bancroft and Bryant are historical democrats who are interested in dead or organized, but not in organizing, liberty. Bancroft would not know George Fox, whom he had so well eulogized, if he should meet him in the street. It is like Lyell's science, who did not know by sight, when George B. Emerson showed him them, the shells he has described in his Geology.

I think four walls one of the best of our institutions. A man comes to me, and oppresses me by his presence; he looks very large and unanswerable. I cannot dispose of him whilst he stays; he quits the room, and passes, not only out of the house, but, as it were, out of the horizon; he is a mere phantom or ghost. I think of him no more. I recover my sanity, the universe dawns on me again.

W. H. Channing thinks that, not in solitude, but in love, in the actual society of beloved persons, have been his highest intuitions. To me it sounds like shallow verbs and nouns; for in closest society a man is by thought wrapt into remotest isolation.

No man can be criticised but by a greater than he. Do not, then, read the reviews.

Wordsworth dismisses a whole regiment of poets from their vocation.

The world is waking up to the idea of Union.[1] . . . [But] the Union is only perfect when all the Unities are absolutely isolated. Each man being the Universe, if he attempt to join himself to others, he instantly is jostled, crowded, cramped, halved, quartered, or on all sides diminished of his proportion, and, the stricter the union, the less and more pitiful he is. But let him go alone, and recognizing the Perfect in every moment with entire obedience, he will go up and down doing the works of a true *member*, and, to the astonishment of all, the whole work will be done with concert, though no man spoke; government will be adamantine without any governor.

Union ideal, — in actual individualism, actual union; then would be the culmination of science, useful art, fine art, and culmination on culmination.

The tongue of flame, the picture the newspapers give, at the late fire in Liverpool, of

[1] The omitted portion of the passage is printed in "New England Reformers" (*Nature, Addresses, etc.*, pp. 266, 267).

the mountains of burning cotton over which the flame arose to twice their height, the volcano also from which the conflagration rises toward the zenith an appreciable distance toward the stars, — these are the most affecting symbols of what man should be. A spark of fire is infinitely deep, but a mass of fire reaching from earth upward into the heaven, this is the fire of the robust, united, burning, radiant fuel.

Fate, yes, our music-box only plays certain tunes, and never a sweeter strain but we are assured that our barrel is not a dead, but a live barrel, — nay, is only a part of the tune, and changes like that.

Conservatism stands on this, that a man cannot jump out of his skin ; and well for him that he cannot, for his skin is the world ; and the stars of heaven do hold him there : in the folly of men glitters the wisdom of God.

This old Bible, if you pitch it out of the window with a fork, it comes bounce back again.

Several Steps. A man's greatness is to advance on a line. Simple recipiency is the virtue of Space not of Man; to him belongs progress, he builds himself on himself. Angelo, Dante, Milton, Swedenborg, Pythagoras, Paracelsus were men of great robustness; they built, not only with energy but symmetry, and their work could be called architecture. Napoleon lately was an architect. . . .

(From E)

December.

The trick of every man's conversation we soon learn. In one, this remorseless Buddhism lies all around, threatening with death and night. We make a little fire in our cabin, but we dare not go abroad one furlong into the murderous cold. Every thought, every enterprise, every sentiment, has its ruin in this horrid Infinite which circles us and awaits our dropping into it. If killing all Buddhists would do the least good, we would have a slaughter of the Innocents directly.

In Orpheus, the Demiurgus interrogates Night, thus, —

" Tell me how all things will as one subsist,
   Yet each its nature separate preserve."

It is the problem proposed to the Fourierist.

The blue sky is a fit covering for a cottage
or a market and for the meeting of supernatural forms and events of magic and of fairy-
land. Could my most poetic dream fall true and
realize itself to my faith in some golden moment
in the presence and by the concurrence of all
gods, I should look upward into the identical
web of blue depth which I see as I trudge along
the road to the Post-Office. And yet no dream
could have that sky. It is like the touch of
God, it discerns between shadow and substance.
The look of the zenith, — would not our friend
Lane reckon that a "*real* experience"?

There was a conversation last evening at our
good Mrs. B.'s on "the Family," which was
quite too narrowing and exclusive. There was a
very unnecessary hostility in a great deal of the
talk. A hostility in the hearers was presumed,
and we were valiant men full of fight, ready
and able to break a lance for our faith. Lane is
so skilful, instant, and witty, there is no loiter-
ing or repetition in his speech, that I delight to
hear him and forgive everything to so much
ability : yet he is very provoking and warlike
in his manner. He rails at trades and cities, and
yet it is obvious in every word he says how

much he is the debtor to both.[1] There is a wisdom of life about them, a toughness and solidity of experience, that makes them always entertaining and makes Alcott's words look pale and lifeless.

I came away from the company in better spirits than from any party this long time, for I did not speak one word. Perhaps the proper reply to the tone of dogmatism should have been, Shall there be no more cakes and ale? Why so much stress?

Two Meals a Day. A poet may eat bread for his breakfast, and bread and flesh for his dinner, but for his supper he must eat stars only.[2]

Romeo was minister of Raymond Béranger, Count of Provence. He managed the affairs of his master so well that each one of his four daughters became a queen. Margaret, the eldest, was married to Louis IX of France; Eleanor,

1 Mr. Lane had been the manager of the *London Mercantile Price Current.*

2 At this period the habit of walking out under the stars before going to rest, shown in "The Poet," was Mr. Emerson's. (*Poems*, Appendix, pp. 312, 315, 317.)

the next, to Henry III, of England; Sancha, the third, to Richard, Henry's brother, and King of the Romans; and Beatrice, the youngest, to Charles I, King of Naples and Sicily, and brother to Louis. The Provençal Barons, enviers of Romeo, instigated the Count his master to demand of him an account of the revenues he had so carefully husbanded, and the Prince as lavishly disbursed. Then Romeo demanded the little mule, the staff, and the scrip, with which he had first entered into the Count's service, a stranger pilgrim from the shrine of St. James in Galicia, and departed as he came, nor was it ever known whence he was, or whither he went. (See Dante, *Paradiso*, Canto VI.)

O what would Nature say?
She spared no speech to-day;
The fungus and the bulrush spoke,
Answered the pine-tree and the oak,
The wizard South blew down the glen,
Filled the straits and filled the wide;
Each maple leaf turned up its silver side.
The south wind blows; I leave my book.

. . . .

I need not bide in nature long,
Could I transfer my life to song;
It needs the lapsing centuries

To tell you the wit of the passing breeze.
And yet the landscape taunts me,
Advancing, then receding. . . .

" Full many a glorious morning have I seen."
That is a bold saying. Few men have seen many
mornings. This day when I woke I felt the
peace of the morning, and knew that I seldom
behold it.

I hear the whistle of the locomotive in the
woods. Wherever that music comes it has its
sequel. It is the voice of the civility of the
Nineteenth Century saying, " Here I am."
It is interrogative : it is prophetic : and this
Cassandra is believed : " Whew ! Whew ! Whew !
How is real estate here in the swamp and wilderness? Ho for Boston ! Whew ! Whew! Down
with that forest on the side of the hill. I want
ten thousand chestnut sleepers. I want cedar
posts, and hundreds of thousands of feet of
boards. Up ! my masters of oak and pine ! You
have waited long enough — a good part of a century in the wind and stupid sky. Ho for axes and
saws, and away with me to Boston ! Whew !
Whew ! I will plant a dozen houses on this
pasture next moon, and a village anon ; and I

will sprinkle yonder square mile with white houses like the broken snow-banks that strow it in March."

History. Something gets possession and elbows all the rest aside. Yet there hang these clouds of dissenters and fanatics and prophets, like Arabs in the horizon or on the mountains waiting their turn and kingdom. Fixtures none. The world is the prey and dominion of thoughts. History is a foolish, pragmatic misstatement. As easily might you survey a cloud, which is now as big as your hat, and before you have measured its first angle, covers ten acres. Thoughts work and make what you call the world. Heroes are the lucky individuals who stand at the pole and are the largest and ripest.

Miracle comes to the miraculous, not to the arithmetician.[1] . . . These [idealists] have no memory, no retrospect, no baggage-waggon of a tradition at their back, but have their eye forward and their foot forward, for their whole attention is to the fact of creation, — of Creation now being and to be.

---

[1] Most of what follows is printed in "Worship" (*Conduct of Life,* p. 238).

The world is too rich for us. We have hardly
set our hearts on one toy, say a house and land,
before a poetic reputation seems the high prize,
then eloquence, then political power, then ascet-
icism, and then art; and thus each of many
things draws us aside from the other. If in choosing one, we could drink a cup of Lethe to the
others, we should not be robbed of satisfaction.

(From Z)

December 10.

A good visit to Boston, and saw Sam Ward
and Ellery to advantage, and my Parian sister.
Ellery has such an affectionate speech, and a
tone that is tremulous with emotion, that he is
a flower in the wind. He says he has an immense dispersing power. Ward is wise and
beautiful : and said and admitted the best things.
He had found out, he said, why people die:
it is to break up their style.

Life would not be worth taking or keeping,
if it were not full of surprises. I wake in the
morning, and go to my window, and see the
day break, and receive from the spectacle a new
secret of Nature that goes to compromise all my
past manner of living, and invite me to a new.

I am filled with a great tranquillity. I seek to express this somehow and find that I have cut out a Hesperus in marble. Wonderful is the Alembic of Nature through which the sentient mind of tranquillity becomes the figure of a youth; but the feeling manages somehow to shed itself over the stone, as if that were porous to love and truth.[1] Yet is not that figure final or adequate; it is a prison rather of the thought, of the emotion, if I am contented with it. The thought scorns it, mocks at it as some wretched caricature; the thought has already transcended it, is already something else, has taken twenty thousand shapes, whilst poor Hans was hammering at this one. The oak leaf is perfect, a kind of absolute realized, but every work of art is only relatively good; — the artist advances, and finds all his fine things naught.

Nature tends to a Fact. She will be expressed. Then scholars are her victims of expression.

You who see the artist, the orator, the poet too near, and find them victims of *partiality*, . . . pronounce them failures[2] . . .

1 Evidently this thought was the origin of the passage in "The Poet" about the sculptor who made the statue of Phosphorus, the morning star (*Essays*, Second Series, p. 24).

2 See "Experience" (*Essays*, Second Series, p. 66).

Very hard it is to keep the middle point. It is a very narrow line.

W. said, that there was a great deal of deferring and a great deal of wondering and quoting, but of calm affirming very little. Cannot a man only communicate that which he knows? But Nature hates calm system-makers, her methods are saltatory, impulsive. Man lives by pulses, all his organic movements are such, and all chemical, and ethereal; even seem to be undulatory or alternate. And so with the mind, it antagonizes ever, and gets on so.

The Yankee is one who if he once gets his teeth set on a thing, all creation can't make him let go; who, if he can get hold anywhere of a rope's end or a spar, will not let it go, but will make it carry him; if he can but find so much as a stump or a log, will hold on to it and whittle out of it a house and barn, a farm and stock, a mill-seat and a village, a railroad and a bank, and various other things equally useful and entertaining, — a seat in Congress or a foreign mission, for example. But these no doubt are inventions of the enemy.

C.'s eyes are a compliment to the human race; that steady look from year to year makes Phidian sculpture and Poussin landscape still real and contemporary.

The harvest will be better preserved and go farther, laid up in private bins, in each farmer's corn-barn, and each woman's basket, than if it were kept in national granaries. In like manner, an amount of money will go farther if expended by each man and woman for their own wants, and in the feeling that this is their all, than if expended by a great Steward, or National Commissioners of the Treasury. Take away from me the feeling that I must depend on myself, give me the least hint that I have good friends and backers there in reserve who will gladly help me, and instantly I relax my diligence. I obey the first impulse of generosity that is to cost me nothing, and a certain slackness will creep over my conduct of my affairs. Here is a bank-note found of one hundred dollars. Let it fall into the hands of an easy man who never earned the estate he spends, and see how little difference it will make in his affairs. At the end of the year he is just as much behindhand as ever, and could not have done at all without that hundred. Let it fall into the hands of a poor and prudent woman, and every shilling and every cent of it tells, goes to reduce debt, or to add to instant and constant comfort, mends a window, buys a blanket or a pelisse, gets a stove instead of the old cavernous fireplace, all chimney.

All the Channings are men of the world; have a little silex in their composition, which gives a good edge, and protects them like a coat of mail. Ellery has the manners and address of a merchant.

Elizabeth Hoar affirms that religion bestows a refinement which she misses in the best-bred people not religious, and she considers it essential therefore to the flower of gentleness.

> Come dal fuoco il caldo, esser diviso
> Non può 'l bel dall' eterno.
> Michel Angelo.

I have no thoughts to-day; What then? What difference does it make? It is only that there does not chance to-day to be an antagonism to evolve them, the electricity is the more accumulated; a week hence you shall meet somebody or something that shall draw from you a shower of sparks.

Travelling is a very humiliating experience to me. I never go to any church like a railroad car for teaching me my deficiencies.

For any grandeur of circumstance length of time seems an indispensable element. Who can attach anything majestic to creatures so short-lived as we men? The time that is proper to spend in mere musing is too large a fraction of threescore years and ten to be indulged to that greatness of behavior. The brevity of human life gives a melancholy to the profession of the architect.

There is a comparative innocence in this country and a corresponding health. We do not often see bald boys and gray-haired girls; children victims of gout and apoplexy; the street is not full of near-sighted and deaf people; nor do we see those horrid mutilations and disgusting forms of disease as leprosy and un-described varieties of plague which European streets exhibit, stumps of men.

Charles Lane said that our people do not

appear to him to have that steadfastness that can be calculated on. Thus, Green may be a trader, or a priest, or a soldier as probably as a progressive reformer. And so Davis and Robbins and the rest. This results from the greater freedom of circumstance. English and Europeans are guided as with iron belt of condition.

The fine and finest young people despise life;[1] . . .

Naming, yes, that is the office of the newspapers of the world, these famous editors from Moses, Homer, Confucius, and so on, down to Goethe and Kant: they name what the people have already done, and the thankful people say, "Doctor, 't is a great comfort to know the disease whereof I die."

AUTHORS OR BOOKS QUOTED OR REFERRED TO IN JOURNAL FOR 1842

Vishnu Sarna; Pythagoras; Æschylus; Sophocles; Euripides; Aristophanes; *Symposium* of Plato, Xenophon, and Phocion; Theophrastus;

Plotinus; Porphyry; Iamblichus; St. Au-

[1] See "Experience" (p. 61).

gustine, *Confessions*; Synesius, *On Providence*; Proclus; Apuleius;

Saadi; Dante, *Paradiso*; Chaucer;

Erasmus; Michel Angelo, *Sonnets*; Sir Thomas More; Rabelais; Cornelius Agrippa, *The Vanity of Arts and Sciences*; Cervantes; Robert Burton;

Chapman; Behmen; Massinger; Ford;

George Fox; Marvell; Molière; Dryden; Otway; Swift; Pope; Doctor Johnson;

Pestalozzi; Goethe; Sheridan; Talleyrand; Richter; Reimer;

Robert Owen; Fourier; Manzoni, *I Promessi Sposi*;

Daniel Webster; Doctor Channing; Edward Everett;

Shelley; Bryant; Carlyle; James P. Greaves; Lyell; John Clare, *Poems descriptive of Rural Life and Scenery*;

Pusey; Bancroft; George B. Emerson; Hawthorne; John Sterling, *Dædalus*;

Disraeli, *Vivian Grey*; Bulwer, *Zanoni*; George Borrow, *The Zincali*;

Tennyson, second volume of *Poems*; Browning, *Paracelsus*; Bailey, *Festus*;

Westland Marston, *The Patrician's Daughter*; George H. Colton, *Tecumseh*;

William Henry Channing; William Ellery Channing, *Poems*; Thoreau, *Poems*;

Alcott; Orestes A. Brownson; Albert Brisbane; Theodore Parker; Margaret Fuller; Charles K. Newcomb;

Balzac, *Peau de Chagrin*;

[English writers, friends of Mr. Alcott] Charles Lane; Henry G. Wright; John A. Heraud; Goodwyn Barmby; Frances Barham;

"*Corporal Spohn*"; *Ernest*, a poem;

The Plain Speaker, edited by Christopher Greene and William M. Chace of Providence.

JOURNAL

LECTURES IN NEW YORK AND
BALTIMORE

VISIT TO WASHINGTON

EDITING DIAL

WEBSTER IN CONCORD

BROOK FARM

JOURNAL XXXIV

1843

(From Journals Z, R, and U)

Καθ' αὐτὸ, μεθ' αὐτοῦ, μονοειδὴς ἀεὶ ὄν.[1]

Secondo alla fede di ciascuno.[2]

And whatsoever soul has perceived anything of truth shall be safe from harm until another period.[3] — PLATO, *Phædrus*.

[IN January, Mr. Emerson set forth on a long lecturing trip. He went to Philadelphia, probably visiting there his friend and loving schoolmate, Rev. William H. Furness; thence by rail to Baltimore, where he gave two lectures, visiting Washington, between them, after an interval of sixteen years. He then gave his course on "New England" in New York, in February before the Berean Society: I, Genius of the Anglo-Saxon Race; II, Trade; III, Manners

1 According to itself, by means of itself, always of one kind.

2 According to each man's faith.

3 This is "The law of Adrastia." (See "Experience," *Essays*, Second Series, p. 84.) Adrastia was a name for Fate or Nemesis.

and Customs of New England; IV, Recent Literature and Spiritual Influences; V, Results.

Meantime Henry Thoreau, chivalrous, universally helpful, witty, and kind, had manned the wall at home for his absent friend, and had also relieved him of much editorial work for the *Dial*. This will appear in the *Familiar Letters of Henry David Thoreau*, edited by Mr. F. B. Sanborn, for that period.[1]]

(From Z)

BALTIMORE, BARNUM'S HOTEL,
January 7, 1843.

Here to-day from Philadelphia. The railroad, which was but a toy coach the other day, is now a dowdy, lumbering country wagon. Yet it is not prosaic, as people say, but highly poetic, this strong shuttle which shoots across the forest, swamp, river, and arms of the sea, binding city to city. The Americans take to the little contrivance as if it were the cradle in which they were born.

AT PHILADELPHIA.

Philosophy shakes hands at last with the simplest Methodist and teaches one fact with him, namely, that it is the grace of God, — all grace,

1 Houghton, Mifflin & Co., 1894.

— no inch of space left for the impertinence of human will. Everything is good which a man does naturally, and nothing else: and sitting in railroad cars, happy is he who is moved to talk, and knows nothing about it; and happy he who is moved to sit still, and knows not that he sits still; but I hate him with a perfect hatred who thinks of himself. Let a man hate eddies, hate the sides of the river, but keep the middle of the stream. The hero did nothing apart and odd, but travelled on the highway and went to the same tavern as the whole people, and was very heartily and naturally there, no dainty, protected person.

"Every bullet will hit its mark if it is first dipped in the marksman's blood."

It makes men very bad to talk good.

An American is served like a noble in these city hotels; and his individuality as much respected; and he may go imperially along all the highways of iron or of water. I like it very well that in the heart of democracy I find such practical illustration of high theories.

Mrs. Siddons said to her niece, Fanny Kemble, "You are an extraordinary girl, but you are

not Mrs. Siddons yet, though many will tell you
that you are."

AT WASHINGTON,
January 11, 12, 13, 14.

" The Winter Arrangement to the South "
advertises "the great central mail route through
from Baltimore to Charleston, with *but three
changes of Person* and Baggage."

January 16.

So much novel-reading ought not to leave
the young men of the land quite unaffected, and
doubtless does idealize them. They must study
noble behavior, and this dignity of hotel arm-
chairs is not quite unsupported by inward dignity.

I understand poverty much better than riches;
and it is odd that one of my friends who is rich
seems to me always accidentally so, and in character made to be poor.

I do not observe that many men can aid others
in the direct way.

Commonly every man occupies every inch of
his ground. The poor or the middle class can
better help than the richer.

Giles Waldo told me of one of his friends who
gambled, not for winnings, but for bread, and

with the members of the Legislature of Indiana; and the men whose money he won liked him so well that they one day made him clerk of the House of Representatives, much to his surprise, and, if he had remained in that country, would have made him Secretary of State.

In Philadelphia, they play chess in all houses. At the Athenæum, a game goes on behind a screen at all hours, and whenever I was in the room I noticed several spectators watching the moves of the players.

NEW YORK, *February* 7.

I am greatly pleased with the merchants. In rail car and hotel it is common to meet only the successful class, and so we have favorable specimens: but these discover more manly power of all kinds than scholars; behave a great deal better, converse better, and have inexpensive and sufficient manners.

Dreamlike travelling on the railroad. The towns through which I pass between Philadelphia and New York make no distinct impression. They are like pictures on a wall. The more, that you can read all the way in a car a French novel.

February 7.

Nature. Nature asked, Whether troop and baggage be two things; whether the world is all troop or all baggage, or whether there be any troop that shall not one day be baggage? Easy, she thinks it, to show you the Universal Soul: we have all sucked that orange; but would you please to mention what is an Individual? She apologized for trifling with you in your nonage, and adding a little sugar to your milk that you might draw the teat, and a little glory afterward to important lessons, but declared she would never tell you another fib, if you had quite settled that Buddhism was better than hands and feet, and would keep that conviction in the presence of two persons. As for *far* and *too far*, she wondered what it meant. She admires people who read, and people who look at pictures, but if they read until they write, or look at pictures until they draw them, she curses them up and down. She has the oddest tastes and behavior. An onion, which is all coat, she dotes on; and among birds she admires the godwit; but when I hinted that a blue weed grew about my house called *Self-heal*,¹ she said, — a coxcomb named

1 See the allusion to this humble little flower, which grew close under his study window, in " Nature" (*Essays*, Second Series, p. 195).

it; but she teaches cobwebs to resist the tempest, and when a babe's cries drove away a lion, she almost devoured the darling with kisses.. She says her office of Dragoman is vacant, though she has been much pestered with applications, and if you have a talent of asking questions, she will play with you all your life; but if you can answer questions, she will propose one, which, if you answer, she will die first. She hates authors, but likes Montaigne.

Webster.[1] Webster is very dear to the Yankees because he is a person of very commanding understanding with every talent for its adequate expression. The American, foreigners say, always reasons, and he is the most American of the Americans. They have no abandonment, but dearly love logic, as all their churches have so long witnessed. His external advantages are very rare and admirable; his noble and majestic frame, his breadth and projection of brows, his coal-black hair, his great cinderous eyes, his perfect self-possession, and the rich and well-modulated thunder of his voice (to which I used to listen, sometimes, abstracting myself from his

1 Mr. Webster was still Secretary of State under President Tyler. He resigned the office in the spring.

sense merely for the luxury of such noble ex-
plosions of sound) distinguish him above all
other men. In a million you would single him
out. In England, he made the same impression
by his personal advantages as at home, and was
called the Great Western. In speech he has a
great good sense, — is always pertinent to time
and place, and has an eye to the simple facts of
nature, — to the place where he is, to the hour
of the day, to the sun in heaven, to his neighborhood to the sea or to the mountains, — but
very sparingly notices these things, and clings
closely to the business part of his speech with
great gravity and faithfulness. " I do not inflame,"
he said on one occasion, " I do not exaggerate ;
I avoid all incendiary allusion." He trusts to his
simple strength of statement — in which he excels all men — for the attention of his assembly.
His statement is lucid throughout, and of equal
strength. He has great fairness and deserves all
his success in debate, for he always carries a
point from his adversary by really taking superior ground, as in the Hayne debate. There
are no puerilities, no tricks, no academical play
in any of his speeches, — they are all majestic men
of business. Every one is a first-rate Yankee.

He has had a faithful apprenticeship to his

position, for he was born in New Hampshire, a farmer's son, and his youth spent in those hardships and privations which add such edge to every simple pleasure and every liberalizing opportunity. The Almanac does not come unnoticed, but is read and committed to heart by the farmer's boys. And when it was announced to him by his father that he would send him to college he could not speak. The struggles, — brothers and sisters in poor men's houses in New England are dear to each other, and the bringing up of a family involves many sacrifices, each for the other.

The faults that shade his character are not such as to hurt his popularity. He is very expensive, and always in debt; but this rather commends him, as he is known to be generous, and his countrymen make for him the apology of Themistocles, that to keep treasure undiminished is the virtue of a chest and not of a man. Then there is in him a large share of good nature and a sort of *bonhomie*. It is sometimes complained of him that he is a man of pleasure, and all his chosen friends are easy epicures and debauchees. But this is after Talleyrand's taste, who said of his foolish wife that he found nonsense very refreshing: so Webster, after he has been pumping his brains in the courts and the Senate, is, no doubt, heartily glad to get among cronies and gossips where he can stretch himself at his ease and drink his mulled wine. They also quote as his *three rules* of living : (1) Never to pay any debt that can by any possibility be avoided ; (2) Never to do anything to-day that can be put off till to-morrow ; (3) Never to do anything himself which he can get anybody else to do for him.

All is forgiven to a man of such surpassing intellect, and such prodigious powers of business which have so long been exerted. There is no malice in the man, but broad good humor and much enjoyment of the hour; so that Stetson said of him, " It is true that he sometimes commits crimes, but without any guilt."

A great man is always entitled to the most liberal interpretation, and the few anecdotes by which his opponents have most deeply stabbed at his reputation admit of explanation. I cannot but think, however, that his speech at Richmond was made to bear a meaning by his Southern backers which he did not intend, and I have never forgiven him that he did not say, Not so fast, good friends, I did not mean what you say.

He has misused the opportunity of making himself the darling of the American world in all coming time by abstaining from putting himself at the head of the Anti-slavery interest, by standing for New England and for man against the bullying and barbarism of the South.

I should say of him that he was not at all majestic, but the purest intellect that was ever applied to business. He is Intellect applied to affairs. He is the greatest of lawyers ; but a very indifferent statesman for carrying his points. He carries points with the bench, but not with the caucus. No following has he, no troop of friends, but those whose intellect he fires. No sweaty mob will carry him on their shoulders. And yet all New England to the remotest farmhouse, or lumberers' camp in the woods of Maine, delights to tell and hear of anecdotes of his forensic eloquence. What he said at Salem, at the Knapp trial ; and how in Boston he looked a witness out of court, — once, he set his great eyes on him, and searched him through and through ; then as the cause went on, and this prisoner's perjury was not yet called for, he looked round on him as if to see if he was safe and ready for the inquisition he was preparing to inflict on him. The witness felt for his hat, and edged towards the door; a third time he looked on him, and the witness could sit no longer, but seized his opportunity, fled out of court, and could nowhere be found, such was the terror of those eyes.

People think that in our license of construing the Constitution, and the despotism of Public Opinion, we have no anchor, and one Frenchman thinks he has found it in our Marriage, and one in our Calvinism. But the fact of two poles is universal; the fact of two forces, centripetal and centrifugal, is universal, and each develops the other, each by its own activity. Wild liberty develops iron conscience; want of liberty strengthens decorous and convenient law, which supersedes in a measure the native conscience.

Queenie makes herself merry with the Reformers who make unleavened bread, and are foes to the death to fermentation. Queenie says, God made yeast as well as wheat, and loves fermentation just as dearly as he loves vegetation; that the fermentation develops the saccharine element in the grain, and makes it more palatable and more digestible.[1] But that they wish

1 Mrs. Emerson had much to bear from the whims of the

the " pure wheat " and will die but it shall not
ferment. Stop, dear Nature, these incessant advances ; let me scotch these ever-rolling wheels.

Earth Spirit, living, a black river like that
swarthy stream which rushes through the human body is thy nature, demoniacal, warm, fruit-
ful, sad, nocturnal.

February 8.

As we go along the street, the eyes of all the
passengers either ask, ask, continually of all they
meet, or else assert, assert to all. Only rarely do
we meet a face which has the balance of expression, neither asking leave to be, nor rudely ego-
tistic, but equally receptive and affirmative.
W. A. Tappan says, that when a man is looked
at, he instantly assumes a new expression, and
strangers whom he meets every day in the street
grow angry at being regarded.[1]

crude reformers who so constantly presented themselves as
guests at her table, and criticized and ate or abstained. Like
her brother, Doctor Charles T. Jackson, the distinguished chemist and geologist, she had a scientific taste, and used the knowledge she learned from him in her household management.

1 William A. Tappan, like Giles Waldo and Edward Palmer,
who have been alluded to, was one of the young " Sons
of the Morning " in whom Mr. Emerson felt an interest. He
wrote some verses for the *Dial.* He married Miss Sturgis, a

Strict conversation with a friend is the magazine out of which all good writing is drawn.

[Here follow the passages from "Experience" on God's delight in isolating us and hiding the past and future; on the eye making the horizon, and the mind's eye deifying persons; and on Skepticisms as limitations of the affirmative. See *Essays*, Second Series, pp. 67, 68; 76, 77; 75.]

Men may affect modesty as much as they will, every speaker wants the most intelligent audience, wants genius to hear him.

It is very funny to go in to a family where the father and mother are devoted to the children. You flatter yourself for an instant that you have secured your friend's ear, for his countenance brightens; then you discover that he has just caught the eye of his babe over your shoulder, and is chirruping to him.

The moral must have its origin from inward fountains, but must have its objects in the variety of social life; how much we are domesticated

valued friend of Mr. and Mrs. Emerson, and, later, moved to Lenox, where he passed his days as a scholar-farmer.

by the *moral*. "I feel at home," said Mrs. B., "more than among my relations, for you are *honest* people." So in my experience with the praying traveller at the hotel. So when I go abroad, if I enter a church, the first godly sentiment makes me truly at home. The source must not be the expectations of others, but a delight in serving, an effusion of good will, a delight in serving and not in being seen to serve, not the feeling of duty, but the wish to make happy.

A man going out of Constantinople met the Plague coming in, who said he was sent thither for twenty thousand souls. Forty thousand persons were swept off, and when the traveller came back, he met the Plague coming out of the city. " Why did you kill forty thousand ? " he asked. " I only killed twenty," replied the Pest ; " Fear killed the rest."

Mr. Adams chose wisely and according to his constitution, when, on leaving the Presidency, he went into Congress. He is no literary old gentleman, but a bruiser, and loves the *mêlée*. When they talk about his age and venerableness and nearness to the grave, he knows better, he is like one of those old cardinals, who, as quick as he is chosen Pope, throws away his crutches and his crookedness, and is as straight as a boy. He is an old *roué* who cannot live on slops, but must have sulphuric acid in his tea.

There is no line that does not return; I suppose the mathematicians will tell us that what are called straight lines are lines with long curves, but that there is no straight line in nature.[1] If, as you say, we are destroying number by affirming the strict infinite, why then I concede that number also is swallowable, and that one of these days we shall eat it like custard.

National characteristics stand no chance beside intellectual. Physicians say every constitution makes a new case of fever. So it is with persons. Our national traits may appear so long as we are drowsy and have headache, but put me in good spirits, search me with thought, and all nations are men together. The first Englishman I met in travelling was a frank, affectionate fellow, and the first Frenchman was a mystic.

Major Davezac at the Carlton House, New

1 Compare the heresy of the Archangel of the Sun in "Uriel" in the *Poems*.

York, told me of Father Antoine at New Orleans, the only man left attached to the Spanish Government when the Americans took possession of the city. He never dined at home, but when the noon came, went into the nearest house wherever he walked, and said, " My child, I have come to dine with you." Then they made festival. After dinner, he smoked a cigar, slept half an hour, blessed the house, and departed.

When he fell sick, hourly bulletins were issued of his health : when he died, all shops were shut, all courts and legislatures adjourned. Two shillings were found in his desk, and his testament begged all his children of all sects — for he would not separate in this instrument those whom in heart he had never separated — to kneel down for five minutes and pray that his term of purgatory might be shortened. And Protestant and Catholic knelt down and prayed. He preached a crusade against the English during the siege. And General Jackson came and thanked him, and told him that his prayers and urgent addresses were as good to him as a thousand men. He had Te Deum sung in the church.

Abbess of the Ursuline Convent and her bell of St. Victoire. A vow of a bell of one thousand pounds' weight, not if the victory, but *because* the victory. The book opened of itself to the prayer of the day, it was the prayer to St. Victoire. General Jackson said, " This was very extraordinary, Major Davezac, and I tell you, sir, that something very remarkable has attended this campaign. Ever since the battle on the night of the 23d, until the retreat of the British, I have had the sense that these things had occurred to me before, and been obliterated; and when I observed it, I was sure of success, for I knew that God would not give me previsions of disaster, but signs of victory. He said, This ditch can never be passed. It cannot be done."

We are all chemists who only know our own gold. Men cast pearls about in large companies where I go, and none but I seems to know that they are pearls.

Society. I feel and own your power, but I lament that your power smothers mine. This I regret, not for my sake, for I am well content to lie hid a year, but for yours, that it prevents me making that just return which your merit demands; and I should like to justify to you your good deed and will towards me.

Democracy with us is charged with being malignant, and I think it seems aimless, selfish resistance, pulling down, and wild wish to have physical freedom, — but for what? Only for freedom; not to any noble end. Vethake[1] thought that society was fast arriving at the excess of democracy, — universal abolition, I think, he called it, which he thought the absolute extinction of the feminine principle. Then woman will say, I cannot stand this death, and will rise in indignation and end that epoch. Mr. V's opinion was that Mahomet had tried power, and Jesus, or, I think, John, persuasion; that Mahomet had felt that persuasion, this John-persuasion had miserably failed, was a pretty poor shift or system of shifts, this expediency or system of coaxing and example and so forth, precisely that against which nowadays we write essays and lectures; and he said, I will try this Oriental weapon, the sword, which never, never will go West; and he said to Ayesha, "I have found out how to work it. This Woman element will not bear the sword; well, I will dispose of woman: she may exist; but henceforward I will veil it:" so he veiled Woman. Then the sword could work and eat. A man and a woman he thought the true social unit, born of

1 An acquaintance in New York.

the community, and that the old and the young could only exist in a state of tutelage or protection; that the only holders of property were the married couple, who should not take either the name of husband or wife, but a new name common to both, and have but one vote. Three ways of killing there were. In the third, I smelt fagots: Society, he said, should not put to death, but should say, this cannot be, and it would cease. I remembered what I have heard or dreamed, that the most terrific of hierarchs would be a mystic. Beware of Swedenborg *in power*. Swedenborg in minority, Swedenborg contemplative, is excellent company; but Swedenborg executive would be the Devil in crown and sceptre. Fagots!

In the capacious leisures of the spirit I think we may beguile the time by the play of the understanding and the use of the hands, and yet be candidates for the divine succors and the use of divine methods as truly as if we should fold our hands and rely on transcendent methods only.

Cheap literature makes new markets. We have thought only of a box audience, or at most of box and pit; but now it appears there is also slip audience, and galleries one, two, three; and back

stairs, and street listeners, besides. Greeley tells
me that *Graham's Magazine* has seventy thousand subscribers, and I may write a lecture, if I
will, to seventy thousand readers.

Like Vethake, Brisbane thought the Democracy did not wish to build, but only to tear down;
"to tear down," as he said, "God and the Bank,
and everything else they could see."

CONCORD, *March* 12.

Home again from my long journey to count
my treasures old and new, and, might it be, to
impart them.

The world has since the beginning an incurable trick of taking care of itself, or every hilltop
in America would have counsel to offer. We sit
and think how richly ornamented the wide cham-
paign and yonder woodlands to the foot of those
blue mountains shall be, and meanwhile here are
ready and willing thousands strong and teachable
who have no land to till. If Government in our
present clumsy fashion must go on, — could it
not assume the charge of providing each citizen,
on his coming of age, with a pair of acres, to enable him to get his bread honestly ? Perhaps one
day it will be done by the State's assuming to

distribute the estates of the dead. In the United States almost every State owns so much public land, that it would be practicable to give what they have, and devise a system by which the State should continue to possess a fund of this sort.

Gypsies and militia captains, Paddies and Chinese, all manner of cunning and pragmatical men and a few fine women, — a strange world made up of such oddities ; the only beings that belong to the horizon being the fine women.

Cheap is the humiliation of to-day which gives wit, eloquence, poetry to-morrow.

All work for me. I and my day. Some persons use my language, but are foreign to me, and others who use a language foreign to me are very near me. Events are the clothes of the Spirit. Why should we try to steal and strip them. And we know God so, as we know each other by our garments. "You flee fast, but the pursuers flee after you as fast." So said to me Mrs. Rebecca Black in New York.

At the Five Points I heard a woman swearing very liberally as she talked with her com-

panions; but when I looked at her face, I saw
that she was no worse than other women; that
she used the dialect of her class, as all others do,
and are neither better nor worse for it; but under this bad costume was the same repose, the
same probity as in Broadway. Nor was she mis-
interpreted by her mates. There is a virtue of
vice as well as of virtue.

And the Spirit drove him apart into a solitary
place. This does the Spirit for every man.

(From R)

I find it easier to read Goethe than Mundt,
and it must always be easier to understand a
sensible than a weak man in a foreign tongue,
because things themselves translate for the one,
and not for the other. Yet very pleasant is the
progress which we make in a new language, the
medium through which we explore the thoughts
ever growing rarer, until at last we become unconscious of its presence in its transparency.

Ellery's verses should be called poetry for
poets, they touch the fine pulses of thought and
will be the cause of more poetry and of verses
more finished and better turned than them-

selves; but I cannot blame the *North Americans* and *Knickerbockers* if they should not suspect his genius. When the rudder is invented for the balloon, railroads will be superseded. And when Ellery's muse finds an aim, whether some passion or some fast faith, any kind of thing on which all these wild and sometimes brilliant beads can be strung, we shall have a poet. Now he *fantasies* merely, as *dilettanti* in music. He breaks faith continually with the intellect. The sonnet has merits, fine lines, gleams of deep thought; well worth sounding, worth studying, if only I could confide that he had any steady meaning before him, that he kept faith with himself; but I fear that he changed his purpose with every verse; was led up and down, to this or that, with the exigencies of the rhyme, and only wanted to write and rhyme somewhat, careless how or what, and stopped when he came to the end of the paper. He breaks faith with the reader; wants integrity. Yet for Poets it will be a better book than a whole volume of Bryant and Campbell. Miss Peabody has beautiful colors to sell, but her shop has no attraction for house-builders and merchants : Mr. Allston and Mr. Cheney will probably find the way to it.

A man of genius is privileged only as far as

he is a genius. His dulness is as insupportable as any other dulness. Only success will justify a departure and a license. But Ellery has freaks which are entitled to no more charity than the dulness and madness of others, which he despises. He uses a license continually which would be just in oral improvisation, but is not pardonable in written verses. He fantasies on his piano.

E. H. said, that he was a wood-elf which one of the maids in a story fell in love with, and then grew uneasy, desiring that he might be baptized. Margaret said, he reminded one of a great Genius with a little wretched boy trotting beside him.

> " For in thee hides a matchless light
>   That splendors all the dreaming night;
>   Thy bark shall be a precious stone
>   In whose red veins deep magic hides,
>   Thy ecstasies be known to none,
>   Except those vast ethereal tides
>   That circulate our being round
>   But whisper not the slightest sound." [1]

> " Away, away, thou starlit breath !
>   On bended knees I pray thee go ;

[1] This and the following verse seem the best of the short extracts from poems by Channing copied on this page of the Journal.

O bind thy temples not with death,
Nor let thy shadow fall on snow."

Jock could not eat rice, because it came west, nor molasses because it came north, nor put on leathern shoes because of the methods by which leather was procured, nor indeed wear a woolen coat. But Dick gave him a gold eagle that he might buy wheat and rye, maple sugar and an oaken chest, and said, This gold-piece, unhappy Jock! is molasses, and rice, and horsehide and sheepskin.[1]

[Here follow sentences from *The Chinese Classical Work*, commonly called *The Four Books*, translated by Rev. David Collier. These and other Oriental religious sayings were printed in the *Dial*, there called " Ethnical Scriptures."]

Criticism. So the Gothic cathedral and the Shakspeare perfection is as wild and unaccountable as a geranium or a rabbit or an ornithorhynchus. It is done, and we must go to work and do something else, that undone something which is now hinting and working and impatient here in and around us.

[1] The superfine abstinences of the Fruitlands projectors are here in mind.

Drawing, M. R. said from Mr. Cheney, was only a good eye for distances; and the descriptive talent in the poet seems to depend on a certain lakelike passiveness to receive the picture of the whole landscape in its native proportions, uninjured, and then with sweet heedfulness the caution of love, to transfer it to the tablet of language.

Health. Health is the most objective of subjects. The Vishnu Sarna said, " It is the same to him who wears a shoe as if the whole earth were covered with leather." So I spread my health over the whole world and make it strong, happy, and serviceable. To the sick man, the world is a medicine chest.

Poet. It is true that when a man writes poetry, he appears to assume the high feminine part of his nature. We clothe the poet, therefore, in robes and garlands, which are proper to woman. The Muse is feminine. But action is male. And a king is draped almost in feminine attire.

The philosophers at Fruitlands have such an image of virtue before their eyes, that the poetry of man and nature they never see; the poetry that is in man's life, the poorest pastoral clown-ish life; the light that shines on a man's hat, in a child's spoon, the sparkle on every wave and on every mote of dust, they see not.

Lectures. " Aristo said, that neither a bath nor a lecture did signify anything unless they scoured and made men clean."

Pride is a great convenience,[1] . . . so much handsomer and cheaper than vanity, but proud people are intolerably selfish, and the vain are gentle and giving.

Translations. I thank the translators.[2] . . .

March 23.

Two brave chanticleers[3] go up and down strip-ping the plumes from all the fine birds, show-ing that all are not in the best health. It makes much unhappiness on all sides; much crowing it occasions on the part of the two cockerels who so shrewdly discover and dismantle all the young

1 Compare " Wealth " (*Conduct of Life*, p. 114).

2 The rest of the passage, telling Mr. Emerson's views and practice, is printed in " Books " (*Society and Solitude*, p. 204).

3 Probably the Englishmen Lane and Wright.

beaux of the aviary. But alas, the two valiant cocks who strip are no better than those who are stripped, only they have sharper beak and talons. In plain prose, I grieved so much to hear the most intellectual youth I have met, Charles Newcomb, so disparaged, and our good and most deserving scholar, Theodore Parker, threatened as a morsel to be swallowed when he shall come to-morrow, and all this by my brave friends, who are only brave, not helpful, not loving, not creative, — that I said, Cursed is preaching, — the better it is, the worse. A preacher is a bully : I who have preached so much, — by the help of God will never preach more.

We want the fortification of an acknowledgment of the good in us. "The girl is the least part of herself" ; God is in the girl. That is the reason why fools can be so beloved by sages ; that, under all the corsets and infirmities, is life, and the revelation of Reason and of Conscience.

Margaret. A pure and purifying mind, self-purifying also, full of faith in men, and inspiring it. Unable to find any companion great enough to receive the rich effusions of her thought, so that her riches are still unknown and seem unknowable. It is a great joy to find that we have underrated our friend, that he or she is far more excellent than we had thought. All natures seem poor beside one so rich, which pours a stream of amber over all objects, clean and unclean, that lie in its path, and makes that comely and presentable which was mean in itself. We are taught by her plenty how lifeless and outward we were, what poor Laplanders burrowing under the snows of prudence and pedantry. Beside her friendship, other friendships seem trade, and by the firmness with which she treads her upward path, all mortals are convinced that another road exists than that which their feet know.[1] The wonderful generosity of her sentiments pours a contempt on books and writing at the very time when one asks how shall this fiery picture be kept in its glow and variety for other eyes. She excels other intellectual persons in this, that her sentiments are more blended with her life; so the expression of them has greater steadiness and greater clearness. I have never known any example of such steady progress from stage to stage of thought and of character. An inspirer of

[1] This and part of the following sentence are used, but not personally applied, in " Manners " (*Essays*, Second Series, p. 150).

courage, the secret friend of all nobleness, the patient waiter for the realization of character, forgiver of injuries, gracefully waving aside folly, and elevating lowness,—in her presence all were apprised of their fettered estate and longed for liberation, of ugliness and longed for their beauty; of meanness and panted for grandeur.

Her growth is visible. All the persons whom we know have reached their height, or else their growth is so nearly at the same rate with ours, that it is imperceptible, but this child inspires always more faith in her. She rose before me at times into heroical and godlike regions, and I could remember no superior women, but thought of Ceres, Minerva, Proserpine, and the august ideal forms of the foreworld.[1] She said that no man gave such invitation to her mind as to tempt her to full expression; that she felt a power to enrich her thought with such wealth and variety of embellishment as would, no doubt, be tedious to such as she conversed with. And there is no form that does not seem to wait her beck,—dramatic, lyric, epic, passionate, pictorial, humorous.

She has great sincerity, force, and fluency as a writer, yet her powers of speech throw her

1 This sentence is used impersonally in " Manners."

writing into the shade. What method, what exquisite judgment, as well as energy, in the selection of her words; what character and wisdom they convey! You cannot predict her opinion. She sympathizes so fast with all forms of life, that she talks never narrowly or hostilely, nor betrays, like all the rest, under a thin garb of new words, the old droning cast-iron opinions or notions of many years' standing. What richness of experience, what newness of dress, and fast as Olympus to her principle. And a silver eloquence, which inmost Polymnia taught. Meantime, all this pathos of sentiment and riches of literature, and of invention, and this march of character threatening to arrive presently at the shores and plunge into the sea of Buddhism and mystic trances, consists with a boundless fun and drollery, with light satire, and the most entertaining conversation in America.

Her experience contains, I know, golden moments, which, if they could be fitly narrated, would stand equally beside any histories of magnanimity which the world contains; and whilst Dante's *Nuova Vita* is almost unique in the literature of Sentiment, I have called the imperfect record she gave me of two of her days, " Nuovissima Vita."

A working King is one of the best symbols. Alfred and Ulysses are such. And we see them now and then in society; — oftener off the throne, of course, than on it. This is the right country for them.[1]

A chamber of flame in which the martyr passes is more magnificent than any royal apartment; and this martyr palace may be built up on any waste place instantly.

Persons are fine things, but they cost so much! for *thee* I must pay *me*.

Fine constellation of people; rare force of character and wealth of truth; they ought to cluster and shine and illuminate the nation and the nations. Alcott said reasonable words about the *Dial*, that it ought to be waited for by all the newspapers and journals, the Abolitionists ought to get their leading from it, and not be able to spurn it as they do. It should lead. Here the sceptre is offered us, and we refuse it from poorness of spirit.

When I see what fine people we have, I think it a sort of King Réné period: there is no do-

1 Compare what is said of a *Working King* in "The Young American" (*Nature, Addresses, etc.*, p. 386).

ing, but rare and shrilling prophecy from bands
of competing minstrels and the age shall not
sneak out, but affirm all the beauty and truth
in its heart.

" *Dial* has not piety."

The same persons should not constitute a
Standing Committee on Reform. A man may
say, I am the chief of sinners, but once. He is
already damned, if having come once to the insight of that condition, he remains there to say
it again. But the Committee on Reform should
be made of new persons every day; of those
just arrived at the power of comparing the state
of society with their own daily expanding spirit.
Fatal to discuss reform weekly! The poorest
poet or young beginner in the fine arts hesitates
to speak of the design he wishes to execute, lest
it die in your cold fingers. And this art of life
has the same pudency and will not be exposed.

It is a great joy to get away from persons, and
live under the dominion of the Multiplication
Table.[1]

1 It should be remembered that Mr. Emerson had been
much at the mercy of Mr. Alcott and his new disciples for
several months, which probably was partly the cause of his

Milton is the most literary man in literature.

We are greatly vexed when poets, who are by excellence the thinking and feeling of the world, are deficient in truth of intellect and of affection. Then is Feeling unfeeling and Thought unwise.

The conversation turned upon the state and duties of Woman. As always, it was historically considered, and had a certain falseness so. For me, to-day, Woman is not a degraded person with duties forgotten, but a docile daughter of God with her face heavenward endeavoring to hear the divine word and to convey it to me.

I read again the verses of Margaret with the new commentary of beautiful anecdotes she had given, freshly in my mind. Of course the poems grew golden, the twig blossomed in my hands: but a poem should not need its relation to life to explain it; it should be a new life, not still half engaged in the soil, like the new created lions in Eden.

long absence from home in the winter, but it was yet some weeks before they moved to the poor farm, which they had "redeemed from human ownership" for their experiment of a new Eden at Harvard, Massachusetts.

Do you know how diamonds and other gems were invented? Rim, wishing to go on the errands of Ormuzd through the Kingdoms of Ariman without discovery, received from Ormuzd in a pod of lupine seven days in the form of seven diamonds. He used each of them as a lamp, which, spent, gave him a sharp and wise light for his path for twenty-four degrees of the way. On other occasions, Ormuzd gave him spring days in the form of emeralds, midsummer days in the shape of rubies, and autumn in topazes. All these stones are Children of Day.

The world must be new as we know it, for see how lately it has bethought itself of so many articles of the simplest convenience; as, for example, wooden clothes-pins to pinch the clothes to the line, instead of metallic pins, were introduced since the Peace of 1783. My mother remembers when her sister, Mrs. Inman, returned from England at that time, and brought these articles with her furniture, then new in this country; then the india-rubber shoe; the railroad; the steamboat; and the air-tight stove; the friction match; and cut nails.

The difference between Talent and Genius is, that Talent says things which he has never heard but once, and Genius things which he has never heard.

Genius is power; Talent is applicability. A human body, an animal, is an applicability; the Life, the Soul is Genius.

"Mamma," said the child, "they have begun again!"[1]

Elizabeth Hoar says, "I love Henry, but do not like him." Young men, like Henry Thoreau, owe us a new world, and they have not acquitted the debt. For the most part, such die young, and so dodge the fulfilment. One of our girls said, that Henry never went through the kitchen without coloring.[2]

Do not mince your speech. Power fraternizes with power.[3] . . .

Montaigne. In Roxbury, in 1825, I read Cotton's translation of Montaigne. It seemed to

1 Louisa Alcott, or one of her sisters, was sent by her mother to find out whether the philosophers had desisted from their speculations and got to some needed task, and came in with this hopeless report.

2 Mr. Thoreau was always most modest and yet chivalrous in his treatment of women of high or low degree.

3 The rest of the paragraph is found in *Natural History of Intellect* (p. 30).

me as if I had written the book myself in some
former life, so sincerely it spoke my thought
and experience. No book before or since was
ever so much to me as that. How I delighted
afterward in reading Cotton's dedication to Halifax, and the reply of Halifax, which seemed no
words, of course, but genuine suffrages. Afterwards I went to Paris in 1833, and to the Père
le Chaise, and stumbled on the tomb of Au-
guste Collignon, who, said the stone, formed
himself to virtue on the essays of Montaigne.
Afterwards John Sterling wrote a loving criticism on Montaigne in the *Westminster Review*,
with a journal of his own pilgrimage to Montaigne's estate and château,[1] — and, soon after,
Carlyle writes me word that this same lover of
Montaigne is a lover of me. Now, I have been
introducing to his genius two of my friends,
James and Tappan,[2] who both warm to him as
to their brother.

1 Some sentences from the above are printed in " Montaigne" (*Representative Men*, pp. 162, 163).

2 Henry James and William A. Tappan, the former a lifelong friend of Mr. Emerson, and a man of great charm, originality, and wit. He early became interested in Swedenborg,
and was the author of several philosophical and religious works,
among them *Substance and Shadow* and *The Secret of Swedenborg*.

Reference. We praise the pine because it looks like a palm, the oriole because it looks like equatorial birds, and all our view of Nature is adjusted to a tropical standard. The man under the line delights as much in the Alpine and Arctic type and dreams of the cool water and the apple and pear and peach of the Temperate climates where Nature serves man. Endless weak reference. Grief and Joy, Charity and Faith get derivative and referring. Dire Necessity is good and strong; — I love him, I hate him; I like, I dislike. Once there was a race that subsisted, but these seeming, spectral fellows that ask even when they curse and swear — or but affect to curse and swear! I wish there was no more good nature left in the world; tomahawks are better. I think the reason why we value mystics so much is, as oaks indicate a strong soil, so a thick crop of mystics shows like redemption from our universal supplication of each other.

Of Books. He is a poor writer who does not teach courage of treatment.

The Brook Farm Community is an expression in plain prose and actuality of the theory of impulse. It contains several bold and consistent philosophers, both men and women, who carry out the theory, odiously enough, inasmuch as this centripetence of theirs is balanced by no centrifugence; this wish to obey impulse is guarded by no old, old Intellect — or that which knows metes and bounds. The young people who have been faithful to this, their testimony, have lived a great deal in a short time, but have come forth with shattered constitutions. It is an intellectual Sansculottism. Happily, Charles Newcomb and George Bradford have been there, and their presence could not but be felt as sanitary and retentive. Charles Newcomb, I hear, was greatly respected, and his conduct, even in trifles, observed and imitated, — the quiet, retreating, demoniacal youth. Nathaniel Hawthorne said that Burton felt the presence of Newcomb all the time.[1]

I read in Ward's Chinese book, the other day, of bards; many sentences purporting that

1 Interesting and almost uniformly pleasant accounts of life at Brook Farm are " Reminiscences of Brook Farm," by George P. Bradford, *Century Magazine*, vol. xxiii; " A Girl of Sixteen at Brook Farm," by Mrs. Sedgwick, *Atlantic Monthly*, vol. lxxxv; and " A Visit to Brook Farm," by Mrs. Kirby, *Overland Monthly*, vol. v.

bards love wine. Tea and coffee are my wine, and I have finer and lighter wines than these.[1] But some nectar an intellectual man will naturally use. For he will soon learn the secret that beside the energy of his conscious intellect, his intellect is capable of new energy by abandonment to the nature of things.[2] . . . All persons avail themselves of such means as they can to add this extraordinary power to their normal powers. One finds it in music, one in war, one in great pictures or sculpture; one in travelling; one in conversation; in politics, in mobs, in fires, in theatres, in love, in science; in animal intoxication. I take many stimulants and often make an art of my inebriation. I read Proclus for my opium; it excites my imagination to let sail before me the pleasing and grand figures of gods and dæmons and demoniacal men. I hear of rumors rife among the most ancient gods, of azonic gods who are itinerants, of dæmons with fulgid eyes, of the unenvying and exuberant will of the gods; the aquatic gods, the Plain of Truth, the meadow, the nutriment of the gods, the paternal port, and all the

1 Mr. Emerson tells of these in his poem "Bacchus."

2 What follows is printed in "The Poet" (*Essays*, Second Series, pp. 26, 27).

rest of the Platonic rhetoric quoted as household words.[1] By all these and so many rare and brave words I am filled with hilarity and spring, my heart dances, my sight is quickened, I behold shining relations between all beings, and am impelled to write and almost to sing. I think one would grow handsome who read Proclus much and well.

But of this inebriation I spoke of, it is an old knowledge that Intellect by its relation to what is prior to Intellect is a god. This is inspiration.

They [the Neoplatonists] speak of the Gods with such pictorial distinctness often that one would think they had actually been present, Swedenborg-like, at the Olympic feasts ; e.g., " This is that which emits the intelligible light, that, when it appeared, astonished the intellectual gods and made them admire their father, as Orpheus says."

How often I have said, what this morning I must say once more, that the conscience of the coming age will put its surveillance on the intellect. We accuse ourselves that we have been useless, but not that we have been thoughtless.

1 These are also alluded to in "Books" (*Society and Solitude*, p. 203).

Thou oughtest to have listened, will it say, so shouldest thou have heard the oracles, which would elevate every day of life.

It is not in the power of God to make a communication of his will to a Calvinist. For to every inward revelation he holds up his silly book, and quotes chapter and verse against the Book-Maker and Man-Maker, against that which quotes not, but is and cometh. There is a light older than intellect, by which the intellect lives and works, always new, and which degrades every past and particular shining of itself. This light, Calvinism denies, in its idolatry of a certain past shining.

Swedenborg, Behmen, Spinoza, will appear original to uninstructed and thoughtless persons.[1] . . . A thinker, or a man through whom shineth that light which is older than intellect and through which alone intellect is a god, will undervalue each reporter when he beholds the splendor of the truth itself. And though such a person will do justice to the good intention of one of these men of God who strove to say truly what they had seen, yet he will see that to such as quote

1 Two sentences immediately following are in " Quotations and Originality " (*Letters and Social Aims*, p. 181).

their words instead of listening to the truth itself, they falsify the truth: for his book is not truth, but truth Swedenborgized or Behmenized or Spinozised.

Much poor talk concerning woman, which at least had the effect of revealing the true sex of several of the party who usually go disguised in the form of the other sex. Thus Mrs, B. is a man. The finest people marry the two sexes in their own person. Hermaphrodite is then the symbol of the finished Soul. It was agreed that in every act should appear the married pair: the two elements should mix in every act.

To me it sounded hoarsely, the attempt to prescribe didactically to woman her duties. Man can never tell woman what her duties are: he will certainly end in describing a man in female attire, as Harriet Martineau, a masculine woman, solved her problem of Woman. No, Woman only can tell the heights of feminine nature, and the only way in which man can help her, is by observing woman reverently, and whenever she speaks from herself, and catches him in inspired moments up to a heaven of honor and religion, to hold her to that point by reverential recognition of the divinity that speaks through her.

I can never think of woman without gratitude
for the bright revelations of her best nature which
have been made to me, unworthy. The angel
who walked with me in younger days shamed my
ambition and prudence by her generous love in
our first interview. I described my prospects.
She said, I do not wish to hear of your prospects.

April 10.

The slowly retreating snow blocks the roads
and wood paths and shuts me in the house. But
yesterday the warm south wind drew me to the
top of the hill, like the dove from the ark, to see
if these white waters were abated, and there was
place for the foot. The grass springs up already
between the holes in the snow, and I walked
along the knolls and edges of the hill wherever
the winter bank was melted, but I thrust my cane
into the bank two feet perpendicular. I greeted
the well-known pine grove which I could not
reach; the pine tops seemed to cast a friendly
gold-green smile of acquaintance toward me, for
it was in my heart that I had not yet quite got
home from my late journey, until I had revisited
and rejoined these vegetable dæmons. The air
was kind and clear, the sky southward was full
of comets, so white and fan-shaped and ethereal

lay the clouds, as if the late visit of this foreign wonder had set the fashion for the humbler meteors. And all around me the new-come sparrows, robins, bluebirds, and blackbirds were announcing their arrival with great spirit.

The Transcendentalist or Realist is distinguished from the Churchman herein, that he limits his affirmation to his perception, and never goes beyond the warrant of his experience (spiritual and sensuous) in his creed. Whilst the Churchman affirms many things received on testimony as of equal value with the moral intuitions.

I told Mr. Means that he need not consult the Germans, but, if he wished at any time to know what the Transcendentalists believed, he might simply omit what in his own mind he added from the tradition, and the rest would be Transcendentalism.

The Church affirms this and that fact of time and place; describes circumstances; a circumstantial heaven; a circumstantial hell. The way of the Spirit is different. It never antedates its revelations, it does not tell you when or how; but it says, *Be thus and thus*, and in our doing, it opens the path, shines in the way we are to go, and creates around us new unpredicted relations.

Daniel Webster is a great man with a small ambition. Nature has built him and holds him forth as a sample of the heroic mould to this puny generation. He was virtual President of the United States from the hour of the Speech on Foot's Resolutions in the United States Senate in 1832, being regarded as the Expounder of the Constitution and the Defender of Law. But this did not suffice; he wished to be an officer, also; wished to add a title to his name, and be a President. That ruined him. He should have learned from the Chinese that " it has never been the case that, when a man in a place where no mulberry trees yet grew could cause the aged to wear silks, and where there were no breeders of fowls or hogs or sheep could cause the aged to eat flesh and the young did not suffer hunger or cold, — he did not become Emperor."

The Drop of Nectar. In Nature the "woodness" or tendency to make an idle savage and idiot of a man, through the seduction of forests, mountains, and waters, is a conspicuous example of the bias or small excess of force which is always added in the vital directions.

Buddhism. Winter, Night, Sleep, are all the invasions of eternal Buddh, and it gains a point every day. Let be, *laissez-faire*, so popular now in philosophy and in politics, that is bald Buddhism; and then very fine names has it got to cover up its chaos withal, namely, trances, raptures, abandonment, ecstasy, — all Buddh, naked Buddh.

Travelling, forsooth! as if every traveller did not feel himself an impertinence when he came among the diligent in their places. Do you suppose there is any country where they do not scald the milkpans, and clout the infants, and burn the brushwood? And yet Humboldt may travel, or any other man, when the state seems to travel in his legs, as these railway levellers whom I met this afternoon.[1]

Nature is the strictest economist,[2] . . .

1 The Fitchburg Railroad was in course of construction, and passed Mr. Emerson's beloved Walden.

2 The rest of the passage thus beginning is in "The Young American" (*Nature, Addresses, etc.,* p. 373).

Ellen wishes to know if she may come and see when the railroad goes by?

"Father, what makes the railroad grow worse?"

I said she must come in, for it was damp, and she would get sick, and I could not spare my little daughter. She answered, "Could you not spare her to God?"

It is a compensation for the habitual moderation of Nature in these Concord fields and the want of picturesque outlines, the ease of getting about. I long sometimes to have mountains, ravines, and flumes like that in Lincoln, New Hampshire, within reach of my eyes and feet; but the thickets of the forest and the fatigue of mountains are spared me and I go through Concord as through a park.

Concord is a little town, and yet has its honors. We get our handful of every ton that comes to the city. We have had our share of Everett and Webster, who have both spoken here. So has Edward Taylor. So did George Bancroft, and Bronson Alcott, and Charles Lane, and Garrison and Phillips, the Abolition orators. We have had our shows and processions, conjurors, and bear-gardens, and here, too, came Herr Driesbach

with his cats and snakes, lying down on a lion-
ess, and kissing a tiger, and rolling himself up,
not in leopard-skins, but in live leopards, and
his companion with his tippet of anacondas.

Hither come in summer the Penobscot Indians, and make baskets for us on the river-bank.

Doctor Channing and Harriet Martineau
were here and — what I think much more —
here was Aunt Mary, Ellen, Edward, and
Charles; here is Elizabeth Hoar; here have
been, or are, Margaret Fuller, Sam and Anna
Ward, Caroline Sturgis, Charles Newcomb,
George Bradford, Ellery Channing, Nathaniel
Hawthorne, Sarah Alden Ripley; Henry Thoreau, James Elliot Cabot.

In the old time, John Winthrop, John Eliot,
Peter Bulkeley; then Whitefield; then Hancock,
Adams and the College were here in 1775.

[Mr. Emerson, years later, added the following: —]

Kossuth spoke to us in the court-house in
1852. Agassiz, Greenough, Clough, Jeffries
Wyman, Samuel Hoar, Lafayette.

April 17.

How sincere and confidential we can be, saying all that lies in the mind, and yet go away feel-

ing that we have spun a rope of sand, that all is
yet unsaid, from the incapacity of the parties
to know each other, *although they use the same
words.*[1] . . . Could they but once understand that
I loved to know that they existed and heartily
wished them Godspeed, yet out of my poverty
of life and thought, had no word or welcome for
them when they came to see me, and could well
consent to their living in another town, from any
claim that I felt on them, — it would be great
satisfaction. Not this, but something like this,
I said, and then, as the discourse, as so often,
touched Character, I added, that they were both
intellectual, they assumed to be substantial and
central, to be the thing they said, but were not;
but only intellectual, or the scholars, the learned,
of the Spirit or Central Life. If they were that,
if the centres of their life were coincident with
the Centre of Life, I should bow the knee, I
should accept without gainsaying all that they
said, as if I had said it: just as our saint (though
morbid), Jones Very, had affected us with what
was best in him, but I felt in them the slight
dislocation of these Centres which allowed them

1 The passage beginning thus forms the conclusion of
"Nominalist and Realist" (*Essays*, Second Series). The
philosophers there alluded to were Alcott and Lane.

to stand aside and speak of these facts *knowingly*. Therefore, I was at liberty to look at them, not as the commanding fact, but as one of the whole circle of facts. They did not like pictures, marbles, woodlands, and poetry; I liked all these, and Lane and Alcott too, as one figure more in the various landscape.

And now, I said, will you not please to pound me a little before I go, just by way of squaring the account, that I may not remember that I alone was saucy? Alcott contented himself with quarrelling with the injury done to greater qualities in my company, by the tyranny of my Taste; — which certainly was very soft pounding. And so I departed from the divine lotuseaters.

Veracity. Almost every writing of a liberal kind when at last it is done assumes the air of an escapade, it is done to get rid of it, done for editors, booksellers, and all miscellaneous occasions, and not out of a dire or divine intrinsic necessity. So much deduction from veracity.

Intellectual race are the New Englanders. Mrs. Ripley [1] at Brook Farm said that the young

1 Mrs. George Ripley. She is not to be confounded with Mr. Emerson's kinswoman by marriage and lifelong friend,

women who came thither from farms elsewhere would work faithfully and do whatever was given them without grumbling, but there was no heart in it, but their whole interest was in their intellectual culture.

" Open the mouth of the cave, and bring out those five kings unto me out of the cave " (Joshua x, 22), was Dr. Frothingham's text on the five points of Calvinism.

Carlyle esteems all living men mice and rats, but that is one of the conditions of his genius. Take away that feeling, and you would possibly make him dumb.

Carlyle in his new book,[1] as everywhere, is a continuer of the great line of scholars in the world, of Horace, Varro, Pliny, Erasmus, Scaliger, Milton, and well sustains their office in ample credit and honor. If the good Heaven have any truth to impart, there he is at his post, a fit organ to say it well. Not a prophet, not a poet, but a master of that cunning art which can clothe any fact with a fine robe of words.

first in Waltham, and, in her later years, in Concord, Sarah Alden Bradford Ripley, wife of Rev. Samuel Ripley.

1 *Past and Present.*

Nature gives me precious signs in such persons as William Tappan, Nathaniel Hawthorne, and now eminently in L. M. W.,[1] that in democratic America, she will not be democratized. How cloistered and constitutionally sequestered from the market and gossips!

Second Advent. I read of an excellent Millerite who gives out that he expects the second advent of the Lord in 1843, but if there is any error in his computation, — he shall look for him until he comes.

The hurts of the husbandmen are many. As soon as the heat bursts his vine-seed and the cotyledons open, the striped yellow bugs and the stupid squash-bug, smelling like a decomposing pear, sting the little plants to death and destroy the hope of melons. And as soon as the grass is well cut and spread on the ground, the thunderclouds, which are the bugs of the haymakers, come growling down the heaven and make tea of his hay.

We cannot forgive you that worst want of tact which incapacitates you from discriminating

1 A writer, not identified, whose offered work interested Mr. Emerson; but he had, once at least, to reject.

between what is to be disputed, and what is to be reverenced or cherished in your friend's communications. The babe of a Choctaw, the cub of a lion, may be strangled by a boy: and the ablest genius, if he trust you with his yet unripe fancies, casts himself helpless on your compassion. Life and death are in your hands, let his power and renown be what they may. There is no part then to be taken but to throw yourself as much as possible into the neutral state of mind and entertain his thought as far as you can ; and where you cannot, be satisfied that you cannot, without criticism. It is, though you can kill it, the babe of a Choctaw, the cub of a lion, and will yet approve its sinewy stock.

I wrote to Thomas Carlyle of his new book, *Past and Present*.[1] . . .

I went to Washington[2] and spent four days. The two poles of an enormous political battery, galvanic coil on coil, self-increased by series on series of plates from Mexico to Canada and from the sea westward to the Rocky Mountains, here

[1] The letter is given in the *Carlyle-Emerson Correspondence* (vol. ii, No. LXVII), and the criticism of the book is on pp. 29, 30.

[2] That is, in January.

terminate and play and make the air electric and violent. Yet one feels how little, more than how much, Man is represented there. I think, in the higher societies of the universe, it will turn out that the angels are molecules, as the devils were always Titans, since the dulness of the world needs such mountainous demonstration, and the virtue is so modest and concentrating.

May 2.

Yesterday I read an old file of Aunt Mary's letters, and felt how she still gains by all comparison with later friends. Never any gave higher counsels, as Elizabeth Hoar most truly said, nor played with all the household incidents with more wit and humor. My life and its early events never look trivial in her letters, but full of eyes, and acquire deepest expression.

In America, out-of-doors all seems a market, in-doors an air-tight stove of conventionalism. Everybody who comes into the house savors of these precious habits: the men, of the market; the women, of the custom. In every woman's conversation and total influence, mild or acid, lurks the *conventional devil*. They look at your carpet, they look at your cap, at your salt-cel-

lar, at your cook and waiting-maid, convention-
ally, — to see how close they square with the
customary cut in Boston and Salem and New
Bedford. But Aunt Mary and Elizabeth do not
bring into a house with them a platoon of conventional devils.

May 7.

Yesterday George Bradford walked and talked
of the Community and cleared up some of the
mists which gossip had made: and expressed
the conviction, shared by himself and his friends
there, that plain dealing was the best defence of
manners and morals between the sexes. I suppose that the danger arises whenever bodily familiarity grows up without a spiritual intimacy.
The reason why there is purity in marriage is, that
the parties are universally near and helpful, and
not only near bodily. If their wisdoms come near
and meet, there is no danger of passion. Therefore, the remedy of impurity is to come nearer.

Many events on the light-winged hours. Alcott and Lane make ready to depart. Channing
has brought his Lares to Concord, and Henry
Thoreau is gone yesterday to New York —
whence come the warm south winds.[1]

1 Mr. Thoreau went to the home of Mr. Emerson's older

At Brook Farm this peculiarity, that there is no head. In every family, a paterfamilias; in every factory, a foreman; in a shop, a master; in a boat, a boatswain; but in Brook Farm, no authority, but each master and mistress of their own actions, — happy, hapless, *sansculottes.*

Yesterday, English visitors, and I waited all day when they should go.

If we could establish the rule that each man was a guest in his own house, and when we had shown our visitors the passages of the house, the way to fire, to bread, and water, and thus made them as much at home as the inhabitant, did then leave them to the accidents of intercourse, and went about our ordinary business, a guest would no longer be formidable.

At Brook Farm again, I understand the authority of Mr. and Mrs. Ripley is felt unconsciously by all; and this is ground of regret to individuals, who see that this particular power is thrown into the conservative scale. But Mr. and Mrs. Ripley are the only ones who have identified themselves with the Community. They

brother William in Staten Island for the summer and autumn as tutor to his son.

have married it, and they are it. The others are
experimenters who will stay by this if it thrives,
being always ready to retire, but these have burned
their ships, and are entitled to the moral consideration which this position gives. The young
people agree that they have had more rapid experiences than elsewhere befel them ; have lived
faster.

May 10.

This morning sent away L. M. W.'s manuscript with some regret that my wild flowers must
ever go back. Their value is as a relief from literature, these unhackneyed fresh draughts from the
sources of sentiment and thought, far, far from
shop and market, or the aim at effect. It is read as
we read in an age of polish and criticism the first
lines of written prose and verse in a nation.

George Bradford yesterday dug with me in the
swamp his young larches, and we sat with the
sphagnum and the budding coptis and the blooming white violet, sweet-scented. He talks happily
of his new friends. But it is not enough that people should be intelligent and interested in themselves. They must also make me feel that they
have a controlling happy Future opening before
them and inevitably bright, and brightening their

present hour. Edward Lowell[1] and Charles Emerson suggested their promise in their salutation, or in the least transaction. Freedom is frivolous beside the tyranny of our genius.

The blue sky in the zenith is the point in which romance and reality meet. If we should be rapt away into all that we dream of heaven, and should converse with Gabriel, Michael, Uriel, the blue sky would be all that would remain of our furniture. — I have written this or the like of this somewhere else, I know not where.

Ellery has reticency, Carlyle has not. How many things this book of Carlyle gives us to think. It is a brave grappling with the problem of the times, no luxurious holding aloof, as is the custom of men of letters, who are usually bachelors and not husbands in the state, but Literature here has thrown off his gown and descended into the open lists. *The gods are come among us in the likeness of men.* An honest Iliad

1 Edward Jackson Lowell, a youth of great promise, the brother of Mr. Emerson's loved classmate Francis Cabot Lowell, and of John Lowell, founder of the Lowell Institute, studied law but died early.

of English woes. Who is he that can trust himself in the fray? Only such as cannot be famil-
iarized, but, nearest seen and touched, is not seen
and touched, but remains inviolate, inaccessible,
because a higher interest, the politics of a higher
sphere bring him here and environ him, as the
ambassador carries his country with him. Love
protects him from profanation. What a book
this is in its relation to English privileged estates![1] . . .

Gulliver among the Lilliputians. This book
comes so near to life and men, that one can hardly
help looking ahead a little and inquiring whether
this strong brain will always be shut up in a scholar's library; whether the most intelligent Englishman will nourish no ambition to do that which
he describes, and when the hour comes that these
volleys of pungent counsels shall have got thoroughly sunk into the ear and heart of the population, and the population is Carlyle's, whether
our vigorous Samson will not have a ruler's part
to play. Yet nobody, neither law-sergeant nor
newspaper, yet cries "Cromwell."

1 *Past and Present.* Then follows the passage (originally
printed in the *Dial*, but to be found on pages 384, 385 of the
Natural History of Intellect) pitying the Queen, the dukes
and lords and bishops, now that Carlyle deals with them.

A Londoner must exaggerate the social problem.

Brook Farm Again! The freaks of the young philosophers show how much life they have, as jockeys, when a horse rolls on the ground, add a gold eagle to his price for every turn he makes. But nothing will take the place of fidelity. The final result will be the same to Mrs. Ripley and the true workers. Yet one would fain say to the dear youths, that pride and bearing will serve for a year or two, but are serpents' eggs, and will end in serpents, though they look now like alabaster and the egg of Jove's eagle; that God has suffered us to be represented in Genius, but in Virtue we must appear in person.

Brook Farm will show a few noble victims, who act and suffer with temper and proportion, but the larger part will be slight adventurers and will shirk work.

May 18.

I set out yesterday, by the hands of Cyrus Warren, nineteen young pine trees west of my house and four in the triangle.

I never see a quite unmusical character. Beautiful results are everywhere lodged.

All intercourse is random and remote, yet what fiery and consoling friendships we have ! The Ideal journeying always with us, the heaven without rent or seam. We never know while the days pass which day is valuable. The surface is vexation, but the serene lies underneath.

Nature lives by making fools of us all, adds a drop of nectar to every man's cup.

Machinery and Transcendentalism agree well. Stage-Coach and Railroad are bursting the old legislation like green withes.

My garden is an honest place. Every tree and every vine are incapable of concealment, and tell after two or three months exactly what sort of treatment they have had. The sower may mistake and sow his peas crookedly : the peas make no mistake, but come up and show his line.

No matter how long you are silent. Silence is only postponement : the retained thought takes a softer form. . . . You must hear the birds sing without attempting to render it into verbs and nouns. Let it lie a while and at night you shall find you have transferred its expression into the history of the day. Our American

lives are somewhat poor and pallid, Franklins
and Washingtons, no fiery grain; staid men,
like our pale and timid flora. We have too
much freedom, need an austerity, need some
iron girth.

The poets, the great, have been illustrious
wretches who have beggared the world which
has beggared them.

Work on; the bee works all day, all summer,
not knowing whom he works for, until the hive
is full. Then comes a higher being, Man, and
takes the store. As long as you feel the vora-
city of reading, read in God's name, asking no
questions of why and whereto. By and by, some
man or men, a continent, or perhaps a higher
sphere of beings, will be served by you.

May 19.

A youth of the name of Ball, a native, as he
told me, of Concord, came to me yesterday,
who towered away in such declamatory talk that
at first I thought it rhodomontade and we
should soon have done with each other. But he
turned out to be a prodigious reader, and writer,
too (for he spoke of whole volumes of prose

and poetry barrelled away), and discovered great
sagacity and insight in his criticisms, — a great
impatience of our strait New England ways, and
a wish to go to the Ganges, or at the least to
live in Greece and Italy. There was little precision in his thinking, great discontent with
metaphysics, and he seemed of a musical rather
than a mathematical structure. With a little
more repose of thought, he would be a great
companion. He thought very humbly of most
of his contemporaries : and Napoleon he thought
good to turn periods with, but that he could see
through him ; but Lord Bacon he could not
pardon for not seeing Shakspeare, for, said he,
" As many Lord Bacons as could stand in Concord could find ample room in Shakspeare's
brain " ; and Pope's mean thought and splendid rhetoric he thought " resembled rats' nests
in kings' closets, made up in a crown and purple robe and regalia." He knows Greek well,
and reads Italian, German, and Spanish. He
spent five hours with me and carried off a pile
of books. He had never known but one person
of extraordinary promise, a youth at Dartmouth
of the name of Hobart.[1]

1 The young man described in the above paragraph was
probably Benjamin West Ball, born in Concord in 1823. The

Critical. Do not write modern antiques like Landor's *Pericles*, or Goethe's *Iphigenia*, or Wieland's *Abderites*, or Coleridge's *Ancient Mariner*, or Scott's *Lay of the Last Minstrel*. They are paste jewels. You may well take an ancient subject where the form is incidental merely, like Shakspeare's plays, and the treatment and dialogue is simple, and most modern. But do not make much of the costume. For such things have no verity ; no man will live or die by them: The way to write is to throw your body at the mark when your arrows are spent, like Cupid in Anacreon. Shakspeare's speeches in *Lear* are in the very dialect of 1843.

High speech of Demiurgus to his gods in the *Timæus*. Goethe's World-Soul is a sequel of the same thought. And that does the Intellect ; it goes *ordering*, distributing, and by order making beauty.

This creative vortex has not spun over London, over our modern Europe, until now in Carlyle. Humboldt is magnificent, too, as a dis-

Editors have not been able to learn more about him. Harrison Carroll Hobart went to Wisconsin, where he took a prominent position in the legislature. He served through the Civil War and became a brigadier-general.

tributing eye. His glance is stratification; geography of plants, etc.

May 20.

Walked with Ellery. In the landscape felt the magic of color; the world is all opal, and those ethereal tints the mountains wear have the finest effects of music on us. Mountains are great poets, and one glance at this fine cliff scene undoes a great deal of prose, and reinstates us wronged men in our rights. All life, all society begins to get illuminated and transparent, and we generalize boldly and well. Space is felt as a great thing. There is some pinch and narrowness to us, and we laugh and leap to see the world, and what amplitudes it has of meadow, stream, upland, forest, and sea, which yet are but lanes and crevices to the great Space in which the world swims like a cockboat in the sea. A little canoe with three figures put out from a creek into the river and sailed downstream to the Bridge, and we rejoiced in the Blessed Water inviolable, magical, whose nature is Beauty, which instantly began to play its sweet games, all circles and dimples and lovely gleaming motions, — always Ganges, the Sacred River, and which cannot be desecrated or made to forget itself. But there below are these farms, yet are the farmers unpoetic. The life of labor does not make men, but drudges. Pleasant it is, as the habits of all poets may testify, to think of great proprietors, to reckon this grove we walk in a park of the noble; but a continent cut up into ten-acre farms is not desirable to the imagination. The Farmer is an enchanted laborer, and after toiling his brains out, sacrificing thought, religion, taste, love, hope, courage at the shrine of toil, turns out a bankrupt as well as the merchant. It is time to have the thing looked into, and with a transpiercing criticism settled whether life is worth having on such terms.[1] . . .

Ellery said, "The village [of Concord] did not look so very bad from our point; — the three churches looked like geese swimming about in a pond."

All the physicians I have ever seen call themselves believers, but are materialists; they believe only in the existence of matter, and not in matter as an appearance, but as substance, and do not contemplate a cause. Their idea of spirit is a chemical agent.

1 These last two sentences are printed in "The Young American" (*Essays*, Second Series, p. 381).

The stars I think the antidotes of pyrrhonism. In the fuss of the sunlight and the rapid succession of moods, one might doubt his identity ; but these expressive points, always in their place so immutable, are the tranquillizers of men. No narcotic so sedative or sanative as this.

Man sheds grief as his skin sheds rain. A preoccupied mind an immense protection. There is a great concession on all hands to the ideal decorum in grief, as well as joy, but few hearts are broken.

Edward Everett did long ago for Boston what Carlyle is doing now for England and Europe, in rhetoricizing the conspicuous objects.

Reform. Chang Tsoo and Kee Neih retired from the state to the fields on account of misrule, and showed their displeasure at Confucius who remained in the world. Confucius sighed and said, " I cannot associate with birds and beasts. If I follow not man, whom shall I follow? If the world were in possession of right principles, I should not seek to change it." See *The Four Books;* translated from the Chinese by Rev. D. Collier, Malacca, 1828.

[Here follow several extracts from the same work.]

I enjoy all the hours of life. Few persons have such susceptibility to pleasure; as a countryman will say, " I was at sea a month and never missed a meal," so I eat my dinner and sow my turnips, yet do I never, I think, fear death. It seems to me so often a relief, a rendering-up of responsibility, a quittance of so many vexatious trifles.

How poetic this wondrous web of property! J. P. sitting in his parlor talking of philanthropy has his pocket full of papers, representing dead labor done long ago, not by him, not by his ancestor, but by hands which his ancestor had skill to set at work and get the certificates of. And now these signs of the work of hands, long ago mouldered in the grave, are honored by all men, and for them J. P. can get what vast amounts of work done by new young hands, — canals, railways, houses, gardens, coaches, pastures, sheep, oxen, and corn.

One great wrong must soon disappear, — this right to burden the unborn with state loans.

It is folly to imagine that there can be anything very bad in the position of woman compared with that of man, at any time; for since
every woman is a man's daughter, and every
man is a woman's son, every woman is too near
to man, was too recently a man, than that possibly any wide disparity can be. As is the man will
be the woman; and as is the woman, the man.

It is greatest to believe and to hope well of
the world, because he who does so, quits the
world of experience, and makes the world he
lives in.

It is very odd that Nature should be so un-
scrupulous. She is no saint;[1] . . .

Luther said he " preached coarsely; that giv-
eth content to all: Hebrew, Greek, and Latin I
spare until we learned ones come together, and
then we make it so curled and finical that God
himself wondereth at us."

Reform, people hate the sound of now that
they have begun to think it is like reading novels, which, when they are done, leave them just
where they were, carpenters, and merchants,

[1] The rest of the passage is printed in "Experience"
(p. 64).

and debtors, and poor ladies — only they dis-
believed the novel, and believed at first the reformer. But with any faith that would give a
new face to the world for poor old eyes, lank
hair, and wrinkled brows — as Millerism and
Fourierism and other of our superstitions attest.

The smallest piece of God in a man makes
him as attractive as loadstone. A scholar shines
and immediately draws many youth around him,
and, if he have not God enough in him to know
how to say No, he finds himself inconveniently
attractive. The Man, the God, is awakening;
the door bolt will be broken, the iron fence
melted in the forge; a man will yet measure his
acres by his need and ability. I can manage ten
and do take ten; I forty, and take forty; I a
hundred, and will farm a hundred. He will
know how to stand in his garden and in his
house as steward, and say, This is right that
you should take; this is wrong; therefore, leave
it, O guest! And by his just standing there, as
a channel of law and not of Self, the human
race will feel that they occupy it by his occupation, they are excluded in his departure.[1]

1 Much of what follows is printed in " The Young American " (*Essays*, Second Series, p. 386).

In dreamy woods, what forms abound
That elsewhere never poet found!
Here voices ring, and pictures burn,
And grace on grace, where'er I turn.[1]

In the dreaming woods, I find what is no-where else, and pictures on pictures whithersoever I turn. Over our little "God's Pond" the birds flitted spectrally ; nothing could look more elysian and unreal. I think that at some Parliament of Beauty, Fire and Water will contend for the apple which mistaken Paris gave, and it will be adjudged to neither but to Animal, who is the child of both. For the red bird is fire and the running horse is water.

It is agreeable and picturesque to see a man drink water and eat bread ; not so, coffee and cake.

It is not travelling, it is not residence, it is relations that make life much or little. A few grand persons coming to us and weaving duties and offices between us and them, shall make our bread ambrosial. — But now it seems to me

[1] These verses were evidently written in later, as the handwriting shows. They come, of course, from the sentence which follows.

that I know persons enough of the first class, if only they were necessarily related. Three, four, five, six, seven, or eight persons, who look at nature and existence with no unworthy eye, but they are players, and rather melancholy players in the world, for want of work. I have seen no one who wore on his face an expression of habitual energy, but rather of indolence, the great faculties lie idle, whilst the hands and feet bustle.

We do not live by times; we do not belong to this or that century; but we live by qualities. A new style of face, a new person, would be a new age and regeneration to us. Nature, a mountain walk, always gives us to suspect the poverty of life, and we believe that we have run along only one thread of experience out of millions of varied threads which we were competent to combine with that single-string of ours.

Life must look forlorn, if we have nothing above us. Paddy values life, and it looks solid to him, because he sees and feels so much and so many above him. It looks to us sad enough that not even a superstition should remain to us, no ghosts in the broad land and social system of millions, no play for the imagination of millions; and yet it has so appeared to all peoples, for no man knew his superstition as superstition. And we who lie under this enchantment of desiring money, may find ours there, when we consider that the net result of the life which is bestowed on drudging for an estate, and of that which is merrily trifled away, does not much vary. The farmer, as we passed, was leading a small company of men in their Eleusinian mysteries along the furrows of the field. One step each and then seeds were dropped and the soil smoothed and then another step and no man lifted his face from the ground.

This country must be filled with incident, and then how will the landscape look! Now our houses and towns are like mosses and lichens, so thin laid on the rock. One day they will get rooted like oaks and be a part of the globe.

I think we are not quite yet fit for Flying Machines, and therefore there will be none.[1] . . .

1 This and the substance of what follows are from "A Letter," first printed in the *Dial*, now included in *Natural History of Intellect* (p. 393); also what is there said of railroads.

The mountains in the horizon acquaint us with more exalted relations to our friends than any we sustain.

Carlyle must write thus or nohow, like a drunken man who can run, but cannot walk. What a *man's book* is that! no prudences, no compromises, but a thorough independence. A masterly criticism on the times. Fault perhaps the excess of importance given to the circumstance of to-day. The poet is here for this, to dwarf and destroy all merely temporary circumstance, and to glorify the perpetual circumstance of men, e.g., dwarf British Debt and raise Nature and social life.

May 25.

Criticism. It is for the novelist to make no character act absurdly, but only absurdly as seen by the others.[1] . . .

The sky is the daily bread of the eyes. What sculpture in these hard clouds; what expression of immense amplitude in this dotted and rippled rack, here firm and continental, there vanishing into plumes and auroral gleams. No crowding; boundless, cheerful, and strong.

1 The rest of the passage is in *Natural History of Intellect* (p. 54).

THOMAS CARLYLE

Men Representative. Nothing is dead. Men and things feign themselves dead.[1] . . .

The gods are jealous, and their finest gifts of men they deface with some shrewd fault, that we may hate the vessel which holds the nectar. And hence men have in all ages suffered the heralds of Heaven to starve and struggle with evils of all kinds; for the gods will not have their heralds amiable; lest men should love the cup and not the nectar.

My friends are leaving the town, and I am sad at heart that they cannot have that love and service from me to which they seem by their aims and the complexion of their minds, and by their unpopularity, to have rich claims. Especially Charles Lane I seem to myself to have treated with the worst inhospitality, inasmuch as I have never received that man to me — not for so much as one moment. A pure, superior, mystical, intellectual, and gentle soul, free and youthful, too, in character, and treating me ever with

[1] The rest of the passage is in "Nominalist and Realist," except that in the Journal are the names Montaigne, Rabelais, Swift, Scaliger, Calvin, and Becket in place of John, Paul, Mahomet, and Aristotle.

marked forbearance, he so formidable, — a fighter
in the ring, — yet he has come, and has stayed so
long in my neighborhood an alien : for his nature
and influence do not invite mine, but always
freeze me. It sometimes seems to me strange
that English and New Englanders should be so
little capable of blending. Their methods and
temperaments so differ from ours. They strike
twelve the first time. Our people have more than
meets the ear. This man seems to me born a
warrior, the most expert swordsman we have ever
seen ; good when the trumpet sounds. Metallic
in his nature, not vegetable enough. No eye for
Nature, and his hands as far from his head as
Alcott's own. — We are not willing to trust the
Universe to give the hospitality of the Omnipresent to the good, but we, too, must assume
to do the honors with offices, money, and clat-
ter of plates.

O Poet, by rock and bird is conferred a new
nobility, and not in palaces any longer. Would
you know the conditions, hard but equal? Thou
shalt leave the world and know the Muse
only. . . .
[This, the concluding passage of "The Poet"
(*Essays*, Second Series) varies, it seems to the

editors for the better, in the Journal, in the following passage : —]

For the time of towns is measured by funeral chimes, and every hour is tolled away from the world, but in Nature the merry hours are dialled by flowers on the hillside and growth of joy on joy. Thou shalt have a new census and calendar; for a long September day between sun and sun shall hold centuries in its rosy and yellow deeps, and thy calendar shall be thoughts and thy action *as thou ought*. God wills also that thou abdicate a manifold and duplex life [1] . . . And a tomb is all that shall be denied thee. For the Universe is thy house to live in and thou shalt not die.

If thou keep these laws, thou shalt have a leader's eye, or live always in the mountain, seeing all the details, but seeing them all in their place and tendency. And thou shalt be greeted by omens that are prosperity and fill thee with light.

And thou shalt serve the God Terminus, the bounding Intellect, and love Boundary or Form; believing that Form is an oracle which never lies.

And every man shall be to thee for all men,

1 For the rest, see last page of "The Poet."

each man being alone in the vast Desart; and thou shalt worship him, for he is the Universe in a mask.

June 10.

Hawthorne and I talked of the number of superior young men we have seen. H. said, that he had seen several from whom he had expected much, but they had not distinguished themselves; and he had inferred that he must not expect a popular success from such; he had in nowise lost his confidence in their power.

I am often refreshed by seeing marks of excellence, and of excellence which makes no impression on people at large, who reckon it a bar-room wit, and swaggering intellect, not presentable, and of no great value. — Then I take comfort that these gifts are so cheap, and it would seem that all men are great, only some are adjusted to the delicate mean of this world and can swim in it wherever put.

June 11.

Pride. Pride is so handsome, pride is so economical, pride eradicates so many vices [1] — . . .

The men show the quality of the land.

[1] The rest of this paragraph is in "Wealth" (*Conduct of Life*, p. 114).

My Chinese book does not forget to record of Confucius, that his night-gown was one length and a half of his body.

There are some persons from whom we always expect fairy gifts. Let us not cease to expect them.

June 18.

Yesterday at Bunker Hill, a prodigious concourse of people, but a village green could not be more peaceful, orderly, sober, and even affectionate. Webster gave us his plain statement like good bread, yet the oration was feeble compared with his other efforts, and even seemed poor and Polonius-like with its indigent conservations. When there is no antagonism, as in these holiday speeches, and no religion, things sound not heroically. It is a poor oration that finds Washington for its highest mark. The audience give one much to observe, they are so light-headed and light-timbered, every man thinking more of his inconveniences than of the objects of the occasion, and the hurrahs are so slight and easily procured. Webster is very good America himself.

Wonderful multitudes: on the top of a house I saw a company protecting themselves from the sun by an old large map of the United States. A charitable lumber merchant near the Bridge had chalked up over his counting-room door " 500 seats for ladies, free " ; and there the five hundred sat in white tiers. The ground within the square at the monument was arranged to hold 80,000 persons.

It was evident that there was the Monument and here was Webster, and he knew well that a little more or less of rhetoric signified nothing :[1] . . . He was there as the representative of the American continent, there in his Adamitic capacity, and that is the basis of the satisfaction the people have in hearing him, that he alone of all men does not disappoint the eye and ear, but is a fit figure in the landscape.

June 22.

I was at Brook Farm and had a cheerful time. Some confidences were granted me; and grief softened the somewhat hard nature of Mrs. George Ripley, so that I had never seen her to such advantage. Fine weather, cheerful uplands, and every person you meet is a character and in free costume. Charles Newcomb I saw, and was

1 This and more that is here omitted is printed in Mr. Emerson's remarkable picturing of Webster, in his speech on the " Fugitive Slave Law," given in New York, March 7, 1854 (*Miscellanies*, p. 221).

relieved to meet again on something of the old footing, after hearing of so much illness and sensitiveness. But Charles is not a person to be seen on a holiday or in holiday places, but one should live in solitude and obscurity, with him for the only person in the county to speak to. Also George Bradford let me a little into the spiritual history and relations that go forward, but one has this feeling in hearing of their spiritualism, — ah! had they never heard of it first! and did not know it was spiritualism.

The scholars are the true hierarchy, only that now they are displaced by hypocrites, that is, sciolists. For is not that the one want of the man, to meet a brother who, being fuller of God than he, can hold him steady to a truth until he has made it his own? O with what joy I begin to read a poem which I confide in as an inspiration.[1] . . .

[Under the ink writing of this page in the Journal can be traced the pencilled lines on "The Poet," beginning —

1 Here follows the long passage in "The Poet" thus beginning (*Essays*, Second Series pp. 12, 13).

> But oh, to see his solar eyes
> Like meteors which chose the way
> And rived the dark like a new day, etc.

which form the end of the first division of the verses with that title printed in the Appendix to the *Poems*.]

The Chinese are as wonderful for their etiquette as the Hebrews for their piety.

Those men who are noised all their lifetime as on the edge of some great discovery, never discover anything. But nobody ever heard of Monsieur Daguerre until the Daguerreotype appeared. And now I do not know who invented the railroad.

Dante's *Vita Nuova* reads like the Book of Genesis, as if written before literature, whilst truth yet existed. A few incidents are sufficient, and are displayed with Oriental amplitude and leisure. It is the Bible of Love.

The Interim. So many things are unsettled which it is of the first importance to settle — and, pending their settlement, we will do as we do.[1] . . .

1 Here follows a long passage printed in "Experience" (pp. 64, 65), thus beginning.

Variety. [Here follows the passage on the successive delights that various authors have given, which is printed in " Experience."] *Però si muove.* And when at night I look at moon and stars, I seem stationary and they to hurry.

THE THREE DIMENSIONS

Room ! cried the spheres when first they shined,
And dived into the ample sky :
Room ! room ! cried the new mankind,
And took the oath of Liberty :
Room ! room ! willed the opening mind,
And found it in Variety.[1]

Life. Fools and clowns and sots make the fringes of every one's tapestry of life, and give a certain reality to the picture. What could we do in Concord without Bigelow's and Wesson's bar-rooms and their dependencies? What without such fixtures as Uncle Sol, and old Moore who sleeps in Doctor Hurd's barn, and the red charity-house over the brook? Tragedy and comedy always go hand in hand.

Life itself is an interim and a transition; this, O Indur, is my one and twenty thousandth form, and already I feel the old Life sprouting

[1] These verses, printed in the *Dial,* were never included by Mr. Emerson in his published poems.

underneath in the twenty thousand and first,
and I know well that he builds no new world
but by tearing down the old for materials.[1]

[In July, Mr. Emerson, by invitation, gave
an address to the Temperance Society at Harvard, Massachusetts. The extract which Mr.
Cabot gives in the Appendix to his Memoir
shows that he treated his subject largely and
by no means in the usual narrow and specific
way.]

July 8.

The sun and the evening sky do not look
calmer than Alcott and his family at Fruitlands. They seemed to have arrived at the fact,
to have got rid of the show, and so to be serene. Their manners and behavior in the house
and in the field were those of superior men, of
men at rest. What had they to conceal? What
had they to exhibit? And it seemed so high an
attainment that I thought, as often before, so
now more, because they had a fit home or the

---

1 When the old world is sterile
    And the ages are effete,
  He will from wrecks and sediments
    A fairer world complete.
            "The World-Soul," *Poems.*

picture was fitly framed, that these men ought
to be maintained in their place by the Country
for its culture. Young men and young maidens,
old men and women, should visit them and be
inspired. I think there is as much merit in
beautiful manners as in hard work.

I will not prejudge them successful. They
look well in July. We will see them in December. I know they are better for themselves
than as partners. One can easily see that they
have yet to settle several things. Their saying
that things are clear, and they sane, does not
make them so. If they will in every deed be
lovers and not selfish; if they will serve the
town of Harvard, and make their neighbors feel
them as benefactors wherever they touch them,
they are as safe as the sun.

We spend our money for that which is not
help and have the inconvenience of the reputation of money without its advantage. Those
who have no appearance to keep up, the dowdy
farmer's wife who meets you at her door, broom
in hand, or pauses at her washtub to answer
your question, — their house is serene and majestic, if their natures are ; but ours is not, let
our ideas be what they may, whilst we may not

appear except in costume, and our immunity at
the same time is bought by money and not by
love and nature.

> And far away the purple morn
> Concealed by intervening fruits and flowers
> Lies buried in the abundance of the hours.

July 10.

Ellery Channing railed an hour in good set
terms at the usurpation of the past, at the great
hoaxes of the Homers and Shakspeares, hinder-
ing the books and the men of to-day of their
just meed. Oh certainly; I assure him that oaks
and horse-chestnuts are entirely obsolete, that
the Horticultural Society are about to recommend the introduction of cabbages as a shade
tree, so much more convenient and every way
comprehensible; all grown from the seed upward to its most generous crumpled extremity
within one's own short memory; past contradiction the ornament of the world, and then so
good to eat, as acorns and horse-chestnuts are
not. Shade trees for breakfast! Then this whole
business of one man taking the praise of all or
more than his share of the praise. As all are
alike in nature and possibility, it is absurd that

any should pretend to exhibit more reason or virtue than I do. A man of genius, did you say? A man of virtue? I tell you both are malformations, painful inflammations of the brain and of the liver and such shall be punishable in the new Commonwealth. And if any such appear they shall be dealt with as all reasonable Spartans and Indians do with lame and deformed infants, toss them into the river and the average of the race improved. Nothing that is not *ex tempore* shall now be tolerated: pyramids and cities shall give place to tents. The man, the skeleton and body, which many years have built up, shall go for nothing: his dinner, the mutton and rice he ate two hours ago, now fast flowing into chyle, that is all we consider; and the problem how to detach new dinner from old man — what we respect from what we scorn — deserves the study of the scientific.

[The poem " Blight " follows.]

The clergy are the etiquette or Chinese Empire of our American Society. They are here that we may not be fed and bedded and die and be buried as dogs, but, in the want of dignity, we may be treated to a sufficiency of parade and gentle gradations of salutation at coming and parting. If anybody dies and grieves us to the heart, so that the people might be melted to tears by a hearty word, the minister shuts his lips and preaches on the miracles, or the parables, or Solomon's Temple, because the family have not *had up their note ;* [1] if any new outrage on law or any pregnant event fills the mind of people with queries and omens, the pulpit is dumb.

Ellery, who hopes there will be no cows in Heaven, has discovered what cows are for, namely, to give the farmers something to do in summertime. All this haying comes at midsummer between planting and harvest, when all hands would be idle, but for this cow and ox, which must be fed and mowed for; and thus Intemperance and the progress of Crime is prevented!

July 16.

Montaigne has the *de quoi* which the French cherubs had not, when the courteous Archbishop implored them to sit down. His reading was Plutarch.

---

1 That is, sent to the minister, by the sexton, a note requesting mention in his prayer.

'T is high time we had a Bible that should be no provincial record, but should open the history of the planet and bind all tendencies and dwarf all the Epics and Philosophies we have. It will have no Books of Ruth and Esther, no Song of Solomon, nor excellent, sophistical Pauls.

As if any taste or imagination could supply identity. The old duty is the old God.

Readiness is youthfulness; to hold the old world in our hand, awaiting our new errand, and to be rebuked by a child, by a sot, by a philistine, and thankfully take a new course. The Moral Sentiment is well called the Newness, for it is never other than a surprise, and the oldest angels are the boys whom it doth whip and scourge, though its scars give the gladness of the Martyr flame.

I have got in my barn a carpenter's bench and two planes, a shave, a saw, a chisel, a vise, and a square. These planes seem to me great institutions, whose inventor no man knoweth, yet what a stroke of genius was each of these tools! When you have them, you must watch a workman for a month, or a year, or seven years, as our boys do, to know all his tricks with them. Great is Tubal Cain. A good pen is a finer, stronger instrument, and a language, an algebra, a calculus, music, or poetic metre, more wondrous tools yet, for this polygon or pentagon that is called Man. Thanks, too, to Pythagoras for the multiplication table.

> To lay down the heavy burden
> Of herself as woman would.

August 5.

Home from Plymouth, where I spent a fine day in an excursion to Half Way Pond, dining at the house of Mrs. R———. Mary and Lucia Russell made the party for us, and Abraham Jackson and Helen Russell accompanied us. Mrs. R. was a genuine Yankee, and so fluent in her provincial English that Walter Scott or Dickens could not desire a better sample of local life. Mr. Faunce, Mr. Swift, and Mr. Stetson, her ministers at " Ponds " (meaning Monument Ponds), baptism by immersion and by sprinkling, Mr. Whitefield's " sarmons," the " Universallers," the Schools, and the Reformation of the Church at Ponds and elsewhere, and the drowning of her son Allen in a vessel loaded with paving-stones which sunk in a tempest near Boston Light, and the marriage of her son's widow, were the principal events of her life, and the topics of her conversation. She lives alone in this pleasing, tranquil scene at the head of a pond, and never is uneasy except in a tempest in the night.[1]

I cannot well say what I found at Plymouth, beyond the uneasiness of seeing people. Every person of worth, man or woman, whom I see, gives me a pain as if I injured them, because of my incapacity to do them justice in the intercourse that passes between us. Two or more persons together deoxygenate the air, apathize and paralyze me. I twist like the poor eel in the exhausted receiver, and my conviction of their sense and virtue only makes matters worse for me by accusing my injustice. I am made for chronic relations, not for moments, and am wretched with fine people who are only there for an hour.

It is a town of great local and social advantages, Plymouth ; lying on the sea with this fine,

---

1 This must have been the old lady whose remark on the latitudinarianism of the times was often quoted by Mr. Emerson. She said that " Arrors [errors] was creepin' into Ponds."

broken, inland country, pine-covered and scooped
into beds of two hundred lakes. Their proverb
is that there is a pond in Plymouth for every day
of the year. Billington Sea is the best of all, and
yet this superb chain of lakes which we pass in
returning from Half Way Pond might content
one a hundred years.

The botany of the region is rare. The Epigæa,
named Mayflower at Plymouth, is now found
elsewhere. The beautiful and fragrant Sabbatia,
the Empetrum, the sun-dew, the Rhinanthus
or Yellow-Rattle and other plants are almost
peculiar to this spot. Great linden trees lift their
green domes above the town, as seen from the
sea, and the graveyard hill shows the monu-
ments of the Pilgrims and their children as far
out to sea as we could see anything of the town.
The virtues of the Russells are as eminent and
fragrant here, at this moment, as ever were the
glories of that name in England : and L—— is
a flower of the sweetest and softest beauty which
real life ever exhibited. These people know so
well how to live, and have such perfect adjust-
ment in their tastes and their power to gratify
them, that the ideal life is necessarily thrown into
the shade, and I have never seen a strong conservatism appear so amiable and wise. We saw

their well-built houses which an equal and generous economy warmed and animated ; and their
good neighborhood was never surpassed : the
use of the door-bell and knocker seems unknown.
And the fine children who played in the yards
and piazzas appeared to come of a more amiable and gentle stock.

[Concord was, until about 1852, a "shire
town" and the courts, later transferred to Lowell, were held there. In the summer of 1843
a somewhat notable case, Commonwealth *vs.*
Wyman, from the eminence of the counsel employed, was tried there, an officer of a Charles-
town bank having been charged with misappro-
priation of its funds. Several passages of this
entry were used by Mr. Emerson in 1854 in his
address in New York on "The Fugitive Slave
Law" ; but it seemed best to keep them here,
not to interrupt the continuity of the text. (See
Miscellanies, pp. 222, 223.)]

August 17.

Webster at Concord. Mr. Webster loses nothing by comparison with brilliant men in the
legal profession : he is as much before them as
before the ordinary lawyer. At least I thought
he appeared among these best lawyers of the
Suffolk Bar, like a schoolmaster among his boys.

His wonderful organization, the perfection of his elocution, and all that thereto belongs, — voice, accent, intonation, attitude, manner, — are such as one cannot hope to see again in a century; then he is so thoroughly simple and wise in his rhetoric. Understanding language and the use of the positive degree, all his words tell, and his rhetoric is perfect, so homely, so fit, so strong. Then he manages his matter so well, he hugs his fact so close, and will not let it go, and never indulges in a weak flourish, though he knows perfectly well how to make such exordiums and episodes and perorations as may give perspective to his harangue, without in the least embarrassing his plan or confounding his transitions. What is small, he shows as small, and makes the great, great. In speech he sometimes roars, and his words are like blows of an axe. His force of personal attack is terrible, he lays out his strength so directly in honest blows, and all his powers of voice, arm, eye, and whole man are so heartily united and bestowed on the adversary that he cannot fail to be felt.

His " Christian religion " is always weak, being merely popular, and so most of his religion. Thus, he spoke of the value of character; it was simply mercantile; it was to defend

a man in criminal prosecutions, and the like; and
bear him up against the inspection of all BUT
the Almighty, etc. And in describing Wyman's
character, he said, he wanted that sternness of
Christian principle which teaches to " avoid even
the appearance of evil." And one feels every
moment that he goes for the actual world, and
never one moment for the ideal. He is the triumph of the Understanding and is undermined
and supplanted by the Reason for which yet
he is so good a witness, being all the time fed
therefrom, and his whole nature and faculty
presupposing that, that I felt as if the children
of Reason might gladly see his success as a
homage to their law, and regard him as a poor,
rude soldier hired for sixpence a day to fight
their battles. I looked at him sometimes with
the same feeling with which I see one of these
strong Paddies on the railroad. Perhaps it was
this, perhaps it was a mark of having outlived
some of my once finest pleasures, that I found
no appetite to return to the Court in the afternoon and hear the conclusion of his argument.
The green fields on my way home were too
fresh and fair, and forbade me to go again.

His splendid wrath, when his eyes became
fires, is as good to see, so intellectual it is, and

the wrath of the fact and cause he espouses, and not at all personal to himself.

Rockwood Hoar said, nothing amused him more than to see Mr. Webster adjourn the Court every day, which he did by rising, and taking his hat and looking the Judge coolly in the face; who then bade the Crier adjourn the Court.

Choate and Webster. Rufus Choate is a favorite with the bar, and a nervous, fluent speaker, with a little too much fire for the occasion, yet with a certain temperance in his fury and a perfect self-command; but he uses the superlative degree, and speaks of affairs altogether too rhetorically. This property of $300,000, the property of a bank, he speaks of as "vast," and quite academically. And there was no perspective in his speech; the transitions were too slight and sudden. But the cast-iron tones of the man of men, the perfect machine that he is for arguing a case, dwarfed instantly Choate and all the rest of the learned counselors.

Webster behaves admirably well in society. These village parties must be dishwater to him, yet he shows himself just good-natured, just nonchalant *enough*, and has his own way without offending any one or losing any ground. He told us that he never read by candle-light.

Judge Allen told me last night that he had great and increasing confidence in juries, and thought that in nine cases out of ten they rendered a satisfactory and a right verdict. He appealed to Mr. Hoar, who thought this true in five cases out of six.

" Sir Walter Raleigh was such a person every way, that, as King Charles I says of the Lord Strafford, a prince would rather be afraid of than ashamed of. He had that awfulness and ascendancy in his aspect over other mortals, that the King—" and here Aubrey's manuscript stops.

Webster quite fills our little town, and I doubt if I shall get settled down to writing until he is well gone from the county. He is a natural Emperor of men; they remark in him the kingly talent of remembering persons accurately, and knowing at once to whom he has been introduced, and to whom not.

He has lately bought his father's farm in

Franklin (formerly Salisbury), New Hampshire, as Waller the poet wished to buy his birthplace, Winchmore Hill, saying to his Cousin Hampden, " A stag, when he is hunted and near spent, always returns home."

Elizabeth Hoar says that she talked with him, as one likes to go behind the Niagara Falls, so she tried to look into those famed caverns of eyes, and see how deep they were, and the whole man was magnificent. Mr. Choate told her that he should not sleep for a week when a cause like this was pending, but that when they met in Boston on Saturday afternoon to talk over the matter, the rest of them were wide awake, but Mr. Webster went fast asleep amidst the consultation.

It seems to me the Quixotism of Criticism to quarrel with Webster because he has not this or that fine evangelical property. He is no saint, but the wild olive wood, ungrafted yet by grace, but according to his lights a very true and admirable man. His expensiveness seems to be necessary to him. Were he too prudent a Yankee it would be a sad deduction from his magnificence. I only wish he would never truckle; I do not care how much he spends.

Webster's force is part of nature and the

world, like any given amount of azote or electricity. . . . After all his great talents have been told, there remains that perfect propriety, which belongs to every world-genius, which animates all the details of action and speech with the character of the whole so that his beauties of detail are endless. Great is life.

I cannot consent to compare him [Webster] with his competitors, but when the Clay men and Van Buren men and the Calhoun men have had all their way and all their political objections have been conceded, and they have settled their little man, whichever it be, on the top of the martin-box of state, then and not before will we begin to state the claims of this world's man, this strong Paddy of the times and laws and state, to his place in history.

Nature. In Nature the doubt occurs whether the man is the cause or the effect. Are beasts and plants degradations of man? or are these the prophecies and preparations of Nature practising herself for her master-piece in Man? Culminate we do not; but that point of imperfection which we occupy — is it on the way *up* or *down?*

Again, is the world (according to the old doubt) to be criticized otherwise than as the best possible in the existing system: and the population of the world the best that soils, climates, and animals permit?

"Will is the measure of Power." — Proclus on *Timæus*.

"Prudence is a medium between intellect and opinion." — *Idem*.

"Intellect is that by which we know terms or boundaries." — Aristotle.

"Beauty swims on the light of forms." [1] — Proclus.

"Intellect," according to Amelius, "is threefold, that which is, that which has, and that which sees." — Proclus.

"Law is the distribution of intellect." — Proclus.

"Every soul pays a guardian attention to that which is inanimate." — Plato, in *Phædrus*.

It is a pathetic thing to meet a friend prepared to love you, to whom yet, from some inaptitude, you cannot communicate yourself with that grace and power which only love will allow. You wish to repay his goodness by showing him

---

1 Compare in the "Ode to Beauty," in the *Poems*, —
Thee, gliding through a sea of form.

the dear relations that subsist between you and your chosen friends, but you feel that he cannot conceive of you whom he knows so slow and cold, under these sweet and gentle aspects.

Confide in your power, whether it be to be a wet-nurse or a wood-sawyer, lion-taming Van Amburgh, or Stewart maker of steam candy, keep your shop, magnify your office. Fear smears our work, and ignorance gilds our neighbor's, but the sure years punish our faint-heartedness.

[Here follow many extracts from the *She-King*, the third member of the pentateuch of most ancient Chinese Classics. A few are here given.]

"The way of Chow is even as a whetstone and as straight as an arrow. Superior men tread in it and inferior men view it as their pattern."

"Sorry sorry is my heart; I am hated by the low herd."

"He who neither errs nor forgets is the man who accords with the ancient canons."

"Let the rain descend first on our public and then on our private fields."

(From U)

Apparent imitations of unapparent natures.[1]

Victurus Genium debet habere liber.[2] — MARTIAL.

I wish to speak with all respect of persons, but sometimes I find it needs much heedfulness to preserve the due decorum, they melt so fast into each other.[3] . . .

August 25.

The railroad whose building I inspected this afternoon brings a multitude of picturesque traits into our pastoral scenery.[4]

There is nothing in history to parallel the influence of Jesus Christ. The Chinese books say

1 The first motto comes from the so-called Chaldean Oracles. Mr. Emerson quotes Thomas Taylor as saying that these were either delivered by Theurgists under the reign of Marcus Antoninus, or by Zoroaster.

2 The book that shall win its way ought to have Genius.

3 The rest of the passage is in "Nominalist and Realist" (*Essays*, Second Series, p. 236).

4 The long passage, almost tragic, about the new-come Irish laborers and their families, camped along the railroad line and working from dark to dark for fifty cents a day, was originally in "The Young American" as printed in the *Dial*, vol. iv. It is not printed here because it is given in full in the notes to that address in the Centenary Edition (vol. i, pp. 451–455).

of Wan Wang, one of their kings, "From the west, from the east, from the south, and from the north there was not one thought not brought in subjection to him." This can be more truly said of Jesus than of any mortal.

Mencius says, "A sage is the instructor of a hundred ages. When the manners of Pih E are heard of, the stupid become intelligent and the wavering determined."

Fourier carries a whole French Revolution in his head, and much more. This is arithmetic with a vengeance.[1]

In the points of good breeding, what I most require and insist upon is deference. I like that every chair should be a throne and hold a king. And what I most dislike is a low sympathy of each with his neighbor's palate.[2] . . . I respect cats, they seem to have so much else in their heads besides their mess. . . . I prefer a tendency to stateliness to an excess of fellowship.

1 See "Life and Letters in New England" (*Lectures and Biographical Sketches*, p. 348).

2 Much of this paragraph is omitted as printed in "Manners" (*Essays*, Second Series, pp. 136, 137, 138).

In all things I would have the island of a man inviolate. No degree of affection is to invade this religion. . . .

The charge which a lady in much trust made to me against her companions was that people on whom beforehand all persons would put the utmost reliance were not responsible. They saw the necessity that the work must be done, and did it not; and it of course fell to be done by herself and the few principals.[1] I replied, that in my experience good people were as bad as rogues, that the conscience of the conscientious ran in veins, and the most punctilious in some particulars were latitudinarian in others.

Henry Thoreau sends me a paper with the old fault of unlimited contradiction. The trick of his rhetoric is soon learned: it consists in substituting for the obvious word and thought its diametrical antagonist. He praises wild mountains and winter forests for their domestic air; snow and ice for their warmth; villagers and wood-choppers for their urbanity, and the wilderness for resembling Rome and Paris. With the constant

1 This apparently refers to members of the Brook Farm Community.

inclination to dispraise cities and civilization, he yet can find no way to know woods and wood-men except by paralleling them with towns and townsmen. Channing declared the piece is ex-cellent: but it makes me nervous and wretched to read it, with all its merits.[1]

The thinker looks for God in the direction of the consciousness, the churchman out of it. If you ask the former for his definition of God, he would answer, "My possibility"; for his defi-nition of Man, "My actuality."

"Stand up straight," said the stage-coachman, "and the rain won't wet you a mite."

We like the strong objectiveness of Homer and of the primitive poems of each country, bal-lads and the Chinese and Indian sentences, but that cannot be preserved in a large and civilized population. The scholar will inevitably be de-tached from the mechanic, and will not dwell in the same house, nor see his handiworks so near by, and must adopt new classification and a more metaphysical vocabulary. Hawthorne boasts that he lived at Brook Farm during its heroic

[1] This probably refers to some paper offered for the *Dial*.

age : then all were intimate and each knew the other's work : priest and cook conversed at night of the day's work. Now they complain that they are separated and such intimacy cannot be ; there are a hundred souls.

It seems as if we had abundance of insight and a great taste for writing in this country : only the describers wanted subjects. But that is deceptive. The great describer is known hereby, that he finds topics.

The farmer whom I visited this afternoon works very hard and very skillfully to get a good estate, and gets it. But by his skill and diligence and that of thousands more, his competitors, the wheat and milk by which I live are made so cheap that they are within reach of my scanty monies, and I am not yet forced to go to work and produce them for myself. Tuttle told me that he had once carried forty-one hundredweight of hay to Boston and received $61.50 for the load. But it is no part of T.'s design to keep down the price of hay or wheat or milk.

> How long shalt thou stay,
> Thou devastator of thy friend's day ?
> Each substance and relation

In Nature's operation
Hath its unit and metre;
And the new compounds are multiples of that.
But the unit of the visit,
Or the meeting of friends,
Is the meeting of their eyes.[1]

. . . .

The founders of Brook Farm ought to have this praise, that they have made what all people try to make, an agreeable place to live in. All comers, and the most fastidious, find it the pleasantest of residences.

If you look at these railroad laborers and hear their stories, their fortunes appear as little controlled as those of the forest leaves. One is whirled off to Albany, one to Ohio, one digs on the levee at New Orleans and one at Walden Pond; others on the wharves in Boston or the woods in Maine, and they have too little foresight and too little money to leave them any more election of whither to go or what to do than the poor leaf which is blown into this dike or that brook to perish. "To work from dark to dark for fifty cents the day," as the poor

[1] This is the poem "The Visit" — a very real issue to Mr. Emerson — in the making.

woman in the shanty told us, is but pitiful wages for a married man.

Few people know how to spend a large fortune. A beauty of wealth is power without pretension, a despotism under the quietest speech and under the plainest garb, neither rich nor poor. . . . The money-lord should have no fine furniture or fine equipage, but should open all doors, be warm, be cool, ride, fly, execute or suspend execution, at his will, and see what he willed come to pass.

Ellery's poetry shows the Art, though the poems are imperfect, as the first Daguerres are grim things, yet show that a great engine has been invented.

Superiority of *Vathek* over *Vivian Grey*.[1] Is life a thunderstorm that we can see now by a flash the whole horizon, and then cannot see our right hand?

Families should be formed on a higher method than by the Intelligence Office. A man will come to think it as absurd to send thither for his nurse or farmer, as for a wife. Domestics

1 Beckford's novel over Disraeli's.

pass in silence through the social rooms and recover their tongues at the kitchen door — to bless you?

September 3.

Representative. We pursue ideas, not persons, the man momentarily stands for the thought.[1] . . .

My friend came hither and satisfied me in many ways, and, as usual, dissatisfied me with myself. She increased my knowledge of life, and her sketches of manners and persons are always valuable, she sees so clearly and steadily through the veils. But best of all is the admonition that comes to me from a demand of beauty so naturally made wheresoever her eye rests, that our ways of life, our indolences, our indulgences, our want of heroic action are shamed. Yet I cordially greet the reproof. When that which is so fair and noble passes, I seem enlarged; all my thoughts are spacious; the chambers of the brain and the lobes of the heart are bigger. How am I cheered always by traits of that "vis superba formæ" which inspires art and genius but not passion: there is

1 This passage occurs in "Nominalist and Realist" (*Essays*, Second Series, p. 225).

that in beauty which cannot be caressed,[1] but
which demands the utmost wealth of nature in
the beholder properly to meet it.

We cannot quite pull down and degrade our
life and divest it of poetry. The day-laborer is
popularly reckoned as standing at the foot of
the social scale: yet, talk with him, he is saturated with the beautiful laws of the world.[2] . . .

Any form of government would content me
in which the rulers were gentlemen, but it is in
vain that I have tried to persuade myself that Mr.
Calhoun or Mr. Clay or Mr. Webster were such;
they are underlings, and take the law from the
dirtiest fellows. In England it usually appears as
if the power were confided to persons of superior sentiment, but they have not treated Russia
as they ought in the affair of Poland. It is true
these fellows should hear the truth from other
quarters than the Anti-slavery papers and Whig
papers and Investigators and all other committed
organs. We have allowed them to take a certain

1 Compare line in "Ode to Beauty."
2 For the rest of the passage on the laborer, and on property, see "Nominalist and Realist" (*Essays*, Second Series,
p. 231).

place in private society as if they were at the head
of their countrymen. They must be told that they
have dishonored themselves and it can be allowed
no longer, they are not now to be admitted to
the society of scholars.

The capital defect of my nature for society (as
it is of so many others) is the want of animal
spirits. They seem to me a thing incredible, as
if God should raise the dead. I hear of what
others perform by thei   , with fear. It is as
much out of my hospitality as the prowess of
Cœur de Lion, or an Irishman's day's work on
the railroad. Animal spirits seem the power of
the Present, and their feats equal to the Pyramids of Karnac. Before them what a base men-
dicant is Memory with his leathern badge. I
cannot suddenly form my relation to my friend,
or rather, can very slowly arrive at its satisfaction. I make new friendships on the old: we shall
meet on higher and higher platforms until our
first intercourse shall seem like an acquaintance
of tops, marbles, and ball-time. I am an architect and ask a thousand years for my probation.
Meantime I am very sensible to the deep flattery of Omens.

Has the South European more animal spirits than we, that he is so joyous a companion?

A visit to the railroad yesterday, in Lincoln, showed me the laborers — how grand they are; all their postures, their air, and their very dress. They are men, manlike employed, and the art of the sculptor is to take these forms and set on them a cultivated face and head. But cultivation never, except in war, makes such forms and carriage as these.

I think it will soon become the pride of the country to make gardens and adorn country-houses. That is the fine art which especially fits us. Sculpture, painting, music, architecture, do not thrive with us.[1] . . .

The other day came C. S., with eyes full of Naushon and Nahant and Niagara, dreaming by day and night of canoes, and lightning, and deer-parks, and silver waves, and could hardly disguise her disdain for our poor cold, low life in Concord, like rabbits in a warren. Yet the interiors of our woodland which recommend the

1 Here follows the passage urging fine gardens in America, to be found in "The Young American" (*Essays*, Second Series, pp. 367, 368).

place to us, she did not see. . . . The great sun equalizes all places, — the sun and the stars. The grand features of Nature are so identical that, whether in a mountain or a waterfall, or whether in a flat meadow, the presence of the great agents makes the presence or absence of the inferior features insignificant. With the sun, with morning and evening.

The difference between men, if one could accept exterior tests, is in power of face. . . .

But it is easy to see that as soon as one acts for large masses, the moral element will and must be allowed for, will and must work. Daniel O'Connell is no saint, yet at this vast meeting on the hill of Tara, eighteen miles from Dublin, of five hundred thousand persons, he almost preaches; he goes for temperance, for law and order, and suggests every reconciling, gentilizing, humanizing consideration. There is little difference between him and Father Mathew, when the audience is thus enormously swelled.

Ellery says that at Brook Farm they keep Curtis and Charles Newcomb and a few others as decoy-ducks.

Life. A great lack of vital energy; excellent

beginners, infirm executors. I should think there were factories above us which stop the water. . . .

God will have life to be real; we will be damned, but it shall be theatrical.

Fear haunts the building railroad, but it will be American power and beauty, when it is done. And these peaceful shovels are better, dull as they are, than pikes in the hands of these Kernes; and this stern day's work of fifteen or sixteen hours, though deplored by all the humanity of the neighborhood, and, though all Concord cries Shame! on the contractors, is a better police than the sheriff and his deputies to let off the peccant humors.

The appeal to the public indicates infirm faith.[1] . . . Yet this must be said in defense of Alcott and Lane, that their appeal to the public is a recognition of mankind as proof of abiding interest in other men, of whom they wish to be saviours.

It is in vain to tell me that you are sufficient to yourself, but have not anything to impart. I know and am assured that whoever is sufficient to himself will, if only by existing, suffice me also.

1 See " Experience " (p. 100).

'Tis a great convenience to be educated for a time in a counting-room or attorney's business; then you may safely be a scholar the rest of your life, and will find the use of that partial thickening of the skin every day as you will of your shoes or your hat. What mountains of nonsense will you have cleared your brain of forever!

We admire the tendency, but the men who exhibit it are grass and waves, until they are conscious of that which they share: then it is still admirable in them, as out of them; yea, how much more dear!

There is no chance for the æsthetic village.[1] . . .

September 26.

This morning Charles Lane left us after a two days' visit. He was dressed in linen altogether, with the exception of his shoes, which were lined with linen, and he wore no stockings. He was full of methods of an improved life: valued himself chiefly just now on getting rid of the animals; thinks there is no economy in using them on a farm. He said that they could carry on their Family at Fruitlands in many respects

1 See *Dial Papers*, "A Letter" (*Natural History of Intellect*, p. 397).

better, no doubt, if they wished to play it well. He said that the clergy for the most part opposed the Temperance Reform, and conspicuously this simplicity in diet, because they were alarmed, as soon as such nonconformity appeared, by the conviction that the next question people would ask, would be, "Of what use are the clergy?" In the College he found an arithmetic class, Latin, German, Hebrew classes, but no Creative Class. He had this confidence, namely, that *Qui facit per alium, facit per se:* that it was of no use to put off upon a second or third person the act of serving or of killing cattle; as in cities, for example, it would be sure to come back on the offending party in some shape, as in the brutality of the person or persons you have brutalized.[1]

1 The farming problem at Fruitlands was hopeless, though only events could convince the members. First of all, they spent large portions of the day in high conversation. Second, the farm is said to have had a northward slope and poor soil. Third, the use of animal manure was abhorrent, and also the enslavement, robbing, or killing of animals. Fourth, commodities produced by slave labor were against conscience. Thus, leaves and green crops, spaded in, must suffice for fertilizers (mineral fertilizers were then unknown); the wheelbarrow, hoe and spade must do duty for cart, plough, etc.; sugar, tea, coffee, chocolate, wine, spices, rice, meat, fish, poultry, eggs, milk, butter,

[Here follow some trial lines for the " Ode to Beauty."]

The poet should walk in the fields, drawn on by new scenes, supplied with vivid pictures and thoughts, until insensibly the recollection of his home was crowded out of his mind, and all memory obliterated, and he was led in triumph by Nature.

When he spoke of the stars he should be innocent of what he said ; for it seemed that the stars, as they rolled over him, mirrored themselves in his mind as in a deep well, and it was their image and not his thought that you saw.

It is of no importance to real wisdom how many propositions you add on the same platform, but only what new forms. I knew somewhat concerning the American Revolution, the action at Bunker Hill, the battle of Monmouth, of Yorktown, etc. To-day I learn new particulars of General Greene, of Lee, of Rochambeau.

cheese, honey, and even fine flour were excluded; also wool and cotton. Hence, corn, rye, buckwheat, unbolted wheat bread without yeast, vegetables and local fruit, unsweetened unless by maple sugar, must serve for diet, and linen for clothing.

But now that I think of that event with a changed mind and see what a compliment to England is all this self-glorification, and betrays a servile mind in us who think it so overgreat an action; it makes the courage and the wit of the admirers suspected, who ought to look at such things as things of course.

Let us shame the fathers by the virtue of the sons, and not belittle us by brag.

We ought to thank the nonconformist for everything good he does. Who has a right to ask him why he compounds with this or that wrong?

Certainly the objection to Reform is the common sense of mankind, which seems to have settled several things; as traffic, and the use of the animals for labor and food. But it will not do to offer this by way of argument, as *that* is precisely the ground of dispute.

Read Montaigne's journey into Italy, which is an important part of his biography. I like him so well that I value even his register of his disease. Is it that the valetudinarian gives the assurance that he is not ashamed of himself? Then what a treasure, to enlarge my knowledge of his friend by his narrative of the last days and the

death of Etienne de la Boëtie. In Boston, when
I heard lately Chandler Robbins preach so well
the funeral sermon of Henry Ware, I thought
of Montaigne, who would also have felt how
much this surface called Unitarianism admits of
being opened and deepened, and that this was
as good and defensible a post of life to occupy
as any other. It was a true cathedral music and
brought chancels and choirs, surplices, ephods
and arks and hierarchies into presence. Certainly
Montaigne is the antagonist of the fanatic reformer. Under the oldest, mouldiest conventions
he would prosper just as well as in the newest
world. His is the common sense which, though
no science, is fairly worth the Seven.

A newspaper lately called Daniel Webster "a
steam engine in breeches," and the people are
apt to speak of him as "Daniel," and it is a sort
of proverb in New England of a vast knowledge
—"if I knew as much as Daniel Webster." *Os,
oculosque Jovi par*.

Henry Ware, with his benevolence and frigid
manners, reminded men how often of a volcano
covered with snow. But there was no deep enthusiasm. . . . All his talent was available, and

he was a good example of the proverb, no doubt a hundred times applied to him, of "a free steed driven to death." He ought to have been dead ten years ago, but hard work had kept him alive. A very slight and puny frame he had, and the impression of size was derived from his head. Then he was dressed with heroical plainness. I think him well entitled to the dangerous style of Professor of Pulpit eloquence, — none but Channing so well, and he had ten times the business valor of Channing. This was a soldier that flung himself into all risks at all hours, not a solemn martyr kept to be burned once and make the flames proud. In calm hours and friendly company, his face expanded into broad simple sunshine; and I thought *le bon Henri* a pumpkin-sweeting.

Plato paints and quibbles, and by and by a sentence that moves the sea and land.

George B. Emerson read me a criticism on Spenser, who makes twenty trees of different kinds grow in one grove, whereof the critic says it was an imaginary grove. George, however, doubts not it was after nature, for he knows a piece of natural woodland near Boston, wherein twenty-four different trees grow together in a small grove.

New England cannot be painted without a portrait of Millerism with the new advent of hymns.

> " You will see the Lord a-coming
>   To the old churchyards,
>   With a band of music, etc.

> " He 'll awake all the nations
>   In the old churchyards.

> " We will march into the city
>   From the old churchyards."

Hard clouds, and hard expressions, and hard manners, I love.

Aristocracy. In Salem, the aristocracy is often merchants; even the lawyers are a second class. In Boston, is aristocracy of families which have inherited their wealth and position, and of lawyers and of merchants. In Charleston, the merchants are an inferior class, the planters are the aristocracy. In England, the aristocracy, incorporated by law and education, degrades life for the unprivileged classes. Long ago they wrote on placards in the streets, "Of what use are the lords?" And now that the misery of Ireland and of English manufacturing counties famishes and growls around the park fences of Lord Shannon, Lord Cork, and Sir Robert Peel, a park and a castle will be a less pleasant abode.[1] ... I must nevertheless respect this *Order* as "a part of the order of Providence," as my good Aunt used to say of the rich, when I see, as I do everywhere, a class born with these attributes of rule. The class of officers I recognize everywhere in town or country. These gallants come into the world to ruffle it, and by rough or smooth to find their way to the top. When I spoke to Nathaniel Hawthorne of the class who hold the keys of State Street and are yet excluded from the best Boston circles, he said, "Perhaps he has a heavy wife."

The Reformer (after the Chinese). There is a class whom I call the thieves of virtue. They are those who mock the simple and sincere endeavorers after a better way of life, and say, These are pompous talkers; but when they come to

1 Here follows the anecdote of the reply of his ambassador to Philip II of Spain: "Your Majesty's self is but a ceremony," given in "The Young American."

act they are weak, nor do they regard what they have said. These mockers are continually appealing to the ancients, and they say, Why make ourselves singular? Let those who are born in this age, act as men of this age. Thus they secretly obtain the flattery of the age. . . . The multitude all delight in them and they confuse virtue.

Chin Seang praised Heu Tsze to Mencius as a prince who taught and exemplified a righteous life. A truly virtuous prince, he added, will plough along with his people, and while he rules will cook his own food.

Mencius. Does Heu Tsze sow the grain which he eats?

Seang. Yes.

M. Does Heu Tsze weave cloth and then wear it?

S. No: Heu Tsze wears coarse hair-cloth.

M. Does Heu Tsze wear a cap?

S. Yes.

M. What sort of a cap?

S. A coarse cap.

M. Does he make it himself?

S. No: he gives grain in exchange for it.

M. Why doesn't he make it himself?

S. It would be injurious to his farming.

M. Does he use earthenware in cooking his victuals, or iron utensils in tilling his farm?

S. Yes.

M. Does he make them himself?

S. No, he gives grain in barter for them.

M. Why does not Heu Tsze act the potter, and take everything from his own shop he wants to use? Why should he be in the confused bustle exchanging articles with the mechanics? He is not afraid of labor, surely?

S. The work of the mechanic and that of the husbandman ought not to be united.

M. Oh, then the government of the Empire and the labor of the husbandman are the only employments that ought to be united. Were every man to do all kinds of work, it would be necessary that he should first make his implements, and then use them: thus all men would constantly crowd the roads. Some men labor with their minds, and some with bodily strength. Those who labor with their strength are ruled by men. Those who are governed by others, feed others. This is a general rule under the whole heavens.

Mencius proceeds to instance Yu, who, after the deluge, was eight years abroad directing the opening of channels to let off the inundation into the sea, and the burning of forests and marshes to clear the land of beasts of prey, so that he had no time to go home even, but passed his own door repeatedly without entering; and asks if he had leisure for husbandry, if he had been inclined? Yu and Shun employed their whole minds in governing the Empire, yet they did not plough the fields. . . .

Gonzalo in the *Tempest* anticipates our Reformers.

Gonzalo. Had I plantation of this isle, my lord,
And were the king of it, what would I do?
In the commonwealth I would by contraries
Execute all things; for no kind of traffic
Would I admit; no name of magistrate;
Letters should not be known; riches, poverty,
And use of service none; contract, succession,
Bourn, bound of land, tilth, vineyard, none;
No use of metal, corn, or wine, or oil:
No occupation; all men idle, all;
And women too; but innocent and pure:
No sovereignty.

   Sebastian.   Yet he would be king on't.

   Gon. All things in common nature should produce
Without sweat or endeavour: treason, felony,
Sword, pike, knife, gun, or need of any engine,
Would I not have; but nature should bring forth,

Of its own kind, all foison, all abundance,
To feed my innocent people.
I would with such perfection govern, sir,
To excel the golden age.

                                        Act II, Scene 1.

Queenie thinks the Fruitlands People far too gross in their way of living. She prefers to live on snow.

Aristocracy. In solitude, — in the woods, for example, — every man is a noble, and we cannot prize too highly the staid and erect and plain manners of our farmers.

Nature seems a little wicked and to delight in mystifying us. Everything changes in ourselves and our relations, and for twenty or thirty years I shall find some old cider barrel or well-known rusty nail or hook, or rag of dish clout unchanged.

The only straight line in Nature that I remember is the spider swinging down from a twig.

The rainbow and the horizon seen at sea are good curves.

For laughter never looked upon his brow.
                                        GILES FLETCHER.

In Saadi's *Gulistan*, I find many traits which comport with the portrait I drew.[1] He replied to Nizan: "It was rumored abroad that I was penitent and had forsaken wine, but this was a gross calumny, for what have I to do with repentance?" Like Montaigne, he learns manners from the unmannerly, and he says "there is a tradition of the prophet that poverty has a gloomy aspect in this world and in the next!" There is a spice of Gibbon in him when he describes a schoolmaster so ugly and crabbed that the sight of him would damage the ecstasies of the orthodox.

Like Homer and Dante and Chaucer, Saadi possessed a great advantage over poets of cultivated times in being the representative of learning and thought to his countrymen. These old poets felt that all wit was their wit, they used their memory as readily as their invention, and were at once the librarian as well as the poet, historiographer as well as priest of the Muses.

"The blow of our beloved has the relish of raisins."

"The dervish in his prayer is saying, O God! have compassion on the wicked; for thou hast

[1] In the poem "Saadi" which Mr. Emerson printed in the *Dial* of October, 1842.

given all things to the good in making them good."

Saadi found in a mosque at Damascus an old Persian of an hundred and fifty years, who was dying, and was saying to himself, "I said, I will enjoy myself for a few moments; alas! that my soul took the path of departure. Alas! at the variegated table of life, I partook a few mouthfuls, and the fates said, Enough!"

"Take heed that the orphan weep not; for the throne of the Almighty is shaken to and fro when the orphan sets a-crying."

[In 1865, at the request of the publishers, Mr. Emerson wrote the Introduction to the American edition of Gladwin's translation of the *Gulistan*. This explains the omission of any account of Saadi in the essay on "Persian Poetry," printed in *Letters and Social Aims*.]

Saadi was long a Sacayi or Water-drawer in the Holy Land, "till found worthy of an introduction to the prophet Khizr (Elias, or the Syrian and Greek Hermes) who moistened his mouth with the water of immortality." Somebody doubted this and saw in a dream a host of angels descending with salvers of glory in their hands. On asking one of them for whom those were intended, he answered, "For Shaikh Saadi of Shiraz, who has written a stanza of poetry that has met with the approbation of God Almighty." "Khosraw of Delhi asked Khzir for a mouthful of this inspiring beverage; but he told him, that Saadi had got the last of it."

"It was on the evening of Friday in the Month *Showal*, of the Arabian year 690, that the eagle of the immaterial soul of Shaikh Saadi shook from his plumage the dust of his body."

No wonder the farmer is so stingy of his dollar.[1] . . .

Ellery says, Wordsworth writes like a man who takes snuff.

Tennyson is a master of metre, but it is as an artist who has learned admirable mechanical secrets. He has no wood-notes. Great are the dangers of education.

I will say it again to-day, — I am very much struck in literature by the appearance that one person wrote all the books.[2] . . .

1 See "Wealth" (*Conduct of Life*, pp. 101, 102).
2 The rest of this passage thus beginning is in "Nominalist and Realist" (p. 232).

Immense benefit of party I feel to-day in seeing how it reveals faults of character in such an idol as Webster.[1] . . . The great men dull their palm by entertainment of those they dare not refuse. And lose the tact of greeting the wits with sincerity, but give that odious brassiness to those who would forgive coldness, silence, dislike,—everything but simulation and duping.

In Goethe is that sincerity which makes the value of literature and is that one voice or one writer who wrote all the good books. In *Helena*, Faust is sincere and represents actual, cultivated, strong-natured Man; the book would be farrago without the sincerity of Faust. I think the second part of *Faust* the grandest enterprise of literature that has been attempted since the *Paradise Lost*. It is a philosophy of history set in Poetry.[2] . . .

FAME

Her house is all of echo made
Where never dies the sound,
And as her brows the clouds invade
Her feet do strike the ground.

BEN JONSON.

1 See " Nominalist and Realist " (pp. 239, 240).
2 The long passage which follows is printed in *Representative Men* (pp. 272, 273).

The skeptic says: how can any man love any woman, except by delusion, and ignorance? Brothers do not wish to marry sisters because they see them too nearly, and all attractiveness, like fame, requires some distance. But the lover of nature loves nature in his mistress or his friend; he sees the faults and absurdities of the individual as well as you. No familiarity can exhaust the chasm. It is not personalities but universalities that draw him. The like is true of life. It seems to me that he has learned its lesson who has come to feel so assured of his well-being as to hold lightly all particulars of to-day and to-morrow, and to count death amongst the particulars. He must have such a grasp of the whole as to be willing to be ridiculous and unfortunate.

Literature is the only art that is ashamed of itself. The poet should be delivered as much as may be from routine, to increase his chances. It is a game of luck that he plays, and he must be liberated and ready to use the opportunities. Every one of them has been a high gambler.

Ellery says, that writers never do anything: they are passive observers. Some of them seem to do, but they do not; H.[1] will never be a writer; he is as active as a shoemaker.

It is vain to attempt to get rid of the children by not minding them, ye parents dear; for the children measure their own life by the reaction, and if purring and humming is not noticed, they begin to squeal; if that is neglected, to screech; then, if you chide and console them, they find the experiment succeeds, and they begin again. The child will sit in your arms if you do nothing, contented; but if you read, it misses the reaction, and commences hostile operations: "*pourvu seulement qu'un s'occupe d'eux*," is the law.

I thought yesterday, as I read letters of Aunt Mary's, that I would attempt the arrangement of them. With a little selection and compiling and a little narrative thinly veiled of the youth of Ellen and Charles, and, if brought far enough, with letters from Charles and later letters from my sweet saint, there should be a picture of a New England youth and education, so connected with the story of religious opinion in New England as to be a warm and bright life picture.

1 Probably Henry Thoreau.

Autobiography. My great-grandfather was Rev. Joseph Emerson of Malden, son of Edward Emerson, Esq., of Newbury(port). I used often to hear that when William, son of Joseph, was yet a boy walking before his father to church, on a Sunday, his father checked him: "William, you walk as if the earth was not good enough for you." "I did not know it, Sir," he replied, with the utmost humility.¹ This is one of the household anecdotes in which I have found a relationship. 'T is curious, but the same remark was made to me, by Mrs. Lucy Brown,² when I walked one day under her windows here in Concord.

What confidence can I have in a fine behavior and way of life that requires riches to bear it out? Shall I never see a greatness of carriage and thought combined with a power that actually earns its bread and teaches others to earn theirs?

1 This was William, the young minister of Concord, and builder of the "Old Manse," eloquent preacher, and eager Son of Liberty, who stirred his people to "stand for the chartered rights of Englishmen" on the village green on the morning of the Nineteenth of April, 1775. Next year he joined the Northern Army at Ticonderoga and died of camp fever at Rutland, Vermont.

2 Mrs. Emerson's sister.

We come down with free thinking into the dear institutions, and at once make carnage amongst them. We are innocent of any such fell purpose as the sequel seems to impute to us. We were only smoking a cigar, but it turns out to be a powder-mill that we are promenading.

If one could have any security against moods! [1] . . .

The best yet, or T. T.'s last. My divine Thomas Taylor in his translation of *Cratylus* (p. 30, note) calls Christianity "a certain most irrational and gigantic impiety," ἀλόγιστος καὶ γιγαντίκη ἀνοσιουργία.

People came, it seems, to my lectures with expectation that I was to realize the Republic I described, and ceased to come when they found this reality no nearer. They mistook me. I am and always was a painter. I paint still with might and main, and choose the best subjects I can. Many have I seen come and go with false hopes and fears, and dubiously affected by my pictures. But I paint on. I count

[1] The rest of the passage is printed in "Nominalist and Realist" (p. 247).

this distinct vocation which never leaves me in doubt what to do, but in all times, places, and fortunes gives me an open future, to be the great felicity of my lot. Doctor C. T. J.,[1] too, was born to his chemistry and his minerals.

"Men who in the present life knew the particular deity from whom they descended, and gave themselves always to their proper employment, were called by the ancient, *divine men*." See Taylor's *Cratylus*, p. 32.

Yet what to say to the sighing realist as he passes and comes to the vivid painter with a profound assurance of sympathy, saying, "He surely must be charmed to scale with me the silver mountains whose dim enchantments he has so affectionately sketched." The painter does not like the realist; sees his faults; doubts his means and methods; in what experiments they make, both are baffled; no joy. The painter is early warned that he is jeopardizing his genius in these premature actualizations.

Very painful is the discovery we are always making that we can only give to each other a rare and partial sympathy; for as much time as we have spent in looking over into our neighbor's field and chatting with him is lost to our

[1] Doctor Charles T. Jackson, Mrs. Emerson's brother.

own, and must be made up by haste and re-
newed solitude.

"*L'esprit est une sorte de luxe qui détruit le
bon sens, comme le luxe détruit la fortune.*"

Alcott came, the magnificent dreamer, brooding, as ever, on the renewal or reëdification of
the social fabric after ideal law, heedless that he
had been uniformly rejected by every class to
whom he has addressed himself, and just as san-
guine and vast as ever;—the most cogent example of the drop too much which Nature adds
of each man's peculiarity. To himself he seems
the only realist, and whilst I and other men wish
to deck the dullness of the months with here and
there a fine action or hope, he would weave the
whole, a new texture of truth and beauty. . . .
Very pathetic it is to see this wandering Emperor from year to year making his round of
visits from house to house of such as do not exclude him, seeking a companion, tired of pupils.

We early men at least have a vast advantage:
we are up at four o'clock in the morning and
have the whole market,—we Enniuses and
Venerable Bedes of the empty American Parnassus.

Wish not a man from England.

Henry V.

It is hardly rhetoric to speak of the guardian angels of children. How beautiful they are, so protected from all infusions of evil persons, from vulgarity and second thought. Well-bred people ignore trifles and unsightly things; but heroes do not see them, through an attention preëngaged to beauty.

"That is musk, which discloses itself by its smell, and not what the perfumers impose upon us," said Saadi.

I began to write Saadi's sentence above as a text to some homily of my own which muttered aloud as I walked this morning, to the effect, that the force of character is quite too faint and insignificant. The good are the poor, but if the poor were but once rich, how many fine scruples would melt away; how many blossoming reforms would be nipped in the bud. I ought to see that you must do that you say, as tomato-vines bear tomatoes and meadows yield grass. But I find the seed comes in the manure, and it is your condition, not your genius, which yields all this democratical and tender-hearted harvest.

November 5.

To genius everything is permitted, and not only that, but it enters into all other men's labors. A tyrannical privilege to convert every man's wisdom or skill, as it would seem, to its own use, or to show for the first time what all these fine and complex preparations were for.

See how many libraries one master absorbs. Who hereafter will go gleaning in those contemporary and anterior books, from each of which he has taken the only grain of truth it had, and has given it tenfold value by placing it? The railroad was built for him; for him history laboriously registered; for him arms and arts and politics and commerce waited, like so many servants until the heir of the manor arrived, which he quite easily administers.

Genius is a poor man and has no house; but see this proud landlord, who has built the great house and furnished it delicately, opens it all to him and beseeches him respectfully to make it honorable by entering there and eating bread.

Some philosophers went out of town, founded a community in which they proposed to pay

talent and labor at one rate, say, ten cents the
hour![1] . . .

Punctuality. On the dinner bell was written,
" I laughed at them and they believed me not." [2]

The sect is the stove, gets old, worn out, there
are a hundred kinds, but the fire keeps its properties. Calvinism is a fine history to show you
how peasants, Paddies, and old country crones
may be liberalized and beatified.

The reformers wrote very ill. They made it
a rule not to bolt their flour, and unfortunately
neglected also to sift their thoughts. But Hesiod's great discovery, πλέον ἥμισυ παντός, is
truest in writing, where half is a great deal more
than the whole. Give us only the eminent experiences.

Alcott and Lane want feet: they are always
feeling of their shoulders to find if their wings

1 This Brook Farm (?) theory is printed in full in " The
Young American" (*Nature, Addresses, and Lectures*, p.
283).

2 Mr. Emerson, who was punctual, used to quote this line
from Scripture when the dinner bell reminded every one of
something they had planned to do before dinner and so dis-
appeared to do it. It was finally engraved on the bell.

are sprouting; but next best to wings are cow-hide boots, which society is always advising them to put on.

Married women uniformly decided against the communities.[1]

November 12.

It is wiser to live in the country and have poverty instead of pauperism. Yet citizens or cockneys are a natural formation also, a second-ary formation, and their relation to the town is organic, — but there are all shades of it, and we dwellers in the country are only half coun-trymen. As I run along the yard from my wood-pile I chance to see the sun as he rises or as he hangs in beauty over a cloud, and am apprised how far off from that beauty I live, how careful and little I am. He calls me to solitude.

Where does the light come from that shines on things? From the soul of the sufferer, of the enjoyer. *Minerva and Telemachus*, PLOTI-NUS, 452.

I have known a person of extraordinary intel-lectual power, on some real or supposed impu-tation of weakness of her reasoning faculty from

1 *Lectures and Biographical Sketches*, p. 365.

another party, enter with heat into a defence of
the same by naming the eminent individuals who
had trusted and respected her genius. The moment we quote a man to prove our sanity, we
give up all. No authority can establish it, and
if I have lost confidence in myself I have the
Universe against me.

Five minutes of to-day, as I used to preach,
are worth as much to me as five minutes a million years hence.

We fathers of American nations should not
set the bad example of Repudiation to the centuries. The Years are the moments of the life
of this nation.

Common sense knows its own, and so recog-
nizes the fact at first sight in chemical experiment. The common sense of Dalton, Davy,
Black, is that common sense which made these
arrangements which now it discovers.

Eternity of the World. The different ages of
man, in Hesiod's *Works and Days*, signify the
mutations of human lives from virtue to vice
and from vice to virtue. There are periods of
fertility and of sterility of souls; sometimes men

descend for the benevolent purpose of leading back apostate souls to right principles. Hades signified the profound union of the soul with the present body. See Taylor's *Cratylus*.

Euclid, Plato, and the multiplication table are spheres in your thought. Bail up with a spoon and you shall get Mrs. Glass or the newspaper: bail up with a bucket and you shall have purer water: dive yourself and you shall come to the immortal deeps.

Therefore, we feel that one man wrote all the books of literature. It will certainly so appear at a distance. Neither is any dead, neither Christ nor Plato.

Each man reserves to himself alone the right of being tedious.

There are many audiences in every public assembly.[1] . . .

[Early in December, Mr. Emerson wrote to his brother William that he had had, for the second time, an application from a bookseller to print a volume of poems.[2] He had, at the re-

1 The rest of this passage is found in "Eloquence" (*Society and Solitude*, p. 66).

2 See Cabot's *Memoir of Emerson*, vol. ii, pp. 480, 481.

quest of Rev. James Freeman Clarke, allowed
him to print several in the *Western Messenger*,
at Louisville, Kentucky ; and he had contributed several to the *Dial*, and many friends urged
their publication.]

December 25.

At the performing of Handel's *Messiah* I
heard some delicious strains and understood a
very little of all that was told me. My ear
received but a little thereof.[1] . . . The genius
of Nature could well be discerned. By right
and might we should become participant of
her invention, and not wait for morning and
evening to know their peace, but prepossess it.
I walked in the bright paths of sound, and liked
it best when the long continuance of a chorus
had made the ear insensible to the music, made
it as if there was none; then I was quite solitary and at ease in the melodious uproar. Once
or twice in the solos, when well sung, I could
play tricks, as I like to do, with my eyes, —
darken the whole house and brighten and trans-
figure the central singer, and enjoy the enchantment.

This wonderful piece of music carried us back

[1] The omitted portion is printed in "Nominalist and
Realist" (p. 233).

into the rich, historical past. It is full of the Roman Church and its hierarchy and its architecture. Then, further, it rests on and requires so deep a faith in Christianity that it seems bereft of half and more than half its power when sung to-day in this unbelieving city.

We love morals until they come to us with mountainous melancholy and grim overcharged rebuke: then we so gladly prefer intellect, the light-maker. Dear sir, you treat these fantastical fellow men too seriously, you seem to believe that they exist.

The solid earth exhales a certain permanent average gas which we call the atmosphere; and the spiritual solid sphere of Mankind emits the volatile sphere of literature of which books are single and inferior effects.

December 31.

The year ends, and how much the years teach which the days never know![1] . . . but the individual is always mistaken.

At the Convention of Socialists in Boston last week Alcott was present, and was solicited to speak, but had no disposition, he said, to do so.

[1] See "Experience" (p. 69).

Although none of the representatives of the "Communities" present would probably admit it, yet in truth he is more the cause of their movements than any other man. He feels a certain parental relation to them without approving either of their establishments. His presence could not be indifferent to any speaker, and has not been nothing to any of them in the past years.

A true course of English literary history would contain what I may read the Wartons and not learn: e.g., of Marlowe's mighty line; of Crashaw's *Musician and Nightingale;* of Ben Jonson's visit to Drummond; of Wotton's list of contemporaries; of the history of John Dennis; of the *Rehearsal;* of the *Critic;* a history of Bishop Berkeley; of the Scriblerus Club; of Wood, and Aubrey; of Shakspeare at the last dates; of Cotton's Montaigne; of the translators of Plutarch; of the forgeries of Chatterton, Landor, and Ireland; of Robert of Gloucester; of the Roxburgh Club; of Thomas Taylor.

We rail at trade, but the historian of the world will see that it was the principle of liberty; that it settled America, and destroyed feudalism, and made peace and keeps peace; that it will abolish slavery.

Belief and Unbelief. Kant, it seems, searched the metaphysics of the Self-reverence which is the favorite position of modern ethics, and demonstrated to the Consciousness that itself alone exists.

The two parties in life are the believers and unbelievers, variously named. The believer is poet, saint, democrat, theocrat, free-trade, no church, no capital punishment, idealist.

The unbeliever supports the church, education, the fine arts, etc., as *amusements*.

But the unbelief is very profound: Who can escape it? I am nominally a believer: yet I hold on to property: I eat my bread with unbelief. I approve every wild action of the experimenters. I say what they say concerning celibacy, or money, or community of goods, and my only apology for not doing their work is preoccupation of mind. I have a work of my own which I know I can do with some success. It would leave that undone if I should undertake with them, and I do not see in myself any vigor equal to such an enterprise. My genius loudly calls me to stay where I am, even with the degradation of owning bank-stock and seeing poor men suffer, whilst the Universal Genius apprises me of this disgrace and beckons me to the martyrs and redeemer's office.[1]

This is belief, too, this debility of practice, this staying by our work. For the obedience to a man's genius is the *particular* of Faith: by and by, shall I come to the *universal* of Faith.

I take the law on the subject of Education to read thus, *The Intellect sees by moral obedience.* (Thomas Taylor's translations.)

Alypius in Iamblichus had the true doctrine of money.

AUTHORS OR BOOKS QUOTED OR REFERRED TO
IN JOURNAL FOR 1843

The *She-King; The Four Books* (Chinese Classics), translated by Rev. D. Collier, Malacca;

Vishnu Sarna; The *Desatir* (Persian), translation of Mr. Duncan, Bombay;

Æschylus, *Prometheus Bound;* Martial; Marcus Terentius Varro; Pliny the Elder;

Plotinus, Iamblichus, Synesius, Proclus (Thomas Taylor's translations);

1 This sympathy with extreme reformers, here confessed, was Mr. Emerson's native hospitality to thought, but also largely a matter of moods as described by him on page 471 of this volume. His saving common sense came to his aid in time.

William Lorris and Jean de Meung, *Roman de la Rose;* Dante; Saadi;

Erasmus; Calvin; Scaliger; Raleigh; Marlowe;

Behmen; Giles Fletcher, *Christ's Victory and Triumph;*

Crashaw, *Musician and Nightingale;* Anthony à Wood; Spinoza; Swift, *Gulliver's Travels;*

Berkeley; Beckford, *Vathek;*

Joseph and Thomas Warton; Beaumarchais; Wieland, *The Abderites;* Goethe, *Iphigenia, Faust* (second part), *Wilhelm Meister;*

Chatterton; William H. Ireland; Thomas Taylor, translations of the *Cratylus* and the Neoplatonists; O'Connell; Campbell; Ludwig Borne; Bettina von Arnim; Webster; Carlyle, *Past and Present;*

Rev. Henry Ware; Rev. Lyman Beecher; Rev. Nathaniel Frothingham; Eugene Bernouf; George Borrow, *The Zincali;* Disraeli, *Vivian Grey;*

Theodore Mundt; John Sterling; Nathaniel Hawthorne;

Rev. Chandler Robbins; Goodwyn Barmby; Margaret Fuller; Thoreau; William Ellery Channing.

JOURNAL

LYCEUM LECTURES
ADDRESSES
END OF THE DIAL
WEST INDIAN EMANCIPATION
THE SECOND ESSAYS

JOURNAL XXXV

1844

(From Journals U and V)

[MR. EMERSON did not begin the year with any course of lectures, but was called, through the winter, to give a lecture — sometimes two — in Boston, Providence, Salem, Fall River, Cambridge, Dorchester, and smaller towns, for Lyceums were everywhere, and well attended. He had to prepare the final issue of the *Dial*, now moribund. The correspondence with Carlyle shows that each was looking after the interests of the other's books and sending proceeds across the ocean.]

(From U)

January, 1844.

There is no expression in any of our poetry, state papers, lecture-rooms, or churches, of a high national feeling. Only the conventional life is considered. I think the German papers greatly more earnest and aspiring. " Conventional worth is intolerable, where personal is wanting," said Schlegel. Who announces to us in journal, or pulpit, or lecture-room —

> " Alone may man
> Do the Impossible " ?

Finish each day before you begin the next, and interpose a solid wall of sleep between two. This you cannot do without temperance.

January 30.

I wrote to Mr. F. that I had no experiences nor progress to reconcile me to the calamity whose anniversary returned the second time last Saturday.[1] The senses have a right to their method as well as the mind; there should be harmony in facts as well as in truths. Yet these ugly breaks happen there, which the continuity of theory does not contemplate. The amends are of a different kind from the mischief.

But the astonishment of life is the absence of any appearances of reconciliation between the theory and practice of life.[2] . . .

1 The death of his child.

2 The rest of the long passage beginning thus is printed in "Montaigne" (*Representative Men*, pp. 178, 179), except its concluding paragraph as to the instability of our opinions, depending on moods, which is in " Nominalist and Realist " (*Essays*, Second Series, p. 247).

Introvert your eye, and your consciousness is a taper in the desart of Eternity. It is the channel, though now demolished to a thread, through which torrents of light roll and flow in the high tides of spontaneity and reveal the landscape of the dusky Universe.

That idea which I approach and am magnetized by — is my Country.

How we love to be magnetized! Ah, ye strong iron currents, take me in also! We are so apologetic, such waifs and straws, ducking and imitating, and then the mighty thought comes sailing on a silent wind and fills us also with its virtue, and we stand like Atlas on our legs and uphold the world.

The magnetism is alone to be respected; the men are steel filings.[1] . . .

I am sorry to say that the Numas and Pythagorases have usually a spice of charlatanism, and that Abolition societies and communities are dangerous fixtures. The manliness of man is a frail and exquisite fruit which does not keep its perfection twenty-four hours. Its sweet fra-

[1] The rest of the paragraph is in " Nominalist and Realist " (*Essays*, Second Series, p. 228).

grance cannot be bottled or barrelled or exported.

Carlyle is an eloquent writer, but his recommendations of emigration and education appear very inadequate. Noble as it seems to work for the race and hammer out constitutions for phalanxes, it can only be justly done by mediocre thinkers, or men of practical, not theoretic faculty. As soon as a scholar attempts it, I suspect him. Good physicians have least faith in medicine. Good priests the least faith in church-forms.

That bread which we ask of Nature is that she should entrance us, but amidst her beautiful or her grandest pictures I cannot escape the *second thought*. . . . We have the wish to forget night and day, father and mother, food and ambition, but we never lose our dualism. Blessed, wonderful Nature, nevertheless ! without depth, but with immeasurable lateral spaces. If we look before us, if we compute our path, it is very short. Nature has only the thickness of a shingle or a slate: we come straight to the extremes; but sidewise, and at unawares, the present moment opens into other moods and moments, rich, prolific, leading onward without end. Impossible to bring her, the goddess, to praise: coquettes with us, hides herself in coolness and generalities: pointed and personal is she never.

The Dead. Ζῶμεν τὸν ἐκείνων θάνατον, τεθνήκαμεν δὲ τὸν ἐκείνου βίον.[1] — HERACLITUS.

The Daguerreotype of the Soul. "The oracles assert that the impressions of characters and other divine visions appear in æther" (τούς τύπους τῶν χαρακτήρων καὶ τῶν ἄλλων θειῶν φασμάτων ἐν τῷ αἰθέρι φαίνεσθαι τὰ λόγια λέγουσιν). *Simplic. in Phys.* apud THOMAS TAYLOR, vol. iii.

"And fools rush in where angels fear to tread." So say I of Brook Farm. Let it live. Its merit is that it is a new life. Why should we have only two or three ways of life, and not thousands and millions? This is a new one so fresh and expensive that they are all homesick when they go away. The shy sentiments are there expressed. The *correspondence* of that place would be a historiette of the Spirit of this Age. They

1 We live their death, but we have died the life of each.

might see that in the arrangements of Brook Farm, as out of them, it is the person, not the communist, that avails.

Ellery Channing is quite assured that he has a natural malice of expression, which is wanting in all the so-called poets of the day. He is very good-natured, and will allow them any merit you choose to claim; but this he always feels to be true. It is infinitely easy to him, as easy as it is for running water to warble, but at the same time impossible to any to whom it is not natural.

The Highest should alternate the two states, of the contemplation of the fact in pure intellect, and the total conversion of intellect into energy: angelic insight alternating with bestial activity: sage and tiger.

When I address a large assembly, as last Wednesday, I am always apprised what an opportunity is there: not for reading to them, as I do, lively miscellanies, but for painting in fire my thought, and being agitated to agitate. One must dedicate himself to it and think with his audience in his mind, so as to keep the perspec-

tive and symmetry of the oration, and enter into
all the easily forgotten secrets of a great nocturnal assembly and their relation to the speaker.
But it would be fine music and in the present
well rewarded; that is, he should have his audience at his devotion, and all other fames would
hush before his. Now eloquence is merely fabulous. When we talk of it, we draw on our fancy.
It is one of many things which I should like to
do, but it requires a seven years' wooing.[1] . . .
Henry Thoreau, with whom I talked of this, last
night, does not or will not perceive how natural is this, and only hears the word Art in a
sinister sense. But I speak of instincts. I did
not make the desires or know anything about
them: I went to the public assembly, put myself in the conditions, and instantly feel this
new craving, — I hear the voice, I see the beck-
oning of this ghost. To me it is vegetation, the
pullulation and universal budding of the plant
Man.

Some men have the perception of difference
predominant, and are conversant with surfaces

[1] Here, and a few pages later in the Journal, follow, but
in different order, the sentences printed in " The Poet,"
there beginning " Art is the path of the Creator to his work "
(*Essays*, Second Series, pp. 39, 40, 41).

and trifles, with coats and coaches, and faces, and cities; these are the men of talent. . . . And other men abide by the perception of Identity; these are the Orientals, the philosophers, the men of faith and divinity, the men of genius. These men, whose contempt of *soi-disant* conservatism cannot be concealed, — which is such a conserving as the Quaker's, who keeps in his garments the cut of Queen Anne's time, but has let slip the fire and the love of the first Friends, — are the real loyalists.

Then I discovered the Secret of the World; that all things subsist, and do not die, but only retire a little from sight and afterwards return again.

The text of our life is accompanied all along by this commentary or gloss of dreams.

Henry Thoreau's lines which pleased me so well were, —

"I hearing get, who had but ears,
  And sight, who had but eyes before;
  I moments live, who lived but years,
  And truth discern, who had but learning's lore."

The question of the annexation of Texas is one of those which look very differently to the

centuries and to the years. It is very certain that
the strong British race, which have now overrun
so much of this continent, must also overrun
that tract, and Mexico and Oregon also, and it
will in the course of ages be of small import by
what particular occasions and methods it was
done. It is a secular question. It is quite necessary and true to our New England character
that we should consider the question in its local
and temporary bearings, and resist the annexation
with tooth and nail. It is a measure which goes
not by right, nor by wisdom, but by feeling. It
would be a pity to dissolve the Union and so
diminish immensely every man's personal importance. We are just beginning to feel our oats.

What a pity that a farmer should not live
three hundred years.

We fancy that men are individuals; but every
pumpkin in the field goes through every point
of pumpkin history.[1] . . .

Ah, if any man could conduct into me the
pure stream of that which he pretends to be.

1 The rest of the paragraph thus beginning is in "Nominalist and Realist" (*Essays*, Second Series, p. 246), and the
passage is immediately followed in the Journal by the opening
paragraphs of the same essay.

Long afterwards, I find that quality elsewhere which he promised me. Intoxicating is to me the genius of Plotinus or of Swedenborg. Yet how few particulars of it can I glean from their books. My debt to them is for a few thoughts. They cannot feed that appetite they have created. I should know it well enough if they gave me that which I seek of them.

Otherness. Henry Thoreau said, he knew but one secret, which was to do one thing at a time, and though he has his evenings for study, if he was in the day inventing machines for sawing his plumbago, he invents wheels all the evening and night also; and if this week he has some good reading and thoughts before him, his brain runs on that all day, whilst pencils pass through his hands. I find in me an opposite facility or perversity, that I never seem well to do a particular work until another is done. I cannot write the poem, though you give me a week, but if I promise to read a lecture day after to-morrow, at once the poem comes into my head and now the rhymes will flow. And let the proofs of the *Dial* be crowding on me from the printer, and I am full of faculty how to make the lecture.

Skeptic. Pure intellect is the pure devil when you have got off all the masks of Mephistopheles. It is a painful symbol to me that the index or forefinger is always the most soiled of all the fingers.

The Two Histories. The question is whether the trilobites, or whether the gods, are our grandfathers; and whether the actual existing men are an amelioration or a degradation arises from the contingence whether we look from the material or from the poetic side.

Railroads make the country transparent.

Somebody said of me after the lecture at Amory Hall, within hearing of A. W., "The secret of his popularity is, that he has a *damn* for everybody " [1]

March 12.

On Sunday evening, 10th instant, at the close of the fifteenth year since my ordination as minister in the Second Church, I made an ad-

[1] Mr. Emerson gave, at Amory Hall, Boston, on February 21, an address, "The Young American," before the Mercantile Library Association, and on Sunday, March 3, read " New England Reformers" to the " Society of Amory Hall," probably a religious society.

dress to the people on the occasion of closing the old house, now a hundred and twenty-three years old, and the oldest church in Boston. Yesterday they began to pull it down.[1]

Bohemian. Intellect is a piratical schooner cruising in all latitudes for its own pot.

Consuelo,[2] as Elizabeth Hoar remarked, was the crown of fulfillment of all the tendencies of literary parties in respect to a certain Dark Knight who has been hovering about in the purlieus of heaven and hell for some ages. The young people have shown him much kindness for some time back. Burns advised him to "take advice and mend"; Goethe inclined to convert him and save his soul in the friendship of Faust; he has, here in America, been gaining golden opinions lately, and now in *Consuelo* he actually mounts the shrine and becomes an object of worship under the name and style of "He to whom wrong has been done."

1 The society were building a new church in Hanover Street. An extract from his address to the congregation, with which he had had so close association, telling how little the years had changed the leading belief of his youth, is found in Mr. Cabot's *Memoir*, vol. ii, p. 413.

2 George Sand's novel.

A capital merit of *Consuelo*, the instant mutual understanding between the great, as between Albert and Consuelo.

Art seems to me to be in the artist a steady respect to the whole by an eye loving beauty in details.[1] . . .

Symmetry. Most lovers of beauty are dazzled by the details. To have seen many beautiful details cloys us and we are better able to keep our rectitude.

The straight line is better than the square: a man is the one; a horse the other.

Poet. Among the "Chaldæan oracles, which were either delivered by Theurgists under the reign of Marcus Antoninus, or by Zoroaster," Taylor inserts the following: —

" Rulers who understand the intelligible works of the Father: these he spread like a veil over sensible works and bodies. *They are standing transporters, whose employment consists in speaking to the Father and to matter ; in producing*

1 The rest of this paragraph is in "Nominalist and Realist" (*Essays*, Second Series, p. 234).

apparent imitations of unapparent natures, and in inscribing things unapparent in the apparent fabrication of the world."

Concerning the universe. "It is an imitation of intellect, but that which is fabricated possesses something of body."

Concerning the light above the empyrean world. "In this light things without figure become figured." See *Monthly Magazine*, vol. iii, p. 509 (A.D. 1797).

It is curious that intellectual men should be most attractive to women. But women are magnetic; intellectual men are unmagnetic: therefore, as soon as they meet, communication is found difficult or impossible.

By acting rashly, we buy the power of talking wisely. People who know how to act are never preachers.

I have always found our American day short. The constitution of a Teutonic scholar with his twelve, thirteen, or fourteen hours a day, is fabulous to me. I become nervous and peaked with a few days editing the *Dial*, and watching the stage-coach to send proofs to printers. If I try to get many hours in a day, I shall not have any.

We work hard in the garden and do it badly and often twice or thrice over, but " we get our journey out of the curses," as Mr. H.'s Brighton drover said of his pigs.

Allston is *adamas ex veteri rupe*, chip of the old block; boulder of the European ledge; a spur of those Apennines on which Titian, Raphael, Paul Veronese, and Michael Angelo sat, cropping out here in this remote America and unlike anything around it, and not reaching its natural elevation. What a just piece of history it is that he should have left this great picture of Belshazzar in two proportions! The times are out of joint, and so is his masterpiece.

Allston and Irving and Dana are all European.

But in America I grieve to miss the strong black blood of the English race: ours is a pale, diluted stream. What a company of brilliant young persons I have seen with so much expectation! the sort is very good, but none is good enough of his sort. Every one an imperfect specimen; respectable, not valid. Irving thin, and Channing thin, and Bryant and Dana; Prescott and Bancroft. There is Webster, but he cannot do what he would; he cannot do Webster.

The Orientals behave well, but who cannot behave well who has nothing else to do? The poor Yankees who are doing the work are all wrinkled and vexed.

The Shaker told me they did not read history, not because they had not inclination, for there were some who "took up a sound cross in not reading." Milton's *Paradise Lost*, he knew, was among Charles Lane's books, but he had never read it. Most of them did not know it was there; he knew. There would be an objection to reading it. They read the Bible and their own publications. They write their own poetry. "All their hymns and songs of every description are manufactured in the Society."

In the actual world, the population, we say, is the best that could yet be. Its evils, as war and property, are acknowledged, which is a new fact, and the first step to the remedying of them. But the remedying is not a work for society, but for me to do. If I am born to it, I shall see the way. If the evil is an evil to you, you are party, chief party to it; say not, you are not covetous, if the chief evil of the world seem to you covetousness. I am always environed by myself : what I am, all things reflect to me. The state of me makes Massachusetts and the United States out there. I also feel the evil, for I am covetous, and I do not prosecute the reform because I have another task nearer. I think substantial justice can be done maugre or through the money of society ; and though it is an imperfect system and noxious, yet I do not know how to attack it directly, and am assured that the directest attack which I can make on it is to lose no time in fumbling and striking about in all directions, but to mind the work that is mine, and accept the facilities and openings which my constitution affords me.

The Peace Society speaks civilly of Trade, in its attacks on War. Well, let Trade make hay whilst the sun shines; but know very well that when the War is disposed of, Trade is the next object of incessant attack, and has only the privilege of being last devoured.

Very sad, indeed, it was to see this half-god driven to the wall, reproaching men, and hesitating whether he should not reproach the gods. The world was not, on trial, a possible element

for him to live in. A lover of law had tried
whether law could be kept in this world, and
all things answered, No. He had entertained the
thought of leaving it, and going where freedom
and an element could be found. And if he
should be found to-morrow at the roadside, it
would be the act of the world.[1] We pleaded
guilty to perceiving the inconvenience and the
inequality of property, and he said, "I will not
be a convict." Very tedious and prosing and
egotistical and narrow he is, but a profound insight, a Power, a majestical man, looking easily
along the centuries to explore *his contemporaries*,
with a painful sense of being an orphan and a
hermit here. I feel his statement to be partial
and to have fatal omissions, but I think I shall
never attempt to set him right any more. It is
not for me to answer him: though I feel the
limitations and exaggeration of his picture, and
the wearisome personalities. His statement
proves too much: it is a *reductio ad absurdum*.
But I was quite ashamed to have just revised
and printed last week the old paper denying the

---

1 After the tragic breaking-down of his Fruitlands endeavor for the ideal life, Mr. Alcott was so grieved that he
was in despair and refused food, and was restored to normal
life and cheer with difficulty.

existence of tragedy, when this modern Prometheus was in the heat of his quarrel with the gods.

Alcott has been writing poetry, he says, all winter. I fear there is nothing for me in it. His overpowering personality destroys all poetic faculty.

It is strange that he has not the confidence of one woman.[1] He would be greater if he were good-humoured, but such as he is, he "enlarges the known powers of man," as was said of Michael Angelo.

A man sends to me for money that he may pursue his studies in theology; he wants fifty or sixty dollars, and says he wants it the "last of this week or the fore part of next."

W. G. dreamed that he had disposed of books and the world in his fontal peace of mind — but did not well know what to do with the reply that the Past has a new value every moment to the advancing mind.

I find it settled that while many persons have attraction for me, these styles are incompatible. Each is mine, but I love one, because it is not

[1] That is, his theories had not. Mrs. Alcott was a loyal wife.

the other. What skepticism is like this? Hence
the philosophers concluded that the Turk was
right: Mahomet was right and Jesus was wrong.

I wish to have rural strength and religion for
my children, and I wish city facility and polish.
I find with chagrin that I cannot have both.

Carlo. I spent the winter in the country.
Thick-starred Orion was my only companion.[1]
I preferred the forest, dry forest. Water made
me feel forlorn.

Writers are so few that there are none: writing
is an impossibility, until it is done. A man gives
you his paper and hopes there is something in
it, but does not know. There is nothing in it:
do not open it. When a man makes what he
calls an answer to a speculative question, he
commonly changes the phrase of the question.
But the only conversation we wish to hear is two
affirmatives, and again two affirmatives, and so on.

Able men do not care in what work a man is
able so only he is able.[2] . . .

1 These two sentences, used in " Worship," are evidently
quoted from Charles K. Newcomb, who, in that essay, is
called Benedict. (See *Conduct of Life,* pp. 234, 235.)

2 See " Goethe " (*Representative Men,* p. 268).

Character brings to whatever it does a great superfluity of strength which plays a gay accompaniment; the air with variations. Hear Daniel Webster argue a jury cause. He imports all the experience of the Senate, and the state, and the man of the world into the county court.

C. inquired why I would not go to B?[1] But the great inconvenience is sufficient answer. If I could freely and manly go to the mountains, or to the prairie, or to the sea, I would not hesitate for inconvenience: but to cart all my pots and kettles, kegs and clothespins, and all that belongs thereunto, over the mountains, seems not worth while. I should not be nearer to sun or star.

May 8.

This morn the air smells of vanilla and oranges.

Our people are slow to learn the wisdom of sending character instead of talent to Congress. Again and again they have sent a man of great acuteness, a fine scholar, a fine forensic orator, and some master of the brawls has crunched him

1 Berkshire ?

up in his hand like a bit of paper. At last they sent a man with a back, and he defied the whole Southern delegation when they attempted to smother him, and has conquered them. Mr. Adams is a man of great powers, but chiefly he is a sincere man and not a man of the moment and of a single measure. And besides the success or failure of the measure, there remains to him the respect of all men for his earnestness. When Mr. Webster argues the case, there is the success, or the failure, and the admiration of the unerring talent and intellectual nature, but no respect for an affection to a principle. Could Mr. Webster have given himself to the cause of Abolition of Slavery in Congress, he would have been the darling of this continent of all the youth, all the genius, all the virtue in America. Had an angel whispered in his young ear, " Never mind the newspapers. Fling yourself on this principle of freedom. Show the legality of freedom; though they frown and bluster, they are already half-convinced and at last you shall have their votes," — the tears of the love and joy and pride of the world would have been his.[1]

1 It is possible that this passage, written in pencil, was of a few years later date.

God, the moral element, must ever be new, an electric spark; then it agitates and deifies us. The instant when it is fixed and made chronic, it is hollowness and cant. It is the difference between poets and preachers.

(From V)

" Concordia res parvæ crescunt."

How finely dost thou times and seasons spin,
And make a twist chequered with night and day!
Which, as it lengthens, winds, and winds us in,
As bowls go on, but turning all the way.
                                    GEORGE HERBERT.

But Jove was the eldest born and knows most.
                                    HOMER.

" I conduct the reader through novel and solitary paths, — solitary, indeed, they must be, since they have been unfrequented from the reign of the Emperor Justinian to the present time; and novel, doubtless, to readers of every description, and particularly to those who have been nursed, as it were, in the bosom of matter, the pupils of *experiment*, darlings of sense, and legitimate descendants of the earth-born race that warred on the Olympian Gods." — THOMAS TAYLOR, " General Introduction " to his *Works of Plato*.

These are they, in Taylor's mind, "whose whole life is a sleep, a transmigration from dream to dream, like men passing from bed to bed." He contrasts ever the knowledge of experiment with that of abstract Science : the former is the cause of a mighty calamity to the soul, extinguishing her principle and brightest eye, the knowledge of divinity. One makes piety, the other atheism. There can be no other remedy for this enormous evil than the philosophy of Plato.

Then follow Taylor's rich apostrophes to the stupid and experimental — "Abandon, then, ye grovelling souls," etc.

Thomas Taylor died at Walworth, near London, November 1, 1835, aged seventy-seven. He was born in London in 1758, and learned the rudiments of Latin and Greek at St. Paul's School. He translated Aristotle, Plato, Proclus, Plotinus, Pausanias, Iamblichus, Porphyry.

Tom Appleton Beckford.[1] Beckford's *Italy and Spain* is the book of a Sybarite of the Talley-

1 Beckford's name was William, — he had just died, — but Mr. Thomas Gold Appleton, of Boston, was a traveller so appreciative of the good things in European travel and so witty a narrator that Mr. Emerson was reminded of him by

rand, Brummel, *Vivian Grey* school, written in
1787–89, and much of the humor consist in
the contrast between the volume of this Johnson - and - Gibbon sentence and the ballroom
petulance it expresses. He delights in classic
antiquity; in sunsets, as associated with that
mythology; in music, in picturesque nature. He
is only a *dilettante*, and before the humblest
original worker would feel the rebuke of a solid,
domestic being, as of a creator of that classic
world, which he only gazes at, but lays no stone
of it. He would affect contempt, but his confidence would be the great foolish multitude, and
that steads him not; for when a man has once
met his master, that is a secret which he cannot keep. Yet the travellers why should we
blame any more than the thousands who stay at
home and do less, or worse?

He loves twilight, and sleep. Many of his
criticisms are excellent. He says of the Duomo
at Florence that the architect seems to have
turned his church inside out, such is the ornate
exterior and so simple is the interior. He says
of Paul Veronese's *Cana in Galilee*, that the

Beckford's book. This heading of the paragraph with the nick-
name is in Mr. Emerson's later handwriting, after he had
known Appleton at the Saturday Club.

people at the table seem to be decent persons accustomed to miracles.

Ole Bull, a dignifying, civilizing influence. Yet he was there for exhibition, not for music; for the wonders of his execution, not as Saint Cecilia incarnated, who would be there to carry a point, and degrading all her instruments into meekest means. Yet he played as a man who found a violin in his hand, and so was bent to make much of that, but if he had found a chisel or a sword or a spyglass, or a troop of boys, would have made much of them. It was a beautiful spectacle. I have not seen an artist with manners so pleasing. What a sleep as of Egypt on his lips in the midst of his rapturous music!

We are impressed by a Burke or a Schiller who believes in embodying in practice ideas; because literary men, for the most part, who are cognizant of ideas, have a settled despair as to the realization of ideas in their own times.

In Boston, I trod the street a little proudly, that I could walk from Allston's Belshazzar's Feast to the Sculpture Gallery, and sit before Michael Angelo's Day and Night, and the Antiques; then into the Library; then to Ole Bull.

We want deference, and, when we come to realize that thing mechanically, we want acres. Scatter this hot, crowded population at respectful distances each from each over the vacant world. Lane and his friends thought the cattle made all this wide space necessary, and that if there were no cows to pasture, less land would suffice. But a cow does not need so much land as my eyes require between me and my neighbor.

For economy it is not sufficient that you make now and then a sharp reduction, or that you deny yourself and your family, to meanness, things within their system of expense; but it needs a constant eye to the whole. You yourself must be always present throughout your system. You must hold the reins in your own hands, and not trust to your horse. The farm must be a system, a circle, or its economy is naught; and the fantastic farmers piece out their omissions with cunning.

The effect of these calamitous pictures of pauperism which obtrude everywhere even in the comic literature, in Punch and Judy, in Hood and Dickens, suggests an admonition not so much to charity as to economy, that we may be self-contained and ready, when the calamity comes nearer, to do our part.

I think Genius alone finishes.

Classifying words outvalue many arguments; —upstart, cockney, granny, pedant, prig, precisian, rowdy, niggers.

Goethe, with his extraordinary breadth of experience and culture, the security with which, like a great continental gentleman, he looks impartially over all literatures of the mountains, the provinces, and the sea, and avails himself of the best in all, contrasts with the rigor of the English, and superciliousness and flippancy of the French. His perfect taste, the austere felicities of his style. It is delightful to find our own thought in so great a man.

The finest women have a feeling we cannot sympathize with in regard to marriage. They cannot spare the exaltation of love and the experiences of marriage from their history. But shall a virgin descend to marry below her? Does she not see that Nature may be trusted for completing her own circle? The true virgin will raise herself by just degrees into a goddess, admirable and helpful to all beholders.

Henry Thoreau's conversation consisted of a continual coining of the present moment into a sentence and offering it to me. I compared it to a boy, who, from the universal snow lying on the earth, gathers up a little in his hand, rolls it into a ball, and flings it at me.

Henry said that the other world was all his art; that his pencils would draw no other; that his jackknife would cut nothing else. He does not use it as a means. Henry is a good substantial Childe, not encumbered with himself. He has no troublesome memory, no wake, but lives *ex tempore*, and brings to-day a new proposition as radical and revolutionary as that of yesterday, but different. The only man of leisure in the town. He is a good Abbot Samson: and carries counsel in his breast. If I cannot show his performance much more manifest than that of the other grand promisers, at least I can see that, with his practical faculty, he has declined all the kingdoms of this world. Satan has no bribe for him.

In America we are such rowdies in church and state, and the very boys are so soon ripe, that I think no philosophical skepticism will make much sensation. Spinoza pronounced that there was but one substance; yes, verily; but that boy yonder told me yesterday he thought the pine log was God! . . . what can Spinoza tell the boy?

Fourier has the immense merits of originality and hope. Whilst society is distracted with disputes concerning the negro race, he comes to prescribe the methods of removing this mask and caricature of humanity, by bringing out the true and real form from underneath.

In the woods, with their ever festal look, I am ever reminded of that parable which commends the merchant, who, seeing a pearl of great price, sold all to buy that: so I could not find it in my heart to chide the Yankee who should ruin himself to buy a patch of heavy-timbered oakland. I admire the taste which makes the avenue to a house, were the house ever so small, through a wood, as it disposes the mind of guest and host alike to the deference due to each. Hail vegetable gods!

I observe two classes very easily among those capable of thought and spiritual life, namely, those who are very intelligent of this matter, and can rise easily into it on the call of conversation, and can write strongly of it, and secondly, those who think nothing else and live on that level, and are conscious of no effort or even variety in experience.

Life is made up of the interlude and inter-labor of these two amicable worlds. We are amphibious and weaponed to live in both. We have two sets of faculties, the particular and the catholic, like a boat furnished with wheels for land and water travel.

It is never strange, an unfit marriage, since man is the child of this most impossible marriage, this of the two worlds.

It is strange that Jesus is esteemed by mankind the bringer of the doctrine of immortality.[1]

The Lyceum should refuse all such pieces as were written *to* it.

Behmen. I read a little in Behmen. In reading there is a sort of half-and-half mixture. The

[1] See " Immortality " (*Letters and Social Aims*, p. 348).

book must be good, but the reader must also be active. I have never had good luck with Behmen before to-day. And now I see that his excellence is in his comprehensiveness, not, like Plato, in his precision. His propositions are vague, inadequate, and straining. It is his aim that is great. He will know, not one thing, but all things. He is like those great swaggering country geniuses that come now and then down from New Hampshire to college and soon demand to learn, not Horace and Homer, but also Euclid and Spinoza and Voltaire and Palladio and Columbus and Bonaparte and Linnæus. . . .

I read in him to-day this sentence, " Men do with truths as children with birds, either they crush them or they let them fly away." Again, " This new wine made the bottle new." Of Adam, " His bones were strengths." " Thus hath this rose of Sharon perfumed our graves."

Jacob Behmen is a great man, but he accepted the accommodations of the Hebrew Dynasty. Of course he cannot take rank with the masters of the world. His value, like that of Proclus, is chiefly for rhetoric.

Theory and Practice in Life. In our recipe, the ingredients are separately named, but in the cup which we drink, the elements are exquisitely mixed ; the heart and head are both nourished, and without fumes or repentance.

Our greatest debt to woman is of a musical character, and not describable. Harriet Martineau solved the problem of woman by describing a man !

Woman. . . . To-day, in our civilization, her position is often pathetic. What is she not expected to do and suffer for some invitation to strawberries and cream? Mercifully their eyes are holden that they cannot see.

Pythagoras was right, who used music as a medicine. I lament my want of ear, but never quite despair of becoming sensible to this discipline. We cannot spare any stimulant or any purgative, we lapse so quickly into flesh and sleep. We must use all the exalters that will bring us into an expensive and productive state, or to the top of our condition. But to hear music, as one would take an ice-cream, or a bath, and to forget it the next day, gives me a humble picture.

Of what use is genius if the organ . . . cannot find a focal distance ?[1] . . .

1 Here follows the passage so beginning in " Experience "

The day of triviality and verbiage. Once "the rose of Sharon perfumed our graves," as Behmen said; but now, if a man dies, it is like a grave dug in the snow, it is a ghastly fact abhorrent to Nature, and we never mention it. Death is as natural as life, and should be sweet and graceful.

> God only knew how Saadi dined;
> Roses he ate, and drank the wind.[1]

And this one thing is certain, that the benefactor of his country shall not propose to himself models, nor content himself with outstripping his neighbors and contemporaries in the race of honor, pausing when he is the best in his little circle; that leads to atheism and despair. New Hampshire and Vermont will in six months let loose some young savage from their wilds who shall take this *petit maître* of virtue and culture like a doll in their hands and shatter the pretty porcelain. All reference to models, all comparison with neighboring abilities and reputations, is

---

(*Essays*, Second Series, pp. 50, 51), and that in the same essay on the pseudo-science, Phrenology (p. 53).

1 At various points in this journal occur lines on the life and experience of the poet under the name of Saadi or Seyd. (See *Poems*, Appendix, pp. 320–326.)

the road to mediocrity.[1] . . . Calm, pure, effectual
service distinguishes the generous soul from the
vulgar great. He is one who without phrase does
what was hitherto impossible.

In general, I am pained by observing the indigence of Nature in this American Commonwealth. Ellen H. said she sympathized with the
Transcendental Movement, but she sympathized
even more with the objectors. I replied that,
when I saw how little kernel there was to that
comet which had shed terror from its flaming
hair on the nations, how few and what cinders of
genius, I was rather struck with surprise at the
largeness of the reflect, and drew a favorable inference as to the intellectual and spiritual tendencies of our people. For there had not yet
appeared one man among us of a great talent.
If two or three persons should come with a high
spiritual aim and with great powers, the world
would fall into their hands like a ripe peach.

Go to hear a great orator, to see how presentable truth and right are, and how presentable
are common facts.[2] . . .

1 For the rest of this passage, see " Aristocracy "(*Lectures
and Biographical Sketches*, p. 61).

2 The rest of this striking passage on the might of right
when bravely presented is in " The Scholar " (*Lectures and
Biographical Sketches*, pp. 281, 282).

"O I did get the rose water
Whair ye wull neir get nane,
For I did get that very rose water
Into my mither's wame."

The new races rise all pre-divided into parties, ready-armed and angry to fight for they know not what. Yet easy it is to see that they all share, to the rankest Philistines, the same idea; . . . The idea rides and rules like the sun. Therefore, then, Philosopher, rely on thy truth; bear down on it with all thy weight; add the weight of thy town, thy country, and the whole world: triumphantly, thou shalt see, it will bear it all like a scrap of down.[1]

I think the best argument of the conservative is this bad one: that he is convinced that the angry democrat, who wishes him to divide his park and château with him, will, on entering into the possession, instantly become conservative, and hold the property and spend it as selfishly as himself. For a better man, I might dare to renounce my estate; for a worse man, or for as bad a man as I, why should I? All the history of man with unbroken sequence of

[1] This is printed in somewhat different form in " Instinct and Inspiration " (*Natural History of Intellect*, p. 81).

examples establishes this inference. Yet it is very low and degrading ground to stand upon. We must never reason from history, but plant ourselves on the ideal.

Men are edificant or otherwise. Samuel Hoar is to all men's eyes conservative and constructive: his presence supposes a well-ordered society, agriculture, trade, large institutions and empire: if these things did not exist, they would begin to exist through his steady will and endeavors. Therefore he cheers and comforts men, who all feel this in him very readily. The reformer, the rebel, who comes by, says all manner of unanswerable things against the existing republic, but discovers to my groping Dæmon no plan of house or empire of his own. Therefore, though Samuel Hoar's town and state are a very cheap and modest commonwealth, men very rightly go to him and flout the reformer.

June 15.

A second visit to the Shakers with Mr. Hecker.[1] Their family worship was a painful spectacle. I could remember nothing but the *Spedale dei pazzi*[2] at Palermo; this shaking of their hands,

1 Rev. Isaac Hecker.   2 Insane Asylum.

like the paws of dogs, before them as they shuffled in this dunce-dance seemed the last deliration. If there was anything of heart and life in this, it did not appear to me: and as Swedenborg said that the angels never look at the back of the head, so I felt that and saw nothing else. My fellow men could hardly appear to less advantage before me than in this senseless jumping. The music seemed to me dragged down nearly to the same bottom. And when you come to talk with them on their topic, which they are very ready to do, you find such exaggeration of the virtue of celibacy that you might think you had come into a hospital-ward of invalids afflicted with priapism. Yet the women were well dressed and appeared with dignity as honored persons. And I judge the whole society to be cleanly and industrious, but stupid people. And these poor countrymen with their nasty religion fancy themselves *the Church* of the world, and are as arrogant as the poor negroes on the Gambia River.

The Long Life. We must infer our destiny from the preparation. We are driven by instincts to higher innumerable experiences which are of no visible value, and which we may revolve through many lives in the eternal whirl of generation before we shall assimilate and exhaust.

It is the rank of the spirit makes the merit of the deed. *Les attractions sont proportionelles aux destinés.* Yes, cries the angel, but my attractions transcend all your system.

Mrs. Snow confessed, when the phrenologist found love of approbation, that "*she did like to suit*."[1]

If I made laws for Shakers or a school, I should gazette every Saturday all the words they were wont to use in reporting religious experience, as "spiritual life," "God," "soul," "cross," etc., and if they could not find new ones next week, they might remain silent.

Be an opener of doors for such as come after thee, and do not try to make the universe a blind alley.

The Right Dandies. We have, it is true, a class of golden young men and maidens, of whom

1 Mrs. Snow was a kind and comforting old-fashioned nurse. The humility of this speech delighted Mr. Emerson and he often quoted it.

we say that for practical purposes they need a grain or two of alloy to make them good coin. If society were composed of such, the race would speedily be extinct by reason of bears and wolves who would eat them up. Granted. But perhaps it is in the great system that society shall have always some pensioners and pets, and how much better that such musical souls as these, worshippers of true beauty, objects of friendship, and monks and vestals in sacred culture, should be the exempts than the present *muscadins* of civilized society, the dandies, namely, who inherit an estate without wit or virtue.

Novels make us skeptical by giving prominence to wealth and social position, but I think them to be fine occasional stimulants, and, though with some shame, I am brought into an intellectual state. But great is the poverty of their inventions. The perpetual motive and means of accelerating or retarding interest is the dull device of persuading a lover that his mistress is betrothed to another. Disraeli is well worth reading; quite a good student of his English world, and a very clever expounder of its wisdom and craft: never quite a master. Novels make us great gentlemen whilst we read them. How generous, how energetic should we be in the crisis described; but unhappy is the wife, or brother, or stranger who interrupts us whilst we read: nothing but frowns and tart replies from the reading gentleman for them. Our novel-reading is a passion for results; we admire parks and the love of beauties, and the homage of parliaments.

Government. A fire breaking out in a village makes immediately a natural government. The most able and energetic take the command, and are gladly obeyed by the rest. The feeble individuals take their place in the line to hand buckets, and the boys pass the empty ones.[1]

I can well hear a stranger converse on mysteries of love and romance of character; can easily become interested in his private love and fortunes; but as soon as I learn that he eats cucumbers, or hates parsnip, values his luncheon, and eats his dinner over again in his talk, I can

1 Mr. Emerson, like most of his neighbors, was a member of the Village Fire Association, and the two leathern buckets, with the green baize bag for saving property, hung always in the east entry of his house, over the stairway. After hand-pumping engines were bought by the town, and fire-companies formed, the necessity for his personal service passed away, but he used to go to fight fire in the woods with a pine bough.

never thenceforward hear that man talk of sentiment.

I rode with a merry sea captain, between whom and the stage-coachman was a continual banter. We stopped at the poor-house. " Mr. Winchester," said the captain, "your passengers say you ought to stop at the poor-house every day." The driver replied, " If we should both stop there, Captain Davis, we should only stop where we started from."

The Fitchburg Road cost $1,100,000, fifty miles. The Worcester $3,000,000, forty miles. New church in Hanover Street cost $65,000.

People seem to me often sheathed in their tough organization. I know those who are the charge each of their several Dæmon, and in whom the Dæmon at intervals appears at the gates of their eyes. They have intervals, God knows, of weakness and folly like other people. Of these I take no heed. I wait the reappearings of the Genius, which are sure and beautiful.[1]

1 Compare the lines " To and fro the Genius flies " in " The Dæmonic Love " (*Poems*, p. 110 ; also in Appendix to *Poems*, p. 352).

The lover transcends the person of the beloved; he is as sensible of her defects and weak-
nesses as another; he verily loves the tutelar and
guiding Dæmon who is at each instant throwing
itself into the eyes, the air and carriage of his
mistress, and giving to them this unearthly and
insurmountable charm.

Do not lead me to question whether what we
call science is help or hurt. Yet unluckily in my
experience of the scientific, it is a screen between
you and the man having the science. He has his
string of anecdotes and rules, as a physician,
which he must show you, and you must endure,
before you can come at the color and quality of
the man. Phrenology, too, I hate. C. adapts his
conversation to the form of the head of the man
he talks with! . . . Alas![1]

Presently the railroads will not stop at Boston, but will tunnel the city to communicate
with each other. The same mob which has beat
down the Bastille will soon be ready to storm the
Tuileries.

[1] The rest of this passage is in " Experience " (*Essays,*
Second Series, pp. 53, 54).

Henry described Hugh[1] as saving every slip and stone and seed, and planting it. He picks up a peach-stone and puts it in his pocket to plant. That is his vocation in the world, to be a planter of plants. Not less is a writer to heed his vocation of reporting.[2] . . .

The vice of Swedenborg's mind is its theologic determination. . . . But a rose, a sunbeam, the human face, do not remind us of deacons.

Life which finishes and enjoys! Life is so affirmative that I can never hear of personal vigor of any kind, great power of performance, without lively sympathy and fresh resolutions.

The power of a straight line is a square, and wisdom is the power, or rather the powers, of the present hour.

We have no prizes offered to the ambition of generous young men. There is with us no Theban Band.[3] . . .

Our mass meetings are a sad spectacle: they show great men put to a bad use, men consent-

1 The gardener.

2 The rest of the passage is printed in " Goethe " (*Representative Men*, pp. 262, 263).

3 The rest is printed in " Aristocracy " (*Lectures and Biographical Sketches*, p. 59).

ing to be managed by committees, and worse, consenting to manage men. The retribution is instant diminution, bereavement of ideas and of power, of all loveliness and of all growth. It is in vain to bawl " constitution " and " patriotism "; those words repeated once too often have a most ironical hoarseness.

In common with all boys, I held a river to be good, but the name of it in a grammar hateful.

Ah! how different it is to render an account to ourselves of ourselves and to render account to the public of ourselves.

> " 'T is the most difficult of tasks to keep
>   Heights which the soul is competent to gain."

Granted; sadly granted; but the necessity by which Deity rushes into distribution into variety and particles, is not less divine than the unity from which all begins. Forever the Demiurgus speaks to the junior gods as in the old tradition of the Timæus, " Gods of gods, that mortal natures may subsist and that the Universe may be truly all, convert [or distribute] yourselves according to your nature to the fabrication of animals," etc.

The use of geology has been to wont the mind to a new chronology.[1] . . .

The progress of physics and of metaphysics is parallel at first; it is lowest instinctive life, loathsome to the succeeding tribes like the generation of sour paste. It is animalcules, earwigs, and caterpillars writhing, wriggling, devouring and devoured. As the races advance and rise, order and rank appear, and the aurora of reason and of love.[2] . . .

Nature will only save what is worth saving, and it saves, not by compassion, but by power. It saves men through themselves. . . . If the black man carries in his bosom an indispensable element of a new and coming civilization, for the sake of that element no wrong nor strength nor circumstance can hurt him, he will survive and play his part. So now it seems to me that the arrival of such men as Toussaint, if he is pure blood, or of Douglass, if he is pure blood,

1 Here follows the passage in " Nature " (*Essays,* Second Series, p. 180) on the vast period from the first breaking of the rock to Plato and the preaching of immortality.

2 See the " Address on the Anniversary of the Emancipation of the Negroes in the British West Indies," delivered in Concord, August, 1844 (*Miscellanies,* pp. 142, 145), only a few passages being here included.

outweighs all the English and American humanity. The anti-slavery of the whole world is but dust in the balance, a poor squeamishness and nervousness; the might and the right is here. Here is the Anti-Slave: here is Man; and if you have man, black or white is an insignificance. Why, at night all men are black. The intellect, that is miraculous. . . . Let us not be our own dupes; all the songs and newspapers and subscriptions of money and vituperation of those who do not agree with us will avail nothing against eternal fact. I say to you, you must save yourself, black or white, man or woman. Other half there is none. I esteem the occasion of this jubilee to be that proud discovery that the black race can begin to contend with the white; that in the great anthem of the world which we call history, a piece of many parts and vast compass, after playing a long time a very low and subdued accompaniment, they perceive the time arrived where they can strike in with force and effect and take a master's part in the music. . . .

But I am struck, in George Sand, with the instant understanding between the great; and in *I Promessi Sposi* with the humility of Fra Cristofero; and in *Faustina* with the silent acquies-

cence of Andlau in the new choice of Faustina;
for truth is the best thing in novels also.

Does he not do more to abolish Slavery who
works all day steadily in his garden than he who
goes to the Abolition meeting and makes a
speech? The Anti-slavery agency, like so many
of our employments, is a suicidal business.
Whilst I talk, some poor farmer drudges and
slaves for me. It requires a just costume, then,
— the office of agent or speaker, — he should
sit very low and speak very meekly, like one
compelled to do a degrading thing. Do not,
then, I pray you, talk of the work and the fight,
as if it were anything more than a pleasant oxy-
genation of your lungs. It is easy and pleasant
to ride about the country amidst the peaceful
farms of New England and New York, and sure
everywhere of a strict sympathy from the intelligent and good, argue for liberty, and browbeat
and chastise the dull clergyman or lawyer that
ventures to limit or qualify our statement. This
is not work. It needs to be done, but it does
not consume heart and brain, does not shut out
culture, does not imprison you, as the farm and
the shoeshop and the forge. There is really no
danger and no extraordinary energy demanded:

it supplies what it wants. I think if the witnesses of the truth would do their work symmetrically, they must stop all this boast and
frolic and vituperation, and in lowliness free the
slave by love in the heart. Let the diet be low,
and a daily feast of commemoration of their
brother in bonds. . . . Let them leave long dis-
courses to the defender of slavery, and show the
power of true words, which are always few. . . .
Let us, if we assume the dangerous pretension
of being Abolitionists, and make that our calling
in the world, let us do it symmetrically. The
world asks, Do the Abolitionists eat sugar? Do
they wear cotton? Do they smoke tobacco? Are
they their own servants? Have they managed
to put that dubious institution of servile labor
on an agreeable and thoroughly intelligible and
transparent foundation? . . . The planter does
not want slaves; give him money; give him
a machine that will provide him with as much
money as the slaves yield, and he will thankfully let them go; he does not love whips, or
usurping overseers, or sulky, swarthy giants
creeping round his house and barns by night
with lucifer matches in their hands and knives
in their pockets. No; only he wants his luxury,
and he will pay even this price for it. It is not

possible, then, that the Abolitionist will begin the assault on his luxury by any other means than the abating of his own. A silent fight, without war-cry or triumphant brag, then, is the new Abolition of New England, shifting the thronging ranks of the champions and the speakers, the poets, the editors, the subscribers, the givers, and reducing the armies to a handful of just men and women. Alas! alas! my brothers, there is never an abolitionist in New England.[1]

October 15.

[Here follows a list of the persons to whom Mr. Emerson is sending his second volume of Essays. Besides his mother, his wife, and Aunt Mary and nearest friends, the following names appear among the fifty-one mentioned: Ogden

1 This was written in the early stages of the Abolition Movement. Yet it should be said that Mr. Emerson, even when Minister of the Second Church, had willingly admitted a speaker against slavery into his pulpit. It was the methods, not the cause, of the Anti-slavery workers that dissatisfied him. When the Fugiive Slave Law was passed, and the matter brought to his own door and heart, his tone was different. He spoke with fire and eloquence and arguments against slavery. (See the two speeches on the Fugitive Slave Law given in *Miscellanies;* also, in the *Poems,* his " Fourth of July Ode," " Voluntaries," and " Boston Hymn.")

Haggerty, Benjamin Rodman, Horace Greeley, Giles Waldo, W. A. Tappan, William M. Prichard, Christopher P. Cranch, Charles K. Newcomb, R. W. Griswold, Sarah Clarke, H. W. Longfellow, George Bemis, J. R. Lowell, W. H. Dennett, Mrs. Lydia Maria Child, C. C. Hazewell, Mrs. Hildreth, Mrs. W. Pope, Miss M. C. Adams, Nathaniel Hawthorne, Warren Burton, Benjamin Peter Hunt, Charles Lane, Harriet Martineau, J. W. Morgan, John Sterling, Cornelius Matthews, John G. Whittier.]

For the fine things, I make poetry of them; but the moral sentiments make poetry of me.

> There are beggars in Iran and Araby;
> Said was hungrier than all.[1]
> . . . .
> Was never form and never face
> So sweet to him as only grace,
> Which did not last like a stone,
> But gleamed in sunlight and was gone.
> Beauty chased he everywhere,
> In flame, in storm, in clouds of air;
> He smote the lake to feed his eye

1 These are fragments of verses, long after mended and filled out. (See *Poems*, Appendix, pp. 320–322.)

With the precious [1] green of the broken wave;
He flung in pebbles well to hear
The moment's music which they gave;
Loved harebells nodding on a rock,
A cabin topped with curling smoke. . . .

The sun and moon are in my way when I would be solitary.

There are many topics which ought not to be approached except in the plentitude of health and playfully.

In Maine they have not a summer, but a thaw.

I understand very well in cities how the Southerner finds sympathy. The heat drives, every summer, the planter to the North. He comes from West and South and Southwest to the Astor and the Tremont Houses. The Boston merchant bargains for his cotton at his counting-house, then calls on him at the hotel, politely sympathizes with all his modes of thinking, — "He never sided with these violent men," — poor Garrison, poor Phillips

1 Later the fortunate word *beryl* was substituted.

are on the coals. Well, all that is very intelligible, but the planter does not come to Concord. Rum comes to Concord, but not the slave-driver, and we are comparatively safe from his infusions. I hardly understand how he persuades so many dignified persons — who were never meant for tools — to become his tools.[1]

Intense selfishness which we all share. Planter will not hesitate to eat his negro, because he can. We eat him in milder fashion by pelting the negro's friend. We cannot lash him with a whip, because we dare not. We lash him with our tongues. I like the Southerner the best; he deals roundly and does not cant. The Northerner is surrounded with churches and Sunday schools and is hypocritical. How gladly, how gladly, if he dared, he would seal the lips of these poor men and poor women who speak for him. I see a few persons in the church, who, I fancy, will soon look about them with some surprise to see what company they are keeping.

I do not wonder at feeble men being strong advocates for slavery. They have no feeling or

---

1 This passage shows that, whatever petulant outbreakings about the Abolitionists' methods and speech Mr. Emerson allowed himself in his journal, the national curse and disgrace of Slavery weighed always on his mind as on theirs.

worthiness which assures them of their own
safety. In a new state of things they are by no
means sure it would go well with them. They
cannot work or facilitate work, or cheer or deco-
rate labor. No; they live by certain privileges
which the actual order of the community yields
them. Take those and you take all. I do not
wonder that such would fain raise a mob, for
fear is very cruel. Instinct of Whigs may shudder at Napoleon. But what does Webster or
Andrew Jackson, or what does Crocker or Bel-
knap, or the Hosmers fear from the elevation
of Irish or negroes? They know they can defy
competition from the best whites or Saxons.
They should be abolitionists.

A gentleman may have many innocent pro-
pensities, but if he chances to have the habit of
slipping arsenic into the soup of whatever person sits next him at table, he must expect some
inconvenience. He may call it his " peculiar institution," a mere way of his ; he never puts it in
his own soup, only in the soup of his neighbor,
and even only in some of his neighbors' ; for
example, he is partial to light hair, and only
spices the dish of such as have black hair, and
he may persuade his chaplain to find him a
text, and be very indignant and patriotic and

quarrelsome and moral-religious on the subject,
and swear to die in defence of this old and
strong habit he has contracted.

The conscience of the white and the improvement of the black coöperated, and the emancipation became inevitable. It is a great deed with
a great sequel, and cannot now be put back.
The same movement goes forward with advantage; the conscience is more tender, and the
black more respectable. Meantime the belly is
also represented, and the ignorant and sensual
feel the danger and resist, so it goes slower.
But it gains, and the haters of Garrison have
lived to rejoice in that grand world-movement
which, every age or two, casts out so masterly
an agent of good. I cannot speak of that gentleman without respect. I found him the other
day in his dingy office.

I have no doubt there was as much intense
selfishness, as much cowardice, as much palter-
ing then [1] as now; many held back and called
the redeemers of their race fanatics and Method-
ists; there were many who with the utmost
dignity and sweetness gave such pepper-corn
reasons, there were church carpets, etc. Then,

1 In England before West Indian Emancipation.

too, died many an old aunt in man's clothes that would nail up her pew to keep Clarkson out.

Bonaparte was sensible to the music of bells. Hearing the bell of a parish church, he would pause, and his voice faltered as he said, "Ah! that reminds me of the first years I spent at Brienne — I was then happy." [1] . . .

Add as much force of intellect again to repair the immense defects of Bonaparte's *morale*, and he would have been in harmony with the ideal world.

Wendell Phillips. I wish that Webster and Everett and also the young political aspirants of Massachusetts should hear Wendell Phillips speak, were it only for the capital lesson in eloquence they might learn of him. This, namely, that the first and the second and the third part of the art is, to keep your feet always firm on a fact. They talk about the Whig Party. There

[1] The sexton, tolling his bell at noon,
Deems not that great Napoleon
Stops his horse and thrills with delight
As his files sweep round yon Alpine height.
Poems, "Each and All."

is no such thing in Nature. They talk about the Constitution. It is a scorned piece of paper. He feels after a fact, and finds it in the money-making, in the commerce of New England, and in the devotion of the Slave States to their interest, which enforces them to the crimes which they avow or disavow, but do and will do. He keeps no terms with sham churches or shamming legislatures, and must and will grope till he feels the stones. Then his other and better part, his subsoil, is the *morale*, which he solidly shows. Eloquence, poetry, friendship, philosophy, politics, in short, all power must and will have the real, or they cannot exist.

The ground of Hope is in the infinity of the World, which infinitely reappears in every particle. I know, against all appearances, that there is a remedy to every wrong, and that every wall is a gate.

Dumont's *Mirabeau*. Mirabeau said of Barnave, " He is a tree growing to become some time the mast of a line-of-battle ship." Target was said to be " drowned in his talents." " I could not puncture his dropsical eloquence," says Dumont.

[After some pages of anecdotes and sayings of Napoleon collected for *Representative Men*, there follows an enumeration of the names and types of men chosen as such ; and the following sentence.]

Jesus would properly be one head, but it requires great power of intellect and of sentiment to subdue the biases of the mind of the age, and render historic justice to the world's chief saint.

Alcott does not do justice to the merits of labor. The whole human race spend their lives in hard work from simple and necessary motives, and feel the approbation of their conscience ; and meet with this talker at their gate, who, as far as they see, does not labor himself, and takes up this grating tone of authority and accusation against them. His unpopularity is not at all wonderful. There must be not a few fine words, but very many hard strokes every day, to get what even an ascetic wants.

P. pleased the Boston people by railing at Goethe, in his Φ B K oration, because Goethe was not a New England Calvinist. If our lovers of greatness and goodness after a local type and standard could expand their scope a little, they would see that a worshipper of truth and a most subtle perceiver of truth like Goethe, with his impatience of all falsehood and scorn of hypocrisy (did he manifest his love of truth and scorn of falsehood to the women whose hearts he broke?), was a far more useful man and incomparably more helpful ally to religion than ten thousand lukewarm church-members who keep all the traditions and leave a tithe of their estates to establish them. But this clergyman should have known that the movement which in America created these Unitarian dissenters, of which he is one, began in the mind of this great man he traduces; that he is precisely the individual in which the new ideas appeared and opened to their greatest extent and with universal application, which more recently the active scholars in the different departments of science, of state, and of the church have carried in parcels and thimblefuls to their petty occasions.

Sarah Alden Ripley is a person externally very successful, . . . with a most happy family around her by whom she is loved and revered, and surrounded, too, by old and tried friends who dearly cherish her. She has quick senses and perceptions and ready sympathies which put her into just relations with all persons, and a tender sense of propriety which recommends her to persons of all conditions.

Her bias is intellectual. It is not her delicacy of moral sentiment that sways her, but the absence of all motive to vice in one whose passion is for the beauty of laws. She would pardon any vice in another which did not obscure his intellect or deform him as a companion. She knows perfectly well what is right and wrong, but it is not from conscience that she acts, but from sense of propriety, in the absence, too, of all motives to vice. She has not a profound mind, but her faculties are very muscular, and she is endowed with a certain restless and impatient temperament, which drives her to the pursuit of knowledge, not so much for the value of the knowledge, but for some rope to twist, some grist to her mill. For this reason it is almost indifferent to her what she studies, — languages, chemistry, botany, metaphysics, — with equal zeal, and equal success, grasping over all the details with great precision and tenacity, yet keeping them details and means to a general end, which yet is not the most general and grand.

I should say that her love of ends is less than

her impartial delight in all means; delight in
the exercise of her faculties, and not her love of
truth, is her passion. She has a wonderful cath-
olicity, not at all agreeable to precisians, in her
creed and in her morality. She sympathizes
with De Staël, and with Goethe, as living in
this world, and frankly regrets that such beings
should die as had more fitness to live in this
world than any others in her experience. In like
manner, whilst she would rapidly appreciate all
the objections which speculative men would
offer to the actual society among us, she would
deprecate any declaration or step which pledged
one of her friends to any hostility to society,
fearing much more the personal inconvenience
to one she loved, than gratified by his opportunity of spiritual enlargement.

This delight in detail, this pleasure in the
work, and not in a result, appears in her conversation, wherein she does not rest for the
tardy suggestions of nature and occasion, but
eagerly recalls her books, her studies, her newest persons, and recites them with heat and
enjoyment to her companion.

[Her] extreme gentleness: [she] excels in
what is called using philosophy against the hurts
of life. She follows Nature in many particulars

of life where others obtrude their own will and
theory. She leaves a dunce to be a dunce, and
rather observes and humors than guides a
scholar. She is necessitarian in her opinions, and
believes that a loom which turns out huckabuck
can never be talked into making damask. This
makes her very despondent in seeing faults of
character in others, as she deems them incurable.
She, however, has much faith in the maturation
and mellowing of characters, which often supplies some early defect.

She will by no means content an abolitionist
by her reliance on principles. She has too much
respect to facts. She delights in French Science
for its precision and experiment, and its freedom from English convention.

Very little taste in the fine arts, — not at all
disposed to hazard a judgment on a picture, or
a statue, or a building, — and only a secondary
taste in music, and even in poetry, — admiring
what those whom she loves and trusts admire,
and so capable of pleasure that she can easily
be pleased by what she is assured by those she
trusts is pleasing: if they say 'T is good, 't is
good; if they say 'T is bad, 't is bad.

She is feminine in her character, though she
talks with men. She has no disposition to preach,

or to vote, or to lead society. She is superior to any appetites or arts. She wishes to please and to live well with a few, but in the frankest, most universal and humane mode ; but in her unselfishness and inattention to trifles, likes very well to be treated as a child and to have her toilette made for her by her young people, too confident in her own legitimate powers of engaging the best, to take any inferior methods. An innate purity and nobility, which releases her once for all from any solicitudes for decorum, or dress, or other appearances. She knows her own worth, and that she cannot be soiled by a plain dress, or by the hardest household drudgery.

She is a pelican mother, and though one might not say of her what was said of the Princess Vaudemont, " Ask any beggar the way to her house ; they all know it," yet of her house and her husband's, it is certain that every beggar and every guest who has once visited it, will never forget it. It is very certain that every young man of parts remembers it as the temple of learning and ideas.

After all, we have not described her, for she is obviously inspired by a great, bright, fortunate Dæmon.

She is of that truth of character that she tor-ments herself with any injustice, real or imagined, she may have done another.

Nature will outwit the wisest writer, though it were Plato or Spinoza, and his book will fall into this dead limbo we call literature ; else the writer were God, too, and his work another nature.

AUTHORS OR BOOKS QUOTED OR REFERRED TO
IN JOURNAL FOR 1844

Zoroaster (?), *Chaldæan Oracles;* Pythagoras ; Heraclitus ; Plato ;

Martial ; Plotinus ; Proclus ;

Dante ; Chaucer ;

Behmen; Spinoza; Voltaire;

Linnæus ; Bausset; Goethe and Schiller, *Correspondence;* Burns ;

Talleyrand ; Dumont, *Souvenirs sur Mirabeau;*

Thomas Taylor, *Translations* from *Plato and Neoplatonists;* Beckford, *Vathek, Italy and Spain;* Dr. Ebenezer Porter ; Schelling ; Schlegel; Fourier; Bettina von Arnim; *Faustina;* Napoleon, and Books on Napoleon, Antommarchi, Bourrienne, etc.; R. Chambers, *Vestiges of Creation;*

Washington Irving; Allston; R. H. Dana (Senior); Bryant; Webster; Everett; William

H. Prescott; Bancroft; Dr. Channing; Rev.
Henry Ware; Alcott; Brisbane; Charles Lane;
George Sand, *Consuelo;* Disraeli, *Vivian Grey;*
Dickens;

William Lloyd Garrison; Wendell Phillips;
Charles K. Newcomb; Henry Thoreau;
W. E. Channing.

END OF VOLUME VI

𝕿𝖍𝖊 𝕽𝖎𝖛𝖊𝖗𝖘𝖎𝖉𝖊 𝕻𝖗𝖊𝖘𝖘
CAMBRIDGE . MASSACHUSETTS
U . S . A